THE
DEPRESSION
SOURCEBOOK

SECOND EDITION

by
Brian Quinn, C.S.W., Ph.D.

LOWELL HOUSE

LOS ANGELES

NTC/Contemporary Publishing Group

The purpose of this book is to educate. It is sold with the understanding that the publisher and author shall have neither liability nor responsibility for any injury caused or alleged to be caused directly or indirectly by the information contained in this book. While every effort has been made to ensure its accuracy, the book's contents should not be construed as medical advice. Each person's health needs are unique. To obtain recommendations appropriate to your particular situation, please consult a qualified health care provider.

Library of Congress Cataloging-in-Publication Data

Quinn, Brian, C.S.W., Ph.D.
     The Depression Sourcebook / by Brian Quinn—2nd ed.
         p.   cm.
     Includes index.
     ISBN 0-7373-0379-4 (pbk.)
         1. Affective disorders—Popular works. 2. Depression, Mental—
         Popular works. I. Title.

RC537.Q56 2000
616.85'27—dc21   00-057940

Published by Lowell House

A division of NTC/Contemporary Publishing Group, Inc.
4255 West Touhy Avenue, Lincolnwood, Illinois 60712, U.S.A.

Design by Robert S. Tinnon Design

Printed in the United States of America

International Standard Book Number: 0-7373-0379-4

00 01 02 03 04 DHD 18 17 16 15 14 13 12 11 10 9 8 7 6 5 4 3 2 1

To my wife and children

CONTENTS

INTRODUCTION

The word *depression* has many meanings. The feeling of sadness we have all experienced from time to time is what most people mean when they use the word. But when used by mental health professionals, the word *depression* (also referred to as *depressive illness*) refers to much more than a feeling of sadness. It is a label for a collection of symptoms such as persistent irritability, excessive guilt, low self-esteem, difficulty experiencing pleasure, and changes in sleep, appetite, and weight. It is a serious medical condition, which adversely affects not only a person's feelings but also his health, his relationships, the ability to work efficiently, and the ability to concentrate and think clearly. It can even lead to death. Fifteen percent of people with depression commit suicide.

Although depression is often treated by mental health professionals, *depression is not a mental illness*. That is to say, it is not primarily an illness of mental or psychological origin. Rather, it is a *biological illness* that manifests itself, in part, in mental or psychological symptoms. Although its origins are not yet fully understood, we do know that genetic factors play a strong role in depressive illness. Depressive illness is associated with changes in brain structure and chemistry, as well as alterations in glandular functioning.

Depressive illness is common. Eighteen million Americans suffer from it each year. Over the course of a lifetime, up to 12 percent of men and 20 to 25 percent of women will suffer from some form of depressive illness.

Episodes of depressive illness can last from several months to many years. Although people with depressive illness can get better with the passage of time, at least 35 percent of people who recover from the worst symptoms of it can be left with residual problems. Residual symptoms can detract from quality of life and make it more likely that another episode of depressive illness will occur.

Depressive illness is highly recurrent. Most patients who have a depressive episode will experience another at some point in their lives.

Depressive illness is on the rise. People born in the decades since 1940 have a higher lifetime incidence of it and other disorders of mood than those born before 1940. Social stresses unique to modern culture such as the increased divorce rate, increased numbers of children born out of wedlock, and the breakdown of social ties in our highly mobile society may be at fault. Biological stresses such as increased drug abuse, industrial toxins, dietary imbalances, alterations in daily and seasonal rhythms of sleep, and decreased exposure to sunlight due to indoor work that may also be partially responsible.

Depressive illness takes a huge toll on the productivity and health of Americans. The World Health Organization (WHO) ranks depression as the number one cause of disability among women. It is the second leading cause of lost days at work for both men and women. By the year 2020, it will be the number-one cause of disability worldwide. A study found that it costs employers about $33 billion a year in absenteeism and lost productivity.

Depressive illness makes sufferers feel worse overall than those with advanced coronary artery disease. It gets in the way of them fulfilling their responsibilities on the job and to their families more often than does diabetes, arthritis, or back problems.

People with untreated depressive illness and other mood disorders have a greater incidence of upper respiratory infections than those without mood disorders.

Women suffering from depressive illness have significantly lower hip-bone and spine density than nondepressed women. As a result, they are at greater risk for osteoporosis and hip fracture.

Those with mood disorders die much more often than do people in the general population from cardiovascular disease. A Danish study revealed that people with symptoms of depressive illness were 70 percent more likely to have had a heart attack than those without them. Other studies have shown depressed patients who have had heart attacks are at much greater risk of dying of a second one than those without depressive illness.

The vast majority of adolescents who commit suicide suffer from some form of mood disorder. Suicide is the second leading cause of death among adolescents. Nearly one-quarter of all adolescent deaths are a result of suicide.

In spite of its prevalence, the suffering it causes, its economic costs, and the increasing number of public information campaigns about depression, it remains one of the most misunderstood of all illnesses.

Here are just some of the misconceptions that get in the way of people identifying depressive illness and getting help for it:

1. *Someone ill with depression is not able to function.* In fact, in milder to moderate cases of the illness, they can often function fairly well, although not to their full potential.

2. *Depressed people are lacking in will-power and are weak. They are not happy unless they can find something about which they can complain.* The implication is that a person with depressive illness chooses to be miserable and that his or her problems are a reflection of some sort of personality weakness or character flaw. In fact, the misery and apparent character flaws are symptoms of an illness not under voluntary control. The depressed person's tendency to complain is no more a conscious choice than a fever is in someone sick with the flu.

3. *A depressed person could help herself, if she really wanted to, if she would only "forget her problems," "stop dwelling on the negative," or "put the past behind her and get on with her life."* Once again, the implication is that the depressed person chooses to dwell on his problems. The ability to temporarily block out or forget painful memories and problems is a useful unconscious defense mechanism all healthy human beings use. Unfortunately, it is not available to the

person with a depressive illness. In fact, the harder he tries to put something painful out of mind, the less likely he is to succeed. Instead, he will feel guilty and ashamed for what is mistakenly believed to be a weakness.

Due to these and many other misconceptions, one-half to two-thirds of patients who suffer from depression will not seek treatment. Surprisingly, even doctors may have trouble identifying the illness. In one study of patients in primary care settings (such as a family doctor's office), 59 percent of those suffering from depressive illness received no treatment for it. Nineteen percent were mistreated with minor tranquilizing drugs. Only 23 percent of the patients with depressive illness were being treated with antidepressants. Even among this group, 40 percent were being treated with inadequate doses of antidepressants. This means less than 14 percent of patients with depressive illness were appropriately treated by their family doctor.

Most alarming of all is the lack of understanding and recognition of depressive illness and related mood disorders among mental health professionals. The problems caused by mood disorders are among the most frequent reasons why people consult therapists.

Most social workers, psychologists, and marriage counselors recognize when patients have a severe depressive illness. The symptoms are obvious: Profoundly disturbed sleep, weight loss, the loss of ability to enjoy life, and thoughts of suicide. But therapists in outpatient practices typically see mildly to moderately ill patients. These patients' symptoms are more subtle and often manifest themselves primarily as low self-esteem, chronic worry, irritability, temper outbursts, and marital problems. Therapists can easily misdiagnose these signs of mood disorder as psychological problems and recommend treatment with psychotherapy alone.

In addition to information on how to recognize depression, this book will provide readers with a comprehensive guide to all the methods used to treat it. There are three kinds of books on the market about depression, all of which are in some way limited: Books by mainstream psychiatrists, which almost exclusively discuss the use of prescription drugs and other medical treatments;

alternative medicine books, which almost solely discuss the use of natural methods of treatment such as amino acids and exercise; and books which guide the reader in applying psychological and behavioral methods of treatment on their own.

Prospective patients need a book to help them evaluate and make sense of the bewildering variety of treatment approaches. Overall, I believe the available evidence best supports the biological approach to the treatment of depression. But the issue needs to be presented in a more balanced fashion.

For instance, given the lack of good scientific data, enthusiastic claims for the safety and efficacy of several natural supplements in the treatment of depression may not be warranted. On the other hand, biological psychiatrists and researchers have virtually ignored the antidepressant potential of some natural compounds.

Psychotherapists and their patients at times blow the risks involved in using prescription antidepressants out of proportion while assuming psychotherapy has no side effects. The fact is, when it is improperly conducted, psychotherapy can do a great deal of harm.

Patients and therapists need to keep in mind that there are risks inherent in *not* treating depressive illness with medication: Persistent irritability that can wreck a marriage or hurt a child, difficulty concentrating that can delay career advancement, and trouble calmly and effectively handling the stresses of everyday life are just some of the problems depressive illness can lead to.

I wrote this book to give the reader hope. Depression and other mood disorders, once recognized, are very treatable. We cannot cure them yet, but we can often eliminate or greatly reduce the symptoms. These illnesses no longer have to destroy a person's ability to lead a long, satisfying, and productive life.

CHAPTER 1

AN OVERVIEW OF DEPRESSION AND OTHER MOOD DISORDERS

T he mood disorders are divided into two groups: unipolar (or depressive) disorders and bipolar disorders. Someone with a unipolar disorder suffers only with depression. Someone with a bipolar disorder experiences ups and downs in mood, energy level, ability to think clearly, and need for sleep, among other symptoms. The highs are called manic episodes or, in less severe cases, hypomanic episodes. Someone affected by bipolar disorder can have not only highs and lows but a mix of both depression and manic symptoms at the same time. He may, for instance, have racing thoughts and yet complain of depressed mood. The mood of a person with mixed symptoms or mania is often irritable or explosive rather than euphoric.

The unipolar disorders include major depression and dysthymia. Bipolar disorders include manic-depressive illness (also known as bipolar I disorder), bipolar II disorder, and cyclothymia.

ABRAHAM LINCOLN

A man who suffers from a lifelong depressive illness is often tortured by feelings of inadequacy. He is convinced he would feel better—and better about himself—if only he could achieve something that others would notice and admire.

I often assure my patient it is his illness that makes him feel terrible about himself and not his lack of achievement. "When you're well," I may say, "you'll no longer feel inadequate and ashamed. You will be able to take pride in yourself, even if your name never goes down in history." I point out that even men who have achieved greatness were made miserable by depressive illness.

Abe Lincoln, for instance, rose from humble beginnings to become the President of the United States. He saved our nation. And yet he was tortured throughout his life by horrible, bleak periods of despair. His life is a lesson for all men with depressive illness: Achievement and success do not guarantee happiness.

In the following story you will note how early in life Lincoln's symptoms began. The early age of onset and his mood swings suggest that he may have had a mild form of bipolar illness.

Abraham Lincoln spent the first years of his life on a poor, hardscrabble farm in Kentucky. Later in life, he could remember little of his childhood, except that he once nearly drowned in a nearby creek and a neighbor waded in to save his life.

By the time he was thirteen, he could entertain friends with hilarious stories. Other times, he could be serious and brooding. Friends were struck by young Abe's similarity to his mother. She was a melancholy woman who accepted adversity as the will of God. Unable to read, she encouraged Abe to get an education. Although accounts vary, one friend said Abe's father, Thomas, thought education would ruin him, and beat him whenever he caught him reading books. Others said that Thomas did not interfere. Regardless, father and son were never close. When Thomas died years later, Abe did not attend his funeral.

As he grew older, Abe became obsessed with death and searched with intensity for the meaning of life. He would often sink into a depression that would plague him for days. In his time, it was called "hypochondria," and throughout his life, friends would talk of his getting "an attack of the hypo."

Always ambitious, he educated himself and built a career as a gifted lawyer and promising politician in the Illinois State Legislature. In 1840, at the age of thirty-one, he met Mary Todd, a fiery, impulsive girl who found him refreshing. She had lost her mother when she was six years old. Pampered by her father, she grew up stubborn and independent. When things didn't go her way, she threw temper tantrums that became legendary among family and friends. She could also be charming and fashionable, and before long they were engaged.

Her family vehemently disapproved of her marrying someone of such low-class origins. Feeling inferior to her, Abe broke off the engagement. He became so depressed, he was in bed for a week. When he finally mustered the strength to return to work, his colleagues were stunned by his emaciated appearance. Abe plunged into his work, but continued struggling with bouts of the hypo.

In the summer of 1842, he started seeing Mary again, and they married a few months later. He told friends he hoped his marriage would make him "less miserable." Abe and Mary loved each other intensely, but she found his mood swings troublesome. He would dote on her whenever she got one of her headaches; other times, he would simply stare off into space. He could brood for days on the meaning of life and the inevitability of death. For her part, she would go on lavish spending sprees and then try to make up for them by being stingy. Still, they formed a loyal partnership.

In 1846, Abe won a seat in Congress by an unprecedented majority but wrote a friend that it had "not pleased me as much as I expected." When he returned home from Congress, he began a self-imposed political exile and focused on his law practice. Though successful, he still got bouts of the hypo. In the middle of a conversation with friends, he would suddenly slip away into moody introspection. Then, just as suddenly, he would snap out of it and joke and quip.

Eventually, he was drawn back to politics and ran for president in 1860. After he was elected, he told newsmen, "Well, boys, your troubles are over now. Mine have just begun."

Though it was a joke, his words couldn't have been truer as the nation plunged into the Civil War. Throughout it, Abe was tormented by self-doubts and depression but was determined to save the Union. Even after the war ended, he suffered from insomnia and nightmares. Writer Harriet Beecher Stowe, who met him in the White House, was struck by his suffering. She later described it as "a dry, weary, patient pain."

Stowe thought he was the safest leader the country could have had during the war. A reckless, bold, or dashing man "would have wrecked our Constitution and ended us in a splendid military despotism." Instead, he had preserved democracy.

What is major depression?

Because it is so prevalent, depression has been referred to as the common cold of mental health problems. If only major depression were as short-lived and easily managed as a cold. At its worst, it is more like a severe bout of the flu than a cold: You do not want to eat, you lose weight, you cannot sleep, you feel fatigued, and you cannot keep your mind on anything except how lousy you feel. In severe depression, you may feel numb as opposed to miserable. You can work only with great effort, or you may not be able to work at all. You do not care about the people you used to love and the things you used to love to do.

Unlike the flu, however, which in most healthy people lasts only a couple of weeks, depression can last months and sometimes years.

And frequently, unlike the flu, it may not go away completely if left untreated. Untreated depression increases the likelihood that the sufferer will have another depressive episode. If you have had one bout of depression, you have a 50 percent likelihood of having another. After two bouts, you have a 70 percent likelihood of having another. After three, there is a 90 percent chance you will have a fourth episode of depression. Finally, people suffering from major depression are at serious risk of committing suicide.

What is the difference between major depression and normal sadness or grief?

The loss of a job, the failure to attain an important goal, the end of a relationship, or the death of a loved one can all lead to intensely painful yet normal feelings of sadness and grief. The early symptoms of intense grief often resemble some of the symptoms of depressive illness. It is not uncommon for someone who has just lost an important relationship to feel sad or empty, cry easily, have trouble sleeping, and lose his appetite.

Depressive illness can and frequently does develop, however, from what began as a normal grief reaction. A clue that depressive illness may have taken over is the persistence or worsening of symptoms. Another clue is a growing impairment in a person's ability to function.

In addition, the appearance of other symptoms suggests that grief may have developed into depressive illness. Depressive illness will lead to a decrease in self-esteem. A depressed person will become pervasively self-critical. Instead of having difficulty falling asleep, the person with depressive illness will have trouble staying asleep. She may begin to wake up early in the morning and be unable to get back to sleep. She will start to have problems thinking clearly, remembering, and concentrating.

Sadness and grief respond to the concern and caring of friends and the passage of time. But in depressive illness, the concern shown by family and friends may not help at all. Family members usually find themselves at a loss as to how to help someone with depressive illness. After a while, in fact, family and friends will begin to feel frustrated and irritated. No matter what they say or do, the person with depressive illness stays stuck in a gloomy, pessimistic mood.

Sadness and grief clear up in a reasonable period of time, and then a person gets back to normal. Some forms of depression do improve temporarily if things go well, but this is usually short-lived. And although depressive illness can improve over time by itself, it usually takes longer to do so than does normal sadness or grief.

In summary, if a depressed mood is hanging on for months, is disrupting your functioning, and is associated with the symptoms mentioned here and in chapter 3, you should seek a professional consultation.

What is dysthymia?

Dysthymia is chronic, mild depression. The person suffering from dysthymia can function, but not at full capacity. Dysthymia is generally associated with a long-standing tendency to be gloomy, sensitive, anxious, worried, and irritable.

If you are dysthymic, you may still have brief periods of happiness. You do not have to be down in the dumps all the time to be dysthymic. You may feel okay at times, but everyday stresses and disappointments may easily push you back into a gloomy or irritable mood. You will tend to feel easily overwhelmed, stressed, and worn out by life's problems. Friends and family may find it hard to sympathize with you since, to them, it seems that you are overreacting to pressures they take in stride. This may lead you to feel both angry and ashamed for being so "weak."

Dysthymia is a serious illness. Yet, if you suffer from it, your symptoms are not so overwhelming as to make it clear that you are ill. As a result, dysthymia often goes unrecognized. It is frequently mistaken for a bad disposition or a personality problem. Up until 1980, even the official position of the American Psychiatric Association (APA) was that dysthymia was a personality problem. (The APA is the national organization of medical doctors specializing in the diagnosis and treatment of illnesses such as depression.) As a result of this confusion, dysthymia is frequently not treated or is inadequately treated, most often with minor tranquilizers or psychotherapy.

I cannot emphasize enough how easily overlooked and misdiagnosed dysthymia is. The manifestations are often so subtle and so much a part of a person's way of being that it seems to be "just the way he is."

Part of the problem in recognizing dysthymia is that the standard list of symptoms for major depression does not capture the subtle manifestations of dysthymia. Three psychiatrists at the University of California, San Diego (Stephen Schuchter, Nancy Downs, and Sidney Zisook), call the subtle manifestations "the language of depression," rather than symptoms. The language is expressed in relationship and work problems and sense of self, rather than in the symptoms we more typically associate with depression—that is, loss of appetite, sleep disturbance, and suicidal thoughts.

For instance, a woman suffering from dysthymia complains repeatedly about her husband's shortcomings. These shortcomings may be real to some extent, but the wife exaggerates them or reacts to them with disproportionate hurt and anger. For a while, her husband tries to accommodate her and attempts to change. After some time, however, he starts to feel as if nothing will please her. If he has shaky self-esteem and a tendency to feel excessively guilty, he may begin to lose perspective. He begins to have trouble discerning where his problem ends and his wife's begins. He may begin to withdraw out of guilt, frustration, a desire to punish, or a sense of helplessness and inability to make things work. Or if he is sensitive to criticism and has poor impulse control, he may end up losing his temper or becoming abusive. Their relationship can spiral down into ugly arguments or, at best, a "cold war" where they rarely talk to each other.

Most couples I see with this pattern have absolutely no idea that one or both of them may have a mood disorder that contributes to their problem. They may believe they have problems communicating or that their spouse has a serious personality problem. They begin to dislike and blame each other for their problems rather than blaming the common enemy: a depressive illness.

Dysthymia has been shown to have clear biological and genetic links to full-blown depressive illness. It is not a personality problem. Proper treatment with a combination of antidepressant medication and appropriate forms of psychotherapy or marriage and family counseling often produces profound improvements in a patient's and family's quality of life.

What is manic-depressive illness?

Manic-depressive illness is the most severe form of bipolar disorder. It is characterized by wide swings in mood, energy level, and need for sleep.

Manic episodes generally develop rapidly, often over the course of a few days or, on occasion, a few hours. Onset is usually more rapid with each succeeding episode. The episodes typically last four to twelve months. Early in the manic phase, a person will feel on top of the world, exuberant, and wildly self-confident. He is more energetic, needs less sleep, and may be quite productive for a time. Thoughts race, and the person is filled with ideas and plans. Speech becomes rapid. As the manic episode goes on, a person usually becomes increasingly agitated, irritable, and eventually hostile and explosive. Thoughts become disorganized. Eventually, a person may begin to have grandiose and paranoid delusions (false beliefs). He may become convinced that he is Jesus Christ or that the mob is after him.

Patients in the depressed phase characteristically become very lethargic and unmotivated and tend to oversleep. They complain of feeling heavy, as if their arms and legs were made of lead. Episodes of depression generally last longer than manic episodes. The switches between episodes of mania and depression are typically rapid.

In bipolar II disorder, a person has major depressive episodes combined with less severe manic episodes referred to as hypomania. Someone with the mild bipolar disorder called cyclothymia has comparatively mild, yet troubling, mood swings. She is often looked upon by others as moody or difficult. As is the case with dysthymia, a person suffering from cyclothymia is often misdiagnosed as having a personality disorder by mental health professionals.

Bipolar disorders were originally considered to be much less prevalent than unipolar disorders. However, if you add up the patients with bipolar II and bipolar I disorders, the breakdown is about two-thirds unipolar and one-third bipolar. Some researchers believe the combined frequency of all forms of bipolar disorder (bipolar I, bipolar II, and cyclothymia) is equal to that of the unipolar disorders.

What causes depression and other mood disorders?

Although depression is a complex illness with many factors playing a role in its development, current scientific evidence indicates that the fundamental problem is a hereditary and biological one. We are not sure of the exact nature of the problem, but it is clear that depression and bipolar illness are due to defects in brain biochemistry and structure, and perhaps the workings of the glandular and immune systems as well.

In this sense, they are not mental illnesses (sicknesses of the mind) but physical illnesses of the brain. With advances in our understanding of the biochemical problems involved in mood disorders, the term *mental illness* will eventually be discarded.

Scientific evidence for the genetic, biochemical, and physical basis of depression comes from several sources:

Identical-Twin Studies   These show that when identical twins (who have the same genetic makeup) are reared apart and one twin has clinical depression, the other twin is more likely to develop depression than would be expected by chance alone.

Adoption Studies   Individuals with depressed parents or other relatives have been found to develop depression more frequently than would be expected by chance alone even if they are brought up by nondepressed adoptive parents.

Biochemical Studies   Depressed individuals have some similar abnormalities in brain biochemistry.

Neuroimaging Studies   Pictures of brain structure and metabolism of people with depression show some similarities. (Imaging techniques may eventually help doctors make a diagnosis in individual patients.)

Medication Response Studies   The majority of people with symptoms of depression respond to medications believed to correct specific brain biochemical imbalances.

This is not to say that the environment an individual was raised in or later unfortunate life circumstances play no role in mood disorders. The current thinking is that the genetic and biochemical dysfunctions in depression are triggered by life events, including problems in the family in which a depressed individual grew up. If a person with a genetic vulnerability to depression is raised by abusive alcoholic parents, for instance, she is more likely to develop depression than is a genetically vulnerabe individual brought up in a stable home.

Someone suffering from depression can usually come up with good reasons for his or her emotional pain. The person might be able to point to a rotten childhood or current problems to explain his troubled mood. But these reasons alone often do not explain why someone would go from *feeling* depressed to developing the many symptoms characteristic of depressive illness. Many people go through profoundly painful traumas of all kinds and do not end up with symptoms of depressive illness.

The prospective patient needs to keep in mind that once a depressive illness takes hold, it can develop a life of its own, regardless of the events that triggered it. Even when depressive illness has clearly been set off by negative events, medical treatment may be needed to help resolve it.

A few studies have suggested that at least some cases of serious depression could be caused by viruses, including a virus called the *Borna virus*. A large percentage of people with bipolar disorder were born in the winter at the height of cold and flu season. The antiviral drug amantadine/Symmetrel has reportedly helped some patients with clinical depression. In addition to being an antiviral drug, however, amantadine also enhances the effectiveness of a neurotransmitter that may be implicated in depression, so its effectiveness could have as much to do with this action as with its antiviral action.

Can medical illnesses
cause symptoms of depression?

Definitely. In fact, before receiving any kind of treatment for depression, you should have a physical exam and blood work-up to rule out so-called medical mimics of depression. One study found that 10 percent of the problems patients came to outpatient mental health clinics for were probably due to medical illness. Another study conducted on a large number of patients in Canada who sought help from outpatient clinics found that roughly 34 percent of these patients had a medical illness that contributed to their psychiatric symptoms. Eighteen percent had an illness that was entirely responsible for the psychiatric problems.

Although there are hundreds of medical illnesses or conditions that can lead to symptoms of depression, only a handful are most common: alcohol or drug abuse, other prescription medications (especially those used to treat cardiovascular disease), glandular problems such as an underactive thyroid, neurological disorders such as multiple sclerosis, and sleep disorders.

Can problems such as low blood sugar
(hypoglycemia) cause depression?

The most common type of hypoglycemia—and the one people are usually referring to when they mention the connection between low blood sugar and mood—is acute reactive hypoglycemia.

When you eat, an organ in your body called the pancreas releases insulin to regulate metabolism of blood sugar. In some people, the pancreas secretes excessive insulin in response to eating a lot of sugary or starchy food quickly. Other people may have defective mechanisms for keeping their level of insulin in check once it is released by the pancreas. In either case, excessive insulin activity causes the blood sugar level to fall into the low-normal or below-normal range. The person may experience transitory symptoms such as anxiety, heart palpitations, restlessness, sweating, fatigue, and weakness. Some people may feel irritable and have other personality changes. These effects may last four to six hours, unless the person eats something.

This type of transient fluctuation in blood-sugar levels, even if repeated frequently, is unlikely to be a cause of depressive illness. In fact, severely depressed patients have generally been found to have a *less than normal reduction in blood-sugar levels in response to insulin, not an exaggerated reduction.* This may be because depressed people often have high levels of cortisol, which suppresses the action of insulin.

Chronic hypoglycemia, caused by an insulin-producing tumor, for instance, *can* mimic depression. Insulin-producing tumors and other causes of chronic hypoglycemia, however, are rare.

To be considered truly hypoglycemic, you must have (a) a glucose tolerance test (GTT) indicating your blood-sugar level is low *and* (b) signs and symptoms such as those indicated above, which coincide with the low blood-sugar level and which are relieved by the ingestion of sugar or other food. The reason *b* is essential for the diagnosis is because 25 percent of individuals taking the GTT have below-normal blood-sugar levels *without any symptoms at all.* Up to 50 percent of women taking a GTT may have below-normal blood-sugar levels without symptoms.

Some doctors interpret the test much more liberally. They will diagnose hypoglycemia if the rate at which the blood-sugar level falls in the GTT is rapid. A number of alternative medicine practitioners swear by the antidepressant effects of an antihypoglycemic diet.

What should the depressed person do? First, you need to understand that the claims of the "hypoglycemic doctors" are just that: claims. There is no good evidence to suggest that hypoglycemia is a frequent cause of depression. In addition, there is no evidence to support the use of antihypoglycemic diets as effective first-line treatment for depression. If you have symptoms suggestive of acute reactive hypoglycemia, you might want to get a GTT. Or, if you have the motivation, you can simply modify your diet by reducing the amount of carbohydrate you eat. This may be especially helpful if you crave sweets or starchy food.

Some depressed patients tend to overeat sweets or starchy foods (those with seasonal depressions and so-called atypical depression— see chap. 3 for details). This may contribute to an increased incidence of acute reactive hypoglycemia in some individuals. It may also precipitate additional episodes of sweet or carbohydrate craving. A person with this problem may find herself gaining unwanted weight, especially in the winter. But all of this is usually a *result* of depression and not its cause. When properly treated, a depressed person's cravings for sweets and junk food decrease.

*Is it true that such things as candida syndrome
(intestinal yeast overgrowth), mercury tooth fillings,
and food allergies can be at the root of depression?*

In the first edition of this book, I pointed out that there was little to no sound research evidence to suggest these and other dietary, metabolic, and biochemical abnormalities were responsible for depressive illness. I stated that a patient would not be well served by a clinician that made the investigation of any of these possibilities a first priority.

There is still little sound research on these issues. The weight of the scientific evidence suggests that someone suffering from dysthymia or a major depressive episode is generally best treated with psychotherapy and/or antidepressant medication (assuming a comprehensive medical workup has shown that no known illnesses are responsible for the depressive symptoms).

However, over the last several years, I have looked into the work of a number of well-trained and respected physicians who approach the treatment of chronic illnesses such as depression from a unique point of view. These physicians point out that just as aspirin reduces a fever but does not cure an underlying infection, antidepressants relieve symptoms without fixing underlying biochemical problems. They do not claim to fully understand the biochemical abnormalities underlying depression or to have a cure for the illness. But they do believe that finding and correcting disturbed bodily functions—ones that do not quite make it to the level of an illness—can help bring about relief on a more fundamental and natural level. For instance, they have found that correcting an overgrowth of yeast in the intestines or desensitizing a patient to food allergies can help relieve symptoms. For more information on this topic, turn to chapter 10.

I tell my patients about all the alternatives for treating depression: Psychotherapy, medication, and natural alternatives. I explain the advantages of each and let them decide how they would like to proceed. But I do suggest—especially to those who are seriously depressed—that we first work on relieving their symptoms with the standard approaches. We can then look for underlying, disturbed bodily functions once they are better.

If I suspect I may have depression or another
mood disorder, whom do I see for an evaluation?

Not every mental-health professional can be counted on to provide a comprehensive evaluation and an accurate diagnosis. Nor can every therapist be counted upon to recommend an appropriate combination of treatments. If you go to two therapists in the same office building with the same problem, you may find that they recommend two entirely different treatment approaches.

Among nonmedically trained psychotherapists (social workers, psychologists, counselors, marriage counselors), there is no one group more likely to conduct a thorough evaluation and recommend appropriate treatment. The chances of good care depend more on individual interests, training, and theoretical orientation.

Psychiatrists as a group are more likely to detect medical mimics of mood disorders and medication-responsive mood disorders than nonmedically trained psychotherapists. However, in my experience, even psychiatrists are prone to missing medical illnesses that can contribute to depression. And unless they specialize in the treatment of mood disorders, they may fail to accurately diagnose people suffering from bipolar disorder.

Some potential patients with mild to moderate mood disorders do not consult psychiatrists because of the mistaken belief that a psychiatrist is needed only if you are "really crazy" or if you need to get into deeply buried emotional issues. This is not true. If your therapist suggests that you have a consultation with a psychiatrist, it is merely an effort to clarify the diagnosis and help decide on appropriate treatment. The psychiatrist you see will probably not probe into any deep emotional issues with you. This will be left to your therapist.

Some mental-health professionals with a doctoral degree (a Ph.D., for instance) are entitled to call themselves "doctor." They are not medically trained, however. Depending on training and orientation, they may or may not consider the possibility that you have a medical illness or a medication-responsive mood disorder.

So what should I do?

If you have insurance or the financial resources, you should try to get a referral from your family doctor, managed-care plan, or employee-assistance program to see someone in private practice. In general, clinicians in private practice have the most years of training and experience.

I recommend that people *not* see a therapist who a relative or friend is seeing or has seen. You may initially feel most comfortable with this kind of referral, but it is a bad idea. Getting a name from a friend when you need a plumber makes sense. You will probably not care a great deal if your friend mentions to the plumber that your bathroom needs a lot of work. And you will not be terribly concerned if the plumber makes a comment to your friend about how old and stained your kitchen sink is. But the potential problems with confidentiality and privacy that can arise with your therapist when he is seeing someone you know are not worth the trouble.

Tell the person making the referral about the nature of your problem. Be sure you get referred to an expert in mood disorders who is knowledgeable about a variety of treatments. Therapists often say that they treat depression, but they may not have specific expertise in treating mood disorders. You should inquire about the therapist's approach to the evaluation and treatment of depression. You should seek another consultation if the therapist fails to provide a comprehensive evaluation, rigidly opposes the use of medication, or strictly adheres to only one theory of treatment.

In metropolitan areas, psychiatrists charge roughly $150 to $200 for forty-five minutes of their time. Clinical psychologists charge from $75 to $125. Clinical social workers charge from $50 to $100. These amounts may be higher in large metropolitan regions like New York City and could be considerably lower in rural areas. Some therapists may charge you on a sliding scale depending on your ability to pay. The differences in fees do not mean one group of professionals is worth more or provides a higher quality of service. Research has clearly demonstrated that academic credentials make no difference in the quality or effectiveness of the *psychotherapy* you receive. Seeing a psychiatrist, however, may make a difference in the diagnosis you receive and the *type* of treatment recommended.

If you do not have insurance or the money to pay for therapy, you can go to a local mental-health agency. These are often run by local charity groups or county and state governments. Their fees are on a sliding scale and are considerably lower than the fees of private therapists. These agencies do not turn people away because of an inability to pay. The advantage of the mental-health agency is that you can usually get all your help (psychotherapy, family counseling, educational seminars, support groups, advocacy services, and medication) under one roof.

There are disadvantages, however: There may be a long wait before you will be able to see a therapist or psychiatrist. Therapists tend to be younger, with less life experience, less professional experience, and less training.

The biggest disadvantage to seeing a therapist in a mental-health agency is that she will often leave the agency after a couple of years. If this happens to you, ask her if she will be working in the area at another agency or in private practice. The therapist might be willing and able to continue with you on a private basis at a reduced fee.

How do mental-health professionals
arrive at a diagnosis? Is there a
blood test for depressive illness?

Everyone would feel more comfortable, of course, if there were some sort of objective physical means, such as a blood test or a brain scan, to verify the diagnosis of depression. Scores of these so-called "biological markers" of depression have been identified and studied. A few are starting to be used to guide the choice of initial antidepressant drug treatment. However, the use of markers to reliably diagnose subtypes of depression and to predict response to specific medications is still in its infancy. The method is not widespread.

The dexamethasone suppression test (DST), for instance, is one tool sometimes used to diagnose depression. A hormone called cortisol is often high in patients with depression. A patient is given a dose of dexamethasone, which normally suppresses production of cortisol. Several hours later, when cortisol should be at a low point, the blood level of cortisol is measured. If it is still high (if cortisol is not suppressed), the patient is considered depressed and should respond to antidepressants. The DST accurately diagnoses some cases of depression, especially in otherwise healthy, young individuals. The problem is that it does not accurately diagnose some individuals with depression and, conversely, diagnoses some people as depressed when they are not.

Dr. Mark Gold, at the University of Florida College of Medicine, believes this reflects a problem with an antiquated system of diagnosis and not with the test itself. In his book, *The Good News About Depression*, he points out that the label "depressed" implies a single disease process from which all patients suffer. But different biochemical derangements in the brain can produce a similar or even identical set of symptoms we call depression. Given this, one would expect that a test of any one biochemical abnormality would be unreliable.

Dr. Gold believes we should discard the current diagnostic system and build a new one from the ground up. That is, identify the various biological abnormalities in depression and then figure out which specific treatments work in cases with particular abnormalities.

To arrive at a proper diagnosis and treatment plan for a patient suffering from depression, Dr. Gold insists that doctors should conduct an exhaustive search for medical illnesses that can mimic depression. If none are found, he advocates the use of laboratory tests to identify a subtype of depression and guide treatment. The need for and the clinical usefulness of this approach for the first-time patient are a matter of some debate. In any case, the practice is not widespread.

For the first-time patient looking for help with depression, a *thorough* traditional workup is likely to be more than adequate. It will properly diagnose and adequately treat depression in the shortest amount of time for the majority of patients.

I emphasize the word *thorough* because many mental-health professionals do not even come close to doing a complete workup. They often fail to pick up on signs of medical illness, substance abuse, and other problems that mimic depression. They may even fail to suspect that the person has a biological illness called depression, especially if it is mild or chronic.

What are the elements of a thorough, traditional evaluation?

A physical exam, blood workup, and medical history forms the foundation of the diagnostic process. The blood workup should include a test of thyroid function called TSH (thyroid stimulating hormone). It would probably be best if everyone seeking help for a mood disorder would get a special test of thyroid function called the TRH (thyrotropin releasing hormone) stimulation test. The TRH stimulation test is sensitive to even the most subtle forms of thyroid disorder. It will pick up thyroid disorders the TSH test will not. However, it requires more than the drawing of a single sample of blood. As a result, it is rarely ordered by doctors. If you have responded to antidepressants but repeatedly slip back into a depression or if you have a form of bipolar illness called rapid-cycling bipolar illness (see chap. 3), you should discuss getting the TRH stimulation test with your doctor.

Your psychiatrist or therapist next looks for the signs and symptoms of a mood disorder. Signs are problems a mental-health professional notices, such as irritability, which you may not recognize as a part of depression. Symptoms are complaints you have or complaints the therapist elicits from you, such as depressed mood. You should be asked about your use of prescription drugs, illicit drugs, and alcohol.

Your doctor or therapist should inquire about any previous episodes of depression, elevated moods suggestive of bipolar illness, or other emotional problems. She will ask about any prior treatment you may have had. She should also ask about your relationships, school and work histories, and other aspects of your personal history. Any family history of psychiatric disorders is taken into account as well. Disorders can run in families, and the presence of specific signs and symptoms in other family members may suggest various diagnoses for your doctor or therapist to consider.

The therapist may do a mental-status exam. This is an equivalent of the physical exam. You may, for example, be given brief verbal and written tests to check on your ability to concentrate and reason. Results of the mental-status exam can suggest the presence of a disease state affecting the brain.

This approach to diagnosis is quite reliable. In fact, the diagnoses of major depression and bipolar disorder are more reliable than are many diagnoses in other branches of medicine. If you can find a doctor or therapist who does all of the above, who keeps in mind the possibilities of medical mimics and knows the subtle manifestations of mood disorders, you will be well served.

You may have many different reactions upon learning that you are suffering from depression. If you have been in a great deal of emotional pain, you may feel relieved to hear that your suffering has a name and a treatment.

If you have a mild to moderate depression and a psychotherapist indicates that you have a depressive illness, you may feel quite shaken up by the diagnosis. You may even feel worse upon hearing the diagnosis than when you first walked into the therapist's office. This is probably because you mistakenly believe depressive illness is a sign of weakness.

Your feelings about the diagnosis may trigger a defensive reaction: You may find yourself looking for reasons why a therapist or doctor who makes such a diagnosis is wrong. For instance, you may find yourself arguing that it is normal for you to be depressed since your marriage is a wreck, your boyfriend or girlfriend dumped you, or you hate your job. Keep in mind that feeling depressed is a normal response when bad things happen to us. But the numerous and persistent symptoms characteristic of depressive illness are not a normal or necessary response to stress. When told about the diagnosis, you may question how the therapist or doctor could suggest such a diagnosis in only one or two sessions. Much work needs to be done, of course, to rule out the possibility that a medical illness may be at the root of your symptoms. The possibility that substance abuse or the use of other prescription drugs could be a factor in your depression also needs to be taken into account. And some time will need to be spent on determining the specific type of depressive illness from which you suffer. But the fact is that a tentative diagnosis of depressive illness can be made in a very short period of time on the basis of your symptoms and family history.

If you react angrily upon hearing the diagnosis, notice that you are uncomfortable with even the idea that you may have a depressive illness. Try to keep an open mind about the possibility of the diagnosis in spite of your anxieties and concerns. Work with your therapist to understand the source of these anxieties.

Sometimes a person with a supportive spouse and a reasonably comfortable life will come to me feeling guilty and ashamed for being depressed. If there have been minor stresses, he may seem to be overreacting to them. Family and friends may have chided the person to "snap out of it." They may have pointed out that the person has "no good reason to be depressed."

But just as someone does not need to have problems with their spouse or family to get the flu, neither does he need a real life problem to get depressed! Overreaction to minor stress is common in depressive illness and is not due to a personality defect.

Occasionally, I see a patient with a depressive illness who does not feel depressed. How is this possible? *Feeling depressed* and *having a depressive illness* are two separate things. These patients are shocked and puzzled by the diagnosis because they do not know that depression is an illness with many symptoms. One of the symptoms someone usually, *but not always*, suffers from is depressed mood. Sometimes a person with depressive illness feels anxious, irritable, dissatisfied, bored, empty, or as if they "just don't care." *Episodes of depression occur in bipolar illness. How does a therapist or doctor know if you have unipolar or bipolar depression?*

The most critical diagnostic task facing a therapist or doctor is determining whether a patient with symptoms of depression has a unipolar or bipolar depression. The distinction has critical treatment implications. Antidepressant medication may cause a number of problems in patients diagnosed as unipolar who actually suffer from bipolar depression: induction of a manic episode (particularly one with irritable mood) and increased cycling of symptoms and depressive symptoms that become increasingly unresponsive to treatment.

This is becoming an especially important issue now that many family doctors are prescribing antidepressants. One study has shown that as many as one-third of depressed patients seen by their primary care physicians actually suffered from bipolar illness.

Psychotherapists are generally poorly trained in sorting out unipolar from bipolar depression. They will often not consider the possibility that their depressed client may have a bipolar disorder. In my experience, even psychiatrists often fail to properly diagnose bipolar depression. One reason is that the patient only comes for help when depressed and will not mention periods in her life when she had hypomanic symptoms. These periods of high energy, inflated self-confidence and self-esteem, and need for less sleep are obviously not thought to be a problem. The therapist or doctor needs to ask about these periods.

Clues suggesting bipolar depression or the presence of a subtle bipolar disorder include:

- Episodes of depression with one or more of the following: oversleeping, overeating, weight gain, extreme lethargy, and fatigue. People with unipolar depression often have trouble staying asleep whereas someone with bipolar depression may sleep ten to eighteen hours per day.
- At least one episode with an "up" mood, high energy, and a decreased need for sleep, especially if it immediately precedes or follows a depressive episode with oversleeping and lethargy. Rapid onset and offset of depressive symptoms is characteristic of bipolar disorder. Unipolar depression tends to come on slowly and dissipate slowly.
- Symptoms of depression that rapidly alternate or mix with periods of intense anxiety, agitation, irritability, restlessness, increased sexual urges, or difficulty falling asleep.
- Seasonal variation in mood (typically winter depression and summer hypomania).
- Symptoms of depression, irritability, or bad temper in some of your siblings and several members of your parents' and grandparents' families.

- Relatives who are unusually energetic, on-the-go, talkative, outgoing, and who regularly get along on little sleep (six hours or less a night).

Please see chapters 2 and 3 for more information on the milder forms of bipolar illness known as cyclothymia and bipolar II disorder.

How is depression treated?

Depressive illness is generally best treated with a combination of medication and psychotherapy. Other methods of treatment, including bright-light therapy, nutritional approaches, dietary supplements, and other promising alternatives, will be discussed in chapter 10.

You should discuss using medication with your therapist if you have moderate to severe depression; suffer from changes in sleep, appetite, or weight; are suicidal; or if you have had mild depression for many years. Markedly decreased ability to experience pleasure is another indication for the use of medication. Misconceptions about the indications for the use of medication keep many people from giving them a try.

A common misconception, for instance, is that medication is only for crazy people or those who cannot function. Nothing could be further from the truth. If you suffer from depression or take medication for it, you are no more crazy than is someone who takes insulin for diabetes. Both diabetes and depression are physical illnesses. You need not feel any shame or embarrassment about treating depression with medication. Many people who function well and who you would never think of as being depressed use and benefit from medication. As you learn more about the illness and begin to feel better about yourself, the embarrassment and shame will fade. You will find more on the common fears and concerns people have about using medication in chapter 8.

When is it appropriate to treat
depression with psychotherapy alone?

This is a matter of some debate among mental-health professionals. The debate will be discussed in detail in chapter 7. As a practical matter and on the basis of clinical experience, if (1) this is your first episode of depression, (2) you have been depressed only mildly or moderately for just a few months, (3) you are not suffering from major sleep or appetite disturbances, and (4) you have no family history of mood disorder, therapy alone is likely to be helpful.

The greatest danger to you as a mental-health consumer lies in getting treated with psychotherapy alone for many months or years when you have signs or symptoms of a depressive illness. If you have been in psychotherapy for more than three or four months without *substantial* improvement in your symptoms of depression, you should seek an evaluation with a therapist familiar with the diagnosis and treatment of mood disorders.

You may find yourself doubting that *any* type of treatment will help *you* feel better. You may think, "What can talking or taking a pill do to fix all of the things wrong in my life?" You may find this hard to believe, but it is true: *When your depression is properly treated, you will feel better, even if your problems do not change.* Keep in mind, too, that hopelessness is a *symptom* of depression. If you are severely depressed, you may not be able to *feel* convinced that there is hope, no matter what anyone says. But keep this *thought* in mind: *The undisputed scientific fact is that if you get treatment, you will in all likelihood begin to feel better within several weeks.*

What will happen if I do not treat an episode
of major depression or some form of bipolar illness?

Depression has traditionally been considered a self-limiting disease. That is, left to itself, it would run its course, and then you would return to normal. As it turns out, that may not be true. Someone suffering from a first episode of depressive illness will likely get somewhat better over time without treatment (although he will suffer more, and it will take longer to get better). But 20 to 35 percent of patients are left with residual symptoms after a depressive episode. These patients are much more likely to have another episode. The more episodes someone has, the more likely they are to have another. Subsequent episodes are likely to be more severe and resistant to treatment. The average patient who does not treat her illness is likely to have seven episodes of depression during her lifetime.

Over time, episodes of untreated bipolar illness are likely to become more severe, more frequent, and more difficult to treat. The risk of suicide in untreated bipolar disorder is high.

What can I do to help myself?

You have already started. Learning that many of your problems are symptoms of an illness and not signs of weakness or a rotten personality can be a relief.

Learning that depression is an illness, however, is also a bit unsettling. It means that you are not in full control of your symptoms and problems. But just because depression is an illness not under your *full* control does *not* mean there is nothing you can do or that you have *no* control.

Learning new ways to think about yourself and your future, practicing new interpersonal skills, modifying your diet, exercising, and the judicious use of dietary supplements will help. (More about all this in chap. 11.)

CHAPTER 2

MILD MOOD DISORDERS THAT MASQUERADE AS PSYCHOLOGICAL PROBLEMS

DYSTHYMIA

Dysthymia is mild, chronic depression. Although less severe in intensity than a major depressive episode, the illness often wreaks greater havoc on the sufferer's life and adjustment than does major depression. Dysthymia has an insidious but pervasive and corrosive effect on self-esteem and self-confidence. It stunts the development of social and interpersonal skills and often robs the person of educational achievement and career success. Since those who suffer with dysthymia can function—albeit with a lot of extra effort and not up to their potential—they usually fail to realize they have a treatable medical illness. Dysthymic disorder often masquerades as or is mistaken for a gloomy, unassertive, and at times irritable personality. Many people with dysthymia have struggled with the disorder for so many years that they and everyone else assumes it is simply "the way they are."

Psychotherapists not trained to recognize the symptoms of dysthymia often end up treating these patients with psychotherapy alone—as if the symptoms were a reflection of psychological or personality problems. This is a mistake that may doom the patient to months or years of needless suffering.

Although it is separated from other forms of mood disorder in diagnostic classifications, some researchers believe that dysthymia may not be a unique form of depression. There is a considerable amount of evidence to support the idea that it is either a variation of major depression or simply a stage of major depressive illness. As a result, dysthymia, like major depressive illness, responds to antidepressant medication and perhaps to specific types of psychotherapy as well.

Some of the symptoms and characteristics of dysthymia include a depressed mood for most of the day, for more days than not, for at least two years, plus two or more of the following:

- Poor appetite or overeating
- Difficulty sleeping or oversleeping
- Low energy or fatigue
- Low self-esteem (feelings of worthlessness, inadequacy, or inferiority)
- Poor concentration or difficulty making decisions
- Feelings of hopelessness and despair

Many people with dysthymia may not have significant problems with appetite, sleep, or concentration. Instead, they may have some or many of the problems listed below. These problems are more subtle and look more like personality flaws or psychological difficulties. But, in fact, they are part and parcel of dysthymia:

- Overly serious; diminished ability to experience pleasure or have fun
- Critical, irritable, complaining
- Prone to worry; pessimistic; engages in worst-case-scenario thinking
- Self-critical; guilt-prone
- Shy, withdrawn, or socially isolated; anxious in social situations
- Difficulty establishing romantic relationships
- Low stress tolerance, easily overwhelmed
- Lacking in self-confidence

- Lethargic, lacking in motivation; decreased effectiveness or productivity
- Cautious; in jobs below his potential
- If somewhat successful, she may feel like a fraud or fake
- Anxious, guilty about expressing anger; worries others will leave if he gets angry
- Difficulty being assertive; lets others be unduly hurtful or take advantage of her
- Overly sensitive to criticism or rejection
- Preoccupied with thoughts of death or the meaninglessness of life
- At times, feels that life is not worth living
- Dependable, conscientious, loyal

Although a person needs to be mildly depressed for only two years to qualify for a diagnosis of dysthymia, many have had the illness since childhood. This is known as "early-onset dysthymia." The onset is often insidious.

Alice remembers being sad as a child. She can recall a lonely feeling while playing by herself with her dolls. "I always felt like a bit of an outsider," she says, "and never really sure that the other kids accepted me. I was painfully self-conscious and lacked self-confidence." Her mother was prone to bouts of irritability and temper outbursts and seemed extremely sensitive to anything her children or husband did, which could be construed as rejection. She needed a great deal of reassurance. Alice recalls her mother as being "hard to please." Alice would learn many years later that her mother had once tried to commit suicide. Alice's father had a drinking problem and would often get verbally abusive to his wife and children when drunk.

Alice often felt inadequate and bad about herself and afraid that she would fail. When she did not do as well as she would have liked in school, she tended to feel grumpy and down. Sometimes kids her age would make fun of her. She did not know how to deal with this and often felt very hurt. She got a reputation as a crybaby. Although attractive, as a teen she did not date because of her lack of self-confidence.

Alice did not complain about being sad and caused no trouble in school. The problems her parents and teachers noticed—her occasional moodiness, irritability, and sensitivity, for instance—they ascribed to her personality. "That's just the way she is," they would say.

Parents and teachers cannot really be blamed for overlooking these early signs of depression. Often they are quite subtle and not easily distinguished from the normal problems of childhood. Most parents are not even aware that children can suffer from depressive illness. In fact, only in recent years have the experts come to realize that children can suffer from depression.

Alice's anxiety about not doing well in school made her avoid the more academically challenging courses. Her anxiety really got in her way when she had to take standardized tests. Test scores did not reflect her true ability. Her mediocre test scores made her feel even worse about herself. She did not try out for athletic teams or become involved in more challenging extracurricular activities. Although she was a good flute player and played in the school band, she avoided playing solos because she was afraid she might not do well. The few friends Alice made were clearly not as bright or talented as she. She felt more competent that way. Although she felt sad and lonely when alone, she preferred solitary activities to those with her friends.

A depressed kid is generally a cautious kid. Shaky self-esteem naturally leads a youngster to avoid social, physical, and intellectual challenges.

It was not until Alice went away to college that she had her first episode of major depression. The change in environment, the social pressures, and the intense academic competition were unsettling for her. "In high school, I was a big fish in a little lake academically. The people I hung out with could not do as well as I did. In college," she says, "everyone was smart and I felt kind of slow." Alice also noticed that everyone seemed to be dating. She was shy and had very poorly developed social skills, so the young men on campus did not pay much attention to her. This made her feel even worse about herself. When a boy who had a passing interest in her did not continue pursuing her (he felt she was kind of grumpy and not much fun), she felt crushed. Her self-confidence and self-esteem plummeted.

Transition points in people's lives often precipitate a mood disorder. The transition from adolescence to young adulthood can be especially stressful. The person has to take on major new responsibilities and challenges. Other major life transitions that can be associated with mood disorders include having children, job loss or career disappointments, divorce, and retirement.

Loss of a relationship is a common trigger for an episode of depression, especially in women.

Alice began to drink. She began thinking life might not be worth living. She overslept yet felt tired during the day. She had a difficult time motivating herself to do her schoolwork. She noticed that she could not concentrate on her reading assignments. Her grades dropped. She overate and gained some weight, but she managed to keep going.

None of Alice's friends suspected that she had developed a depressive illness. They figured she was just upset about the relationship that did not work out. When she spoke to her mother and mentioned how lousy she was feeling, her mother became concerned but did not realize her daughter was ill. She did not see the connection between her own symptoms and her daughter's. She did feel guilty and ashamed, however, thinking she was responsible for her daughter's pain.

A friend told Alice about the college mental-health center and suggested it might help to talk to someone. Although nervous about it, Alice called for an appointment. The therapist she spoke to was kind and seemed to understand what she was going through. She asked about Alice's family. Alice felt somewhat uncomfortable talking about her mother and father. She felt as if she were betraying them. Her mother had always taught her to keep the family's business to herself. When the therapist discovered Alice's father was an alcoholic, she pointed out that it was an unwritten rule in alcoholic families to keep painful feelings inside.

Alice felt quite a bit of relief after speaking to the therapist. But the gloom settled over her again in several hours. In later sessions, the therapist talked about how Alice's being so disappointed in herself both academically and socially was related to having grown up with a mom who was hard to please and a dad who, when he was drinking, was impossible to please. The boyfriend who rejected her brought all this up again for her.

Although the therapist inquired about thoughts of suicide, she did not ask Alice about other symptoms of depression. She also did not inquire in more depth about a family history of mood disorder.

This therapist's training emphasized psychological models for understanding people's problems. She saw Alice's depression as understandable in light of having grown up with an alcoholic father and a depressive mother. This kind of an early environment certainly did nothing to protect Alice from a probable inherited vulnerability to depression. In fact, the stress of the early environment may well have triggered the onset of her dysthymia in childhood. But there is no research evidence to suggest that growing up in an alcoholic household will by itself cause depressive illness, even though it may lead to feelings of depression.

It is often possible to discern connections between early life experiences and adult problems. But this does not prove that the early life experiences are the cause of the adult problems. More important, it does not mean that exploring early traumas and losses will resolve clinical depression.

Alice's depressive episode gradually diminished in intensity during the remainder of her freshman year and the first part of her sophomore year in college. Her natural intellectual curiosity and desire to learn returned. Her mood improved, and she felt more confident about herself. She began to date and discovered with some surprise that boys were attracted to her. This boosted her self-esteem.

It is impossible to say what factors might actually have caused Alice's depression to get better. Therapy probably played a part in her recovery. But it is also possible that the depression had simply run its course.

Alice graduated from college with good grades. She went on to graduate studies in English. She was not troubled by depression for her last two years in college and while in graduate school. After finishing graduate school, she got a job as a grade-school teacher. Early on, she became rather critical of the teaching methods used by her colleagues. She did not do well with the suggestions her supervisors and colleagues gave her. She reacted defensively by pointing out how they, too, were making mistakes. Relations with her colleagues grew tense. She began to grow impatient with her students. She also began to feel overly responsible for how well they did. She began to question her ability to be a teacher. She felt like a fraud. Her motivation to teach waned and reviews of her teaching grew increasingly critical. As her dissatisfaction mounted, she began to wonder if she had made the right career choice.

Alice had met a man in graduate school, Roger, whom she later married. Although both Alice and her husband were intelligent and caring people who genuinely enjoyed each other's company, they had a lot of arguments in the first several years of their relationship. Little things that Roger did or forgot to do irritated Alice. She let him know it. Being rather sensitive himself and prone to feeling guilty, Roger had a hard time understanding what was wrong. He began to snap back at her.

Alice became increasingly preoccupied with what was wrong with her life. She complained that she was overwhelmed by the demands of work and home and that she needed Roger to help more. Roger soon began to feel that nothing he did was good enough. He resented her constant whining about how tough life was. From what he could see, she actually had it pretty good. He pointed out that she worked in a good school district, was well paid, and got the whole summer off. What was there to be overwhelmed about? If she hated her job so much and felt it was so stressful, why not just quit and do something else? He also said that he was getting tired of having her come home and go to bed so early. They had little social life and virtually no sex life anymore.

Neither Alice, her husband, nor her colleagues thought she might be suffering from a depressive illness. Alice figured that if her husband and colleagues did things the right way, she would not be in such a bad mood. After awhile, though, she started to wonder if she was just a nasty person. She tried hard to be friendly and personable, but her short fuse and increasing irritability kept getting in the way. Her husband concluded he had married a bitchy woman. Her colleagues diagnosed Alice as a snob and a know-it-all.

CYCLOTHYMIA

Cyclothymia is a type of bipolar disorder characterized by periods of mild hypomania (cheerfulness, talkativeness, decreased need for sleep) alternating or mixing with mild or low-level symptoms of depression (gloominess, withdrawal, lack of energy, increased need for sleep). Irritability and, in some cases, explosive temper outbursts may occur. Only 15 percent of patients with mild forms of bipolar disorder such as cyclothymia have clear family histories of bipolar illness. Many of those with cyclothymia will, however, have multiple-generation family histories of relatives with a variety of mood symptoms. Relatives are often described as irritable and critical. A family history of bad tempers appears to be common as well. Cyclothymia often begins in childhood or adolescence with depressive episodes. The mood switches in cyclothymia are sudden and often seem to come out of the blue. Up to half of people with cyclothymia will develop more serious forms of bipolar disorder with wider and more debilitating mood swings.

The symptom pattern seen in cyclothymia, as described by psychiatrist Hagop Akiskal and colleagues in the professional journal *Psychiatric Clinics of North America* (volume 2, 1978), is alternating patterns of:

- Oversleeping vs. decreased need for sleep
- Withdrawal vs. sociability
- Being taciturn vs. being talkative
- Unexplained tears vs. laughter or joking
- Lethargy or lack of motivation vs. increased energy or productivity
- Dulling of thinking processes vs. clarity of thought or creativity
- Low self-confidence and neediness vs. overconfidence and arrogance
- Worry vs. feeling carefree

Mood instability along with the impulsiveness and poor judgment of the hypomanic phases of the illness often leads cyclothymic disorder to be mistaken for an unpredictable and unstable personality. Dr. Akiskal and colleagues have observed that cyclothymic individuals frequently have the following characteristics:

- Difficulty sustaining interest in and completing activities and plans; frequent shifts in interests; restless; easily bored
- Uneven work performance; unusual work hours
- Multiple job or career changes
- Promiscuous

• Stormy relationships with many breakups; multiple marriages
• A history of drug or alcohol abuse

John is a fifty-three-year-old salesman who is married with one child from a previous marriage and two from his current marriage.

John has been working for his current employer for eight months. For periods of time, John can feel excited by his job and certain he is one of his company's best sales representatives. He comes across as cheerful and self-confident. Sometimes, however, he gets on everyone's nerves with his know-it-all attitude. His cheerfulness can quickly turn to impatience and irritability if someone frustrates him or is demanding and hard to please. There are times when he feels bored, uncertain of his abilities, and thinks he might like to work for a different company. He has worked for six different companies in the last eight years.

His irritability and temper outbursts have been a problem at home as well. His first wife filed for divorce after being subjected to several years of criticism, complaining, and verbal abuse. Occasionally he would lose control of his temper and would threaten his wife. He grabbed her hard enough on one occasion to leave bruises on her arms. He had several affairs while with his first wife and currently has a girlfriend he sees from time to time. He drinks only occasionally, but at times he drinks to the point of intoxication.

His current wife, having grown up with an abusive alcoholic father and being inclined to feel excessively guilty and depressed, tolerates his irritability without much fight. Her feelings for him have withered over the years. John has noticed this, but always blames it on her being a cold person. Although he has expressed regret for having lost his temper with his wife, it always happens again. At times it just erupts over seemingly inconsequential things. For instance, he has lost patience with his wife for not flattening cardboard cereal boxes before putting them in the recycling pile and for leaving lights on when he has told her "a million times" to turn them off before leaving the room. He sometimes feels embarrassed after these outbursts but generally tends to rationalize his behavior as being understandable given how "stupid" his wife has been.

He went to a therapist at the insistence of his first wife. Although initial sessions went well, John's irritability kept creating problems in the marriage. The therapist surmised that his perfectionism and drive for success were unconsciously designed to win his father's love. John made great demands on himself and was tortured by his inability to please his inner parent. The therapist felt that John was hard on others in direct proportion to how hard he was on himself.

The therapist conceptualized John's problems in purely psychological terms. The therapist knew well enough what major depression was and that it was a disorder needing medical attention. But since John had no serious symptoms of depression such as waking up early in the morning, he did not consider the possibility that John had a mood disorder. He ascribed John's problems to personality difficulties.

The counseling seemed to get bogged down after three or four months. John's irritability waxed and waned. The therapist was a bit confused by this. Just when it seemed that John was beginning to feel more satisfied with his marriage and had learned some ways to deal with his anger more appropriately, he would suddenly become bitter, resentful, critical, and emotionally volatile. The therapist would confront him with how destructive this behavior was and urge him to redouble his efforts to learn the tools to manage it. At times John felt as if the counseling was helping him a lot. He praised the therapist's skill. But at other times, he would voice his impatience and say he was losing hope that counseling could help him. He wondered if the therapist was on the right track.

After another temper outburst, the therapist insisted John get involved in group treatment for men who have problems controlling their tempers. John initially refused, but after losing his temper yet again, he felt so ashamed that he agreed to go. He went to the group for sixteen weeks. He found it useful but still had periods where he got very irritable with his wife. He did not grab his wife in anger while he was in the program. He seemed to have learned to walk away. His wife was becoming more assertive with the help of counseling. About a month after the men's group ended, John's wife told him she was going out with some friends that night. He said that he had other plans and she could not go. She insisted, and when she started to leave their home, he pushed her out the door and told her not to come back.

Then John lost his temper and got into a shouting match with a customer. His sales manager called him in for a meeting to discuss the incident and his uneven performance. John explained his behavior by saying that he was under a lot of stress because of his marriage problems. His boss was sympathetic but insisted that John had to get his act together. He asked John if he had ever thought about getting any professional help. When John answered that he had been going to marital counseling for a while, the sales manager suggested that maybe the counseling was not working. He recommended that John get another opinion from the counselor who had recently been hired through the company's employee assistance program (EAP).

John was alternately denying his problem and feeling terribly guilty and ashamed that he could not get a handle on it. On this particular day, he was rather desperate and appreciated his sales manager's concern, so he agreed to see the EAP counselor. The counselor asked a lot of questions about John's drinking and about his experiences growing up in an alcoholic household. He got John to talk about some of the emptiness and loneliness he felt inside. John cried during the first session and felt relieved.

He went home that night feeling better and feeling somewhat closer to his wife. When he walked in the door, however, he could not help but notice that his wife had left the kitchen a mess after dinner and had left lights on all around the house. His good mood suddenly changed to one of irritation. He noticed this and decided to sit on his irritation and not say anything. But the annoyance just about dripped out of his pores. His wife could tell he was irritated and asked him what was wrong. John said he did not want to talk about it. His wife pressed him. This irritated him further. Finally, he let her know that he was in a good mood coming home but that she had ruined it by the mess in which she had left the place. No longer willing to take this kind of criticism from her husband, she counter-attacked by pointing out that lately he had not exactly been doing a lot around the house. A rather nasty argument ensued. John stormed out of the house. He went to a local bar and had several drinks before returning home.

John discussed all this in the next meeting with the employee counselor. The counselor suggested that John's problems really lay in his alcohol abuse and the character defects that went along with it. He said that John needed to stop drinking and attend Alcoholics Anonymous meetings. John was shocked and argued with the counselor about his assessment. Since John was under no mandate to follow the EAP counselor's recommendations, he refused to go to AA and stopped seeing the counselor. John seemed to do quite a bit better for a while. He came out of his slump and impressed his sales manager with how well he was doing. "The EAP," he thought, "must have really done him some good." But a few months later, John lost his temper with a customer again. This time his boss was less understanding. He insisted that John receive further EAP counseling and follow whatever advice he was given.

John decided to go ahead and give AA a try. He managed to stop drinking for several months, but his moodiness and irritability came and went. His sponsor urged him to work harder at looking at his character defects and to really work the program's twelve steps. Still, his irritability persisted.

While John used alcohol inappropriately as a coping tool, it was not the cause of his problems. The EAP counselor put the cart before the horse. The fundamental problem was John's mood instability. It is certainly not the case that alcohol abuse is always secondary to a mood disorder. Even if it is, it can become a problem in its own right that needs attention as much as the mood disorder.

John, during one of his depressive episodes, saw his doctor because he was feeling restless and edgy. His doctor did a complete physical and blood tests. Everything appeared normal. His doctor gave him a prescription for tranquilizers.

This happens more often than you might believe. A minority of patients with symptoms of major depression are correctly diagnosed and properly treated by their family doctors.

John began to lose his temper more frequently while taking the tranquilizers.

Tranquilizers will do this on occasion. They produce what is referred to as disinhibition in some patients.

John's doctor then referred him to a psychiatrist. The psychiatrist put John on the antidepressant Prozac. John responded quickly. He soon said he was feeling better than he had in years. At the urging of his psychiatrist, John went back into individual therapy. He told his therapist that he was feeling quite well. He seemed happy and energetic. The therapist noted that John spoke rapidly and loudly in the sessions. He laughed a great deal.

In spite of the good mood he seemed to be in, however, John continued to mention irritable outbursts he had with his wife. John rationalized these as normal given his wife's irritating habits, but they seemed excessive to the therapist. The therapist suggested to John that he needed to view these outbursts as problems; they were hurting his wife and his relationship with her. The patient eventually agreed with his therapist and said he would attempt to suppress his anger. For the next few weeks, John was rather depressed. He stayed in bed all day one weekend and was again talking about how his sales work was getting boring. The psychiatrist increased the dosage of Prozac. A month or so later John was out of his depression but had had another temper outburst with his wife. He then told his therapist that he had stayed up for most of the night working on some sales strategies that he was sure would boost sales considerably. He said he just loved his work at times and could not get enough of it.

John had begun to cycle between highs and lows more often with more clearly pronounced hypomanic episodes. It is by no means uncommon for bipolar patients—even severely ill ones—to be treated with antidepressants first since they come for help only when depressed. Although some psychopharmacology experts say that this is not a problem for cyclothymic or bipolar II patients, others insist that any patient with bipolar symptoms should be started on a mood stabilizer first.

TEMPERAMENT, PERSONALITY, AND MOOD

Any mother or father with more than one child knows that babies are born with different temperaments or dispositions. One baby may be relaxed and easygoing and the next edgy and easily irritated. Although not fixed for all time and modifiable to some extent by environmental influences, temperament is a relatively constant and consistent influence on the growing child. It affects personality development, influences how parents and others feel about and react to the baby, and is something to which the growing child must adapt.

If a child or an adult is excessively anxious, gloomy, impatient, and irritable, we can say that there is a temperament disorder. The symptoms and problems caused by this temperament disorder may not be severe enough to warrant a diagnosis of dysthymia or cyclothymia. But they can lead to interpersonal and other problems. Frequently, children with these temperament problems grow up in households with parents having similar temperament problems. Parents who are ill-tempered, explosive, or anxiety ridden can severely tax the limited coping abilities of a temperamentally vulnerable child.

Until recently, mental health professionals virtually ignored how temperament contributes to patients' personalities and interpersonal difficulties. Instead, they have focused their attention almost exclusively on how early relationships with parents and learned habits of thinking and behavior shaped their patients personality and emotional problems.

In 1921, Emil Kraepelin, a German psychiatrist, described what he referred to as four "fundamental states" of mood or temperament: depressive, manic, irritable, and cyclothymic. Kraepelin's depressive temperament is similar to the modern concept of dysthymic disorder, while his manic temperament corresponds to individuals who would currently be considered to have hypomanic or milder states.

An interesting variation of Kraeplin's manic temperament is the hyperthymic temperament. Hyperthymic individuals are blessed with a persistent "up" mood. They do not cycle into depressed moods. They often become highly successful sales people and entrepreneurs. They are attractive people, are fun to be around, and can infuse others with a sense of energy and mission. Our culture places a high value on these traits. The hyperthymic's enthusiasm can be wearing, however, and at times they turn others off with their brash self-confidence and strong opinions. Although friendly, they may get easily irritated when frustrated or if they feel you are standing in their way. Following are some characteristics of individuals with hyperthymia, according to Dr. Akiskal and colleagues:

- Cheerful and exuberant
- Talkative, articulate, and witty
- Overly optimistic and carefree
- Overly confident, boastful, and grandiose

- Extroverted, charming, engaging
- Energetic, full of plans (some of which may impress others as risky or far-fetched)
- Broad range of interests
- Unihibited or promiscuous
- Habitual short sleeper (six hours or less a night)

People with hyperthymia rarely seek help. Why would they when they feel so good? In middle age, however, people with hyperthymia sometimes do begin to experience depression. They may then seek psychotherapy.

Kraepelin observed that individuals with major depressions and manic episodes (he referred to them as "attacks") often displayed one of the four fundamental states *between* episodes. He believed that full-blown depression and mania arose out of these fundamental states and that these seemingly "permanent personality peculiarities" are actually subtle manifestations of mood disorder.

Dr. Akiskal and others have garnered an increasing amount of evidence that the "personality peculiarities" of many patients who today seek psychotherapy are, as Kraepelin suspected, intimately related to depression and mild forms of bipolar illness. Moodiness, excessive worry, a tendency to be critical and complaining, irritability, impulsiveness, promiscuity, explosive anger, and interpersonal problems are all symptoms that can stem from a temperament disorder. Patients with these temperament disorders are common in alcohol and drug treatment settings, as well. There is a growing realization, however, that these fundamental mood states are in many cases difficult if not impossible to modify with psychotherapy alone.

Akiskal has also gathered evidence to support another observation Kraepelin made: Given sufficient stress, individuals with disorders of temperament are particularly vulnerable to full-blown episodes of depression and manic-depressive illness. Patients suffering from depression and manic-depressive illness can often recall subtle manifestations of their illness going back as far as early childhood.

CHAPTER 3

MAJOR DEPRESSION, BIPOLAR I DISORDER (MANIC-DEPRESSION), AND BIPOLAR II DISORDER

MAJOR DEPRESSION

Look over the following list of symptoms of major depression:

- Depressed mood
- Loss of interest in previously enjoyable activities
- Feelings of worthlessness or excessive guilt
- Loss of appetite, an increase in eating, especially carbohydrates and sweets, or weight loss/weight gain
- Trouble staying asleep, waking up early in the morning and being unable to get back to sleep, or oversleeping
- Restlessness or sluggishness (when feeling sluggish, the person may actually move and talk more slowly; the face will be much less expressive—as if the person is wearing a mask)
- Fatigue and loss of energy
- Inability to think clearly, concentrate, or make decisions
- Thoughts of death or suicide

Have you had the first or second symptom and five or more of the rest for more than two weeks? If so, and you do not abuse alcohol or drugs and have been found to otherwise be in good health (a doctor has determined that no known medical illness is causing these symptoms), then it is likely you are suffering from a major depressive episode. If you are having trouble working, parenting, or doing schoolwork, you may well have a severe depression. Do you have the first or second symptom and between one and four of the rest? If so, you may have a mild to moderate major depression.

Be careful about letting your mind dismiss the symptoms as a normal response to current problems in your life. It is certainly normal to feel depressed when things are not going well, but it is not normal or necessary to suffer from these symptoms, even if things are terribly wrong. Keep in mind that even if current problems clearly triggered these symptoms (e.g., you are going through a divorce), the depressive illness may well have taken on a life of its own and may require treatment.

The following vignette represents one way in which a major depression may develop and describes the symptoms a sufferer may experience.

If your symptoms are not the same as those found in this or other case examples, do not be too quick to conclude that you do not have a mood disorder. Lists or even detailed descriptions of your symptoms may not fully capture your individual experience.

George, a married, thirty-five-year-old computer programmer with two children, has been going through a rough time at his job. His dad is dying of terminal cancer. He has been feeling down for weeks. He has not thought much of it, since he has been under a lot of stress. He figures he will snap out of it.

But as the weeks pass, he feels worse. First the gloom begins to envelop more of the day. He used to be able to put it out of his mind for awhile by watching TV or reading. But now George finds that the gloom is not as easy to get rid of.

He starts to feel confused and unsure about his work. He spends a lot of time redoing things. Then work begins to get boring, even though he has usually enjoyed programming. George finds himself—more days than not—not wanting to go to work.

If you are temporarily sad or blue because something has gone wrong in your life, you will normally be able to get relief by burying yourself in work or by forcing yourself to do things to take your mind off your problems. But as normal sadness passes over into depression, the lousy moods may become more pervasive and less responsive to your efforts to distract yourself.

At this point, you might begin to realize something is wrong. You begin to search for explanations for your problems and may try various self-help measures.

> George thinks he may need a vacation. He takes a week off but has a hard time enjoying himself. Sitting down and reading a book no longer seems as enjoyable as it has in the past. Besides, he feels a little restless and finds himself rereading parts of his book. For some reason he cannot recall what he has been reading. Well, he thinks, maybe it's not as great a book as my friend told me it was.

George's loss of enjoyment in previously pleasurable activities is referred to as hypohedonia. Agitation and anxiety are common in depression. Sixty percent of depressed patients have significant problems with anxiety. Intense anxiety increases the risk of suicide. Depression also affects your brain's ability to process information. Many people develop problems with memory and concentration.

> Back at work, he briefly thinks he might be getting out of his slump. He notices he is not feeling down. But he then realizes that he is not feeling like his normal self, either. In fact, he feels kind of numb or dead, except maybe for the restlessness and waves of anxiety that hit him periodically. He becomes increasingly unmotivated to do his work.

As depression deepens, hypohedonia may give way to anhedonia, a complete loss of interest in things that were previously enjoyable. In an effort to explain this lack of interest, you may begin to question whether you have chosen the right path in life. If you have been working at the same career for many years, you may wonder if you are getting burned out.

He tells himself that maybe he should have become an engineer. Hadn't a part of him always wanted to go into engineering? Life, he thinks, seems to be getting kind of pointless. People at work begin to remark that he looks tired and tense. But they just pass it off as the type of anxiety that a lot of people are having over the company restructuring. At home, his wife notices that he is not eating as much as he used to. She assumes that he is finally sticking to his diet. He begins to lose weight. His friends and family compliment him because he has always had trouble keeping off those extra pounds.

Depression's effects on your mood, thoughts, and behavior are often not seen by others as telltale signs of a developing illness. Symptoms of illness are often assumed to be normal reactions to what you are going through. If the intensity or duration of your problems seem to go beyond the norm, others will often draw the wrong conclusions. They will assume that you are *letting* yourself get too caught up in whatever is troubling you. You may be urged to "forget about it and just get on with your life." You may be chided for not being able to "let go of the past." If only you could.

The truth is, if you are severely depressed, it is often difficult if not impossible to get problems off your mind. If you try, you may well fail and will then feel guilty, ashamed, and even more depressed.

Consider this: If you broke your leg, would you beat yourself up for not being able to walk on it right after you broke it? Would you think yourself weak? Would you think there is something wrong with you as a person? Trying to force yourself to "get on with your life" and failing when you are severely depressed is no more a reflection of you as a person than is your inability to walk on a broken leg.

Friends tell George that he should take some extra vitamins, exercise, or take classes. He tries to exercise but then gets upset with himself because he does not have the energy to stick with it. He becomes increasingly irritable with his wife and children. He and his wife begin fighting more. He does not feel close to his wife and children. Maybe, he thinks, I do not love my wife anymore. Maybe this is what they mean by a midlife crisis, he tells himself. He feels both resentment for being trapped and guilt for being a horrible husband and father.

A lack of warm, loving feelings toward family and friends is a symptom of depression, as is irritability. You may feel that you want to be left alone. This symptom often contributes to a deepening spiral of depression because you end up feeling so guilt-ridden.

George starts to think his family might be better off without him. He does not see a way out of his problems. His sleep is really terrible now. He can fall asleep okay because he is exhausted by the end of the day. But he wakes up after an hour or two and is not able to go back to sleep for a couple of hours. He sometimes wakes up at four in the morning and is not able to get back to sleep at all. He is smoking a lot more and begins to drink more frequently, too.

Hopelessness and helplessness are routine in severe depression. In severe depression, you will either have a number of middle-of-the-night awakenings or awaken early in the morning. Sometimes you may not sleep at all.

If you smoke, you will probably find yourself doing more of it. You may begin drinking more heavily, even if you have not had a history of alcohol abuse. Alcohol and drug abuse can also cause depression, either directly, through biochemical changes, or indirectly, through problems your use will create for you. This kind of depression most often clears up once you stop drinking. If you are in recovery from alcohol or drug abuse and you still feel depressed after two to four weeks of abstinence, you should get an evaluation for clinical depression.

> At work, George feels as if he is getting senile. He cannot keep his mind on his work. He finds himself completely forgetting important assignments. He feels as if his mind is in slow motion. His grandfather had Alzheimer's disease. Could he be getting that already? His supervisor is beginning to get frustrated and impatient with him.

Depression can lead to what is referred to as "pseudodementia." It is a scary experience resembling the cognitive difficulties some elderly people get with senile dementia or Alzheimer's disease. Unlike true dementia, however, depressive pseudodementia is fully reversible with proper treatment.

Variations in the Severity of Depression

Major depressive episodes are rated by mental-health professionals as mild, moderate, or severe. The rating depends on the kind and number of symptoms, the extent and severity of suicidal thoughts or urges, and by the degree to which the depression disrupts your functioning.

Variations in the Main Symptoms of Depression

Melancholic Depression   This is a severe form of depression characterized by a profound loss of pleasure in all or almost all activities and at least three of the following: awakening at least two hours earlier than usual, extreme agitation or loss of energy, loss of appetite or significant weight loss, excessive guilt and the feeling that your depression is worse in the morning.

Depression with Catatonic Features   Patients with catatonic depression may appear immobile, rigid, or in a trance. They may make peculiar repetitive movements like grimacing or adopt odd postures. They may repeat other people's words or imitate their body movements.

Double Depression   Some patients develop a major depressive episode after a long period of low-grade chronic depression. It is not clear if this reflects the imposition of a new illness on top of an old one or merely the worsening of chronic, low-grade depression.

Agitated Depression   The agitated patient is restless and cannot sit still. Some clinicians believe that this is a more severe form of depression with anxiety features. Others believe that patients with prominent agitation actually have a so-called "mixed mood disorder" with both bipolar and unipolar features.

Atypical Depression and Bipolar Depression   The symptoms described as characteristic of depression represent only one particular kind of depression. Some individuals with so-called atypical depressions (which are actually very common) have some symptoms that are the reverse of the ones described above. Instead of being unable to sleep, patients with atypical depression sleep too much and have a hard time getting out of bed. Rather than losing their appetite and weight, their appetite increases (particularly for sweets and carbohydrates), and they gain weight. They usually feel fatigued and lethargic and may suffer from a feeling of being weighted down (so-called "leaden paralysis"). Patients with atypical depression may also complain of anxiety and suffer from phobias.

The typical depressive, especially when the depression is severe, will not feel better if good things happen. In contrast, a primary feature of atypical depression is so-called "mood reactivity." The atypical patient will temporarily feel better when good things happen, especially if she is loved or admired. The patient may flourish with the attention of others and may not seem the least bit depressed. In fact, she may feel a bit high. Because of this, clinicians unfamiliar with the condition will fail to recognize it as a mood disorder. Unfortunately, the periods of normal mood are not stable, and when criticized or rejected, those suffering from atypical depression will feel devastated and quickly relapse.

The person with pronounced rejection sensitivity often runs into a great deal of interpersonal difficulty. He overreacts to perceived slights with bitter disappointment and anger. The anger may only be expressed indirectly, through sullen withdrawal. All of this tends to drive others away, thereby contributing to the very rejection he dreads.

Atypical depression symptoms usually have an earlier age of onset. Although they can be less debilitating in the short run than a typical major depression, the chronicity of the symptoms may lead to worse overall psychosocial adjustment. A person with atypical symptoms may still experience episodes of more typical, severe major depression.

Bipolar depression refers to the depressive phase of manic-depressive illness. The symptoms of bipolar depression are often atypical. The person suffering from a bipolar depression is often very slowed down, lethargic, fatigued, and unmotivated. She may sleep twelve to fourteen hours a day and still not feel rested.

It is important for a doctor to determine whether you have symptoms of atypical, unipolar, or bipolar depression. Critical decisions about which medications to use hinge on the diagnosis.

Psychotic Depression   A depressed individual can become ill enough to lose touch with reality. He can develop hallucinations—hearing voices saying that he deserves to die or seeing people or animals that are not really there. Delusions—false beliefs—such as the belief that his body is rotting can also develop. Sometimes the psychotic features are subtle and not easily detected without careful questioning.

These patients are at higher risk for suicide than are those without psychosis. They may be misdiagnosed as schizophrenic.

Schizoaffective Illness   Schizoaffective illness is a term used to describe patients with a mixture of schizophrenic and mood-disorder symptoms, which makes them hard to place in one category or another.

Current thinking is that this group of patients is probably best thought of as mood disordered. Patients with depressive symptoms should be treated with antidepressants. Manic symptoms should be treated with mood stabilizers. Psychotic symptoms, even subtle ones, and particularly ones that persist beyond resolution of manic or depressive symptoms, should be treated with antipsychotics.

The atypical antipsychotic medications, such as clozapine/ Clozaril and risperidone/Risperdal, appear to be useful in treating these patients.

Pseudounipolar Depression and Recurrent Depression   Clinicians suspect pseudounipolar depression when depressed patients without current or past hypomania have certain features seen more typically in patients with bipolar illness. These include (a) early onset of illness, (b) many episodes of depression, (c) atypical symptoms, such as overeating, weight gain, oversleeping, and lethargy, and (d) relatives with hypomanic symptoms or frank bipolar illness.

Patients who have recurrent depressive episodes in spite of ongoing antidepressant treatment or those with treatment-resistant depression that once responded well to antidepressants may also be suspected of having a bipolar illness.

The danger in misdiagnosing these patients as unipolar is the possibility of producing hypomanic episodes and rapid cycling if they are treated with antidepressants.

Masked Depression   The symptoms and behavioral problems listed below have sometimes been referred to as masked depression. They do not look like depression but are hypothesized to be related disorders. Some of these problems may crop up at times when you might expect a person to become depressed. Masked depression may respond to antidepressant medication.

1. Chronic aches and pains.
2. Compulsive social activities: partygoing, dating, avoidance of being alone, workaholism, and thrill seeking. These are all behaviors designed to keep someone from feeling depressed.
3. Impulse-control problems: rage attacks, sexual compulsions, shoplifting, and gambling.
4. Repeated accidents.
5. Multiple surgeries for vague complaints.

Variations In Time of Onset of Depression

Postpartum Depression (PPD)   Roughly half of mothers experience "baby blues" after delivery. The mother's mood is typically labile or changeable. The mother retains the ability to experience pleasure. She does not have suicidal thoughts, and does not usually have thoughts of harming the baby. Self-esteem is not usually affected. The baby blues can occur even if the mother is in a stable marriage with a supportive husband. Moodiness peaks around four days after childbirth and then subsides within a few weeks at most.

PPD is a major depressive episode that begins three to six months after delivery. It occurs in about one in ten mothers. It may last months or years. Women with a prior history of mood disorder are at greater risk of getting depressed after the birth of a baby than are women without such a history. The symptom picture is more like that seen in other depressive episodes: Mood is usually depressed and not labile; there is a loss of the ability to experience pleasure; sleep is disrupted; the mother feels inadequate and guilt-ridden, may have thoughts of suicide, and frequently has thoughts of harming the baby.

Lack of support from the husband or other family members or significant family conflicts increase the likelihood of PPD.

Untreated postpartum depression may increase the risk for subsequent episodes of depression.

Treatment for PPD is similar to that for other depressions.

Women with manic symptoms or mixtures of manic and depressive symptoms or pronounced irritability can be treated with divalproex/Depakote.

Couples' counseling and interpersonal psychotherapy may also be of use in PPD.

Women with PPD may wish to join a support group with other women (see the appendix for resources).

Seasonal Affective Disorder (SAD)   SAD has been included in official psychiatric diagnostic criteria just since 1987, but seasonal variations in mood disorders have been recognized for centuries. The most intensely studied form is winter SAD. In this form, patients will begin to show symptoms of atypical depression in October or November (in the northern hemisphere). Their mood is depressed, and they become lethargic with a tendency to oversleep, overeat (craving of sweets and carbohydrates is common), and gain weight. They may become quite dysfunctional and have suicidal thoughts. By March or April, they begin to feel better and may become somewhat hypomanic in the summer. Summer SAD (summer depression, winter hypomania) does exist but is perhaps only one-fifth as prevalent as winter SAD. The summer depressions apparently show more typical features of depression: difficulty sleeping and loss of appetite and weight, for example.

This pattern emerges for most patients in their twenties and thirties and occurs more frequently at higher latitudes (closer to the poles of the planet). Over half of these patients have close relatives with major mood disorders. Some patients with SAD have a mild form of bipolar illness.

Many patients with SAD also complain that they feel worse during periods of cloudy and dreary weather or if they are stuck inside at any time of the year.

Perhaps half or more patients with SAD respond to treatment with bright light therapy (see chap. 10).

Premenstrual Dysphoric Disorder (PMDD)   Although somewhat controversial as a diagnosis, some 5 percent of women experience marked distress, interference in relationships, and impairment of their ability to function in the week or two prior to menstruation. Emotional symptoms include extreme moodiness, tension, and irritability.

The cause of PMDD is not clearly understood, but it is not simply due to excess or deficiency of hormones. Fortunately, effective treatments are available. The most effective are suppression of ovulation (although this may be associated with long-term risks) and the SSRI medications Prozac, Zoloft, and Paxil. The effectiveness of these medications does not appear to be due to their antidepressant effect. The medications work almost immediately in PMDD, whereas in depression they take several weeks.

Other treatments seem to work well for a number of women with less severe symptoms (referred to as premenstrual syndrome, or PMS), including diet, exercise, and cognitive-behavioral therapy. Vitamin B_6 at doses between 50 and 150 milligrams per day may also be useful, as well as magnesium supplements, tryptophan supplements (6 grams per day), evening primrose oil, and prescription diuretics when bloating and irritability are a problem. Oral contraceptives do not appear to be effective and may even contribute to depression.

Menopausal Depression   Also referred to as involutional melancholia, this diagnosis has been discarded. Menopause does not automatically mean a woman will become depressed. However, women as a group do experience an increased incidence of depression in the premenopausal years. Estrogen levels begin to decline during these years.

Some menopausal women who have had only a partial response to an antidepressant respond fully when they take supplemental estrogen. Very high doses of estrogen may help a woman with depression that has not responded to other treatments.

The incidence of depression in women as a group declines after menopause.

VINCENT VAN GOGH

Many of humankind's greatest artists, writers, and composers have suffered from depressive or manic-depressive illness. Do the illnesses lead individuals to become creative? The jury is still out, since good scientific evidence is lacking. Creative individuals often report, however, that their mood disorder can be a source of inspiration, as well as misery.

Vincent Van Gogh was born and died on March 30, 1852. Exactly one year later, on March 30, 1853, another boy was born to the Van Goghs. They also named him Vincent, and in his early years he grew up around the corner from his dead brother's grave.

Vincent's family was a hardworking, middle-class Dutch family that was plagued with depression and manic depression. His younger brother Theo suffered from recurrent depressions. His sister Wilhelmina suffered from a chronic psychotic illness. And their youngest brother, Cornelius, died at the age of thirty-three; an acquaintance said he committed suicide.

According to biographies of Van Gogh, Vincent had a gloomy, sterile childhood. He suspected that his chronic melancholy had its roots in his family history. But he also believed in the value of suffering and sorrow. A deeply religious man, he felt that he learned from it.

He also felt that it fired his creativity. He worked constantly and frenetically at his art, as a way of avoiding his own melancholy. Over his lifetime, Vincent produced hundreds of paintings and drawings. Once, in an art class in Antwerp, he painted so feverishly that the other students in his class were stunned. Some critics have said that his use of vivid colors and bold strokes was a way of brightening the darkness within, his way of triumphing over his own manic depression.

His manic periods alternated with depressions. Although he longed for sympathy from others, his own behavior often repelled those he wished to attract. He would fly into a rage over a perceived insult. Vincent's brother Theo was his steadfast ally throughout his life, supporting him financially and emotionally. But for Vincent, it was never enough, and he would accuse his brother of being cruel.

His relationships with women were fraught with disaster; rarely did they return his affection. And although his own correspondence reveals no loving references to his own mother, he was the one who nursed her back to health after she hurt her hip. The suffering of others always aroused Vincent's compassion.

Suffering was a theme of his art. One of his earliest paintings, *Bearers of the Burden*, depicts a procession of women, each carrying a heavy sack of coal on her bent back. Darkness and light, earth and heaven, and death and rebirth were other themes of his work.

Vincent was preoccupied with death. He gravitated toward cemeteries and felt an affinity for ghosts. Fellow artist Paul Gauguin, with whom Vincent had a troubled friendship, said Vincent called himself a ghost before he mutilated his ear in 1888. It was Christmas Eve, and Vincent was agitated. He cut off a piece of his ear and brought it to a prostitute in a brothel. A policeman arrived, and Vincent was hospitalized. A local newspaper reported the incident, saying it had been committed by "an unfortunate maniac."

It was not the first time that Vincent hurt himself. Early in his childhood, he had exhibited a masochistic streak. He saw himself as an ugly, unloved outsider. Identifying with the crucified Jesus Christ, he ate sparingly and often dressed in rags. He often had stomach trouble and suffered from a loss of appetite, headaches, and dizzy spells. After his hospitalization for cutting off his ear, Vincent improved and started eating voraciously.

But the recovery was brief. He continued to have "attacks," in which people seemed to be at a distance and voices seemed to be coming from far away. He would become violent and rageful. He tried to commit suicide several times.

In 1890, he succeeded. Theo was having trouble raising funds for him and was at odds with his employers, who disapproved of his interest in the Impressionists. He was also trying to cope with a sick child and a serious illness of his own. Vincent was deeply worried about Theo and feared aging himself. He did not fear death, however, and he shot himself on a Sunday in the middle of the summer. Six months later, Theo died.

MANIC-DEPRESSIVE ILLNESS (BIPOLAR I DISORDER)

Manic-depressive illness, like depressive illness, has many causes. But it clearly has genetic underpinnings. Bipolar disorder is up to ten times more common in the immediate relatives of those affected than in the general population.

The age of onset of the illness has come down over the last few generations. According to psychiatrist Frederick Goodwin, there may be a number of reasons for this. They include genetic factors and the stress that vulnerable children and adolescents are placed under with divorce, single-parent homes, and increasingly frequent moves. Alcohol and drug use probably also play a role. Bipolar-disordered patients who use drugs or alcohol have an earlier age of onset of their illness than do those who do not use any drugs or alcohol. They may set off a vulnerability to bipolar disorder with their substance abuse.

Sixty percent of bipolar I patients meet criteria for alcohol or drug abuse. Forty percent of bipolar I patients are alcoholic or drug dependent. Alcohol is the most commonly abused drug in bipolar I patients. A study done in the 1970s showed that alcoholic bipolar patients have nearly twice the rate of suicide attempts as do nonalcoholic bipolar patients. Cocaine tends to be used more by patients with other forms of bipolar disorder.

The prognosis is poor for manic-depressive illness when substance abuse or dependence is not controlled. Substance abuse may increase the likelihood of the patient developing rapid-cycling bipolar illness. Especially in the alcoholic and drug-dependent group, the substance abuse should not be expected to clear up when the mood disorder is controlled. Even if alcohol and drug abuse were initially a response to mood problems, once the manic patient becomes addicted, he will need simultaneous treatment for both problems. Manic-depressive illness is nearly always recurrent. A person who has had a manic episode has a 90 percent chance of having another. Manic episodes that start suddenly appear to presage multiple episodes.

Manic-depressive illness is frequently precipitated by some sort of stress, but subsequent episodes may require less and less stress to set them off. Eventually, episodes of bipolar I disorder may occur spontaneously on a regular basis and be more difficult to control. For this reason, it is important to intervene in the illness early and aggressively.

Unfortunately, this is often difficult to do, partly because the manic patient denies the illness. Although a patient may accept treatment when he is depressed, the patient often stops taking medication when he feels well. Patients hate to lose the high. Younger people especially may have to go through a couple of episodes before they are ready to stick to treatment.

Another reason bipolar disorder tends not to be treated early on is because the initial signs of it in children and adolescents can easily be missed. The onset of bipolar disorder in children typically begins with symptoms such as irritability, temper outbursts, and conduct problems (see chap. 4). There tends to be an eight- to ten-year lag between the onset of symptoms and correct diagnosis. The typical bipolar patient may see three or four doctors or other mental- health professionals before the diagnosis is made. Women with bipolar disorder have three times as many depressive episodes as do men with bipolar disorder. Male bipolar patients tend to have more episodes with symptoms of mania. Following is a description of the main symptoms of the manic phase of bipolar I disorder:

- *Elevated, expansive, or irritable mood.* You have been feeling unusually "up," "high" or euphoric. Those closest to you may tell you your good cheer and expansive mood is excessive. It may be annoying others. You believe there is nothing wrong with the way you feel. In fact, to you, everything seems great. You think everyone else needs to improve their outlook. You may feel that they envy your good mood and are just trying to bring you down.

  Your mood may be irritable instead of up. Little things annoy you. You have a hard time being patient, especially if your efforts are frustrated. You are increasingly cynical and ill-humored. You may find yourself increasingly sensitive to sound. Others may say you are overly critical or complaining. You think you would not be so irritable if everyone would just get out of your way or do things the way you think are best.

- *Inflated self-esteem.* You feel unusually good about yourself. You believe your ideas, abilities, or plans for changing things are extraordinary or brilliant. You may feel that you are a special person with insights others fail to appreciate. You find yourself trying to convince others to consider your plans or ideas for

improving things. Others may say you think too highly of yourself or your plans. You think they are fools for dismissing you.

You may have an intense sense of physical or emotional
well-being. You may feel an exquisite sense of communion
with nature, mankind, or God. You may feel as if you have
a great deal in common with a famous person or group
of persons.

- *Decreased need for sleep.* You find that you are energetic and
  alert even though you are sleeping much less than you usually
  do. You may feel that you have so many exciting ideas and
  plans that sleep is a waste of time. Your family may express
  surprise or concern about the hours you are keeping. You may
  begin to feel restless, driven, and agitated.
- *More talkative than usual.* You talk a lot more, talk more
  quickly or more loudly than usual. You may feel pressured to
  keep talking or you may find yourself unable to stop talking
  when you should. You may make jokes at times others consider inappropriate. You may feel angry others do not want to
  hear you out. Others may say you talk too much or they
  "can't get a word in edgewise." They may describe you as ob-
  noxious or intrusive.
- *Racing thoughts.* You may notice your mouth cannot keep up
  with the flow of ideas in your head. You may feel that all issues, no matter how remotely related to your main point, are
  important to mention. Others may say you are "jumping all
  over the place."
- *Distractibility.* You find it hard to focus your attention. You
  are becoming increasingly distracted by things that should
  not grab your attention such as the faint ring of a distant
  telephone.
- *Increased sex drive.* You may feel a sexual tension that is nearly
  unbearable. Your partner may complain that you want too
  much sex. You think your partner is undersexed. You may be
  having sex indiscriminately or with multiple partners

- *Increased capacity for work.* People may say that you are getting to be a "workaholic," that you have taken on too many projects at home or at the office. They may caution you about "burning the candle at both ends." You find yourself calling people at all hours of the night with notions you are excited about. As the mania intensifies, you will notice that you are jumping from one project to the next, without finishing anything.
- *Increased risk-taking.* You are feeling carefree, uninhibited. The risks you are taking may be self-destructive. You may be spending money, taking business risks, drinking or doing drugs, or having casual sexual relations. Others will caution you or express concern about the chances you are taking. In spite of their warnings, you throw caution to the wind, act on impulse, and do whatever comes to mind.

  You will probably find yourself minimizing the risks of your behavior and rationalizing your actions: You will insist everyone is worrying too much. You may criticize the people who caution you to watch your step as being too "straight-laced or uptight" to let themselves have a good time.

If you have had a persistently elevated, expansive, or irritable mood and three or more of the symptoms listed, then it is likely that you are suffering from a manic episode. Drug use and some medical conditions can cause manic symptoms.

Albert is a twenty-six-year-old publishing assistant and part-time graduate student who was brought to a hospital emergency room by the police. Albert had always been moody as a child. He did exceptionally well in school in spite of difficulty concentrating. When he was twelve, his family moved from a rural town to a large metropolitan area. Shortly after the move, he became unusually withdrawn and irritable. This lasted about nine months and then went away on its own.

He became depressed when he was seventeen after a girlfriend broke up with him. She complained that he was too often critical and easily angered. He became very depressed and slept for eleven or twelve hours a day. For a short while he expressed a concern his heart might be rotting. Medical workups revealed no problems. This belief seemed to last only a month or so. When asked about it later he said it was "a silly idea that I got carried away with. I guess I just had a broken heart." He began abusing alcohol and cocaine at that point, and continued doing so in college.

He had a third episode of depression when he was twenty-one, after being rejected from a graduate program he had hoped to attend. He lost all his energy and motivation. Although he slept nine hours a day, he felt exhausted all the time. He received no treatment for any of these episodes.

Albert had frequent depressions starting at an early age characterized by atypical symptoms. During the second episode, he may have had a psychotic delusion. Between episodes, he showed signs of having an irritable temperament. These are all signs of a bipolar illness, but could easily have been mistaken for a recurrent unipolar depression.

Albert's uncle was alcoholic. Albert's mother had always been ill-tempered. She had had a postpartum depression after each of the births of her two children. Albert's grandmother had once spent time in a mental hospital, and his aunt had thyroid problems.

For reasons that are not quite clear, postpartum depressions and thyroid illness are common on the maternal side of bipolar patients' families. The family histories of patients with bipolar illness are frequently loaded with relatives with alcohol and emotional problems as well.

Albert's current problems began when he was given an important project to work on. It was more responsibility than he had been given on other projects. He was nervous he might not be capable of doing the tasks assigned to him. He worked long hours and stayed up late several nights in a row. At times he insisted on being left alone and got testy if his girlfriend, Julie, interrupted him. At other times he wanted her to sit down and talk with him about the project. He would speak rapidly and at length about some aspect he found especially interesting. At first Julie tried to indulge Albert, even though she felt as though their talks were becoming more like lectures on his part. She figured that he would get back to normal once he was finished with the project.

Julie began to worry as Albert became more consumed by the project. It was getting to the point where he hardly took time out for a meal. When he talked to her it was always about the project. He called her at two o'clock in the morning to tell her one of his ideas. He was sure that his idea would make the publishing house millions. He said he would be famous, and they would live in a mansion in a fancy part of the city.

He insisted on presenting some of his marketing ideas at staff meetings, even though that was not his role in the project. He then took to calling his associates late at night, saying he had ideas that he just had to run by them. When they started to object to his late-night calls, he got angry and said that they were sleeping their lives away and were just jealous that he had so many great ideas. He began to tell Julie that he thought he should be the one running the marketing department. The current department head did not seem to know half as much as he did.

It was beginning to get difficult for Julie—and Albert's colleagues—to follow his train of thought. Whereas his colleagues had previously felt that his ideas were good, they now worried that he was branching out into too many areas and not getting his main assignment completed. When his boss brought this up to him, he said that he had realized he was much too talented to be wasting his time on his regular assignment. He stated that he was "an idea man" and he wanted his special talents to be recognized.

At home Albert was growing increasingly agitated. He began to
drink more. He also bought expensive new computer equipment
and software even though he had little money and little need for it.
He insisted, however, that he would make the money back a thou-
sand times with the plans he had in mind.

His colleagues were beginning to avoid him. He thought that
they were so jealous of him that they were plotting to ruin his reputation in the publishing world (even though he had no reputation).
One day he was so frightened that he did not go to work. When his
boss called him at home, he threatened to hire a hit man if the publishing firm did not leave him alone. His boss called his girlfriend.
She went to his apartment, but he would not let her in. That was
when she called the police.

Types of Manic-Depressive Illness

Euphoric In this form of mania, the patient is unusually cheerful
or has an unusually elevated and expansive mood. Less than 40 percent of all bipolar patients have euphoric mania. Euphoric patients
have inflated self-esteem, are grandiose, and are overconfident.
They may develop delusions about having powers, abilities, or
knowledge they do not possess or about having relationships with
famous or powerful people. If the mania is not too severe or in its
early stages, manic individuals can be charismatic, persuasive, and
often very funny. Their mood can be infectious.

The euphoric mood can be quite changeable, however, especially if the manic patient is thwarted in his efforts or frustrated in
any way. They can suddenly become irritable.

Classic euphoric mania typically progresses through three
stages. The first stage is characterized by euphoria: overconfidence;
racing and somewhat aimless thoughts; and increased activity,
spending, and sociability. In stage two mania, the patient becomes
increasingly driven. Mood becomes a mixture of euphoria, agita-

tion, and hostility. The person can have an explosive temper and even become assaultive. Thinking becomes increasingly disorganized, and speech becomes more rapid and pressured. In stage three, the manic individual may be violent and panic-stricken. Thinking becomes incoherent, and behavior is bizarre. One-third of patients develop hallucinations and delusions.

Mixed Strictly defined, these patients demonstrate a combination of manic and depressive features. However, there may be a unique quality to the mood state, which is difficult to describe and not captured by the terms *manic* and *depressed*. The words that perhaps come closest to capturing the mood are *irritable, easily angered, hostile, agitated, anxious, discontented, dissatisfied,* or *displeased with everything, sullen, and surly.* Unlike the euphoric manic, the patient in a mixed state feels miserable. At least 40 percent of bipolar I patients have mixed episodes. When women with bipolar disorder have a manic episode, it is more likely to be mixed than euphoric. Mixed episodes are associated with a high rate of substance abuse and suicide. Patients with milder mixed states are frequently misdiagnosed as personality disordered.

Rapid Cycling Patients with manic-depressive illness show a great variability in the length of time between onset of illness episodes (referred to as cycle length). In general, however, cycle length tends to shorten over time (episodes occur more frequently), and then levels off after three to five episodes. At that point, episodes occur roughly every year.

In contrast, rapid-cycling patients have, by definition, at least four manic or depressed episodes per year. Rapid cyclers account for up to 20 percent of bipolar patients. Ultra-rapid cyclers may have episodes every forty-eight hours. Ultradian cyclers have mood episodes on a daily basis.

Only one-fifth of rapid cyclers have an early age of onset. Most patients evolve into a rapid-cycling pattern over time. This may be due, in part, to treatment with antidepressants, which appears to shorten cycle length in bipolar patients. One investigator concluded that 25 percent of rapid cyclers got that way because of antidepressant treatment. Rapid-cycling patients can have periods of nonrapid cycles.

Rapid-cycling occurs three times more frequently in women than in men. Hypothyroidism (low thyroid gland activity) is associated with rapid cycling. The hypothyroidism may be detectable only through the special test of thyroid function mentioned in chapter 1—the TRH stimulation test.

MARGAUX AND ERNEST HEMINGWAY

Margaux Hemingway's story is a good example of how friends and family often view manifestations of a mood disorder as an expression of personality. It is publicly known that Margaux suffered from not one but several psychiatric illnesses. In addition, she suffered from epilepsy, an illness that may be linked with symptoms of bipolar disorder. She could be full of life or terribly depressed. Some people knew her as gentle and sweet while others described her as critical and angry. Her grandfather, Ernest, probably suffered from a bipolar disorder.

Yet her problems were not explained, at least publicly, as manifestations of a hereditary, biological illness. Interviews with family and friends reveal that these were seen as expressions of her personality and her unusual life experiences.

Margaux Hemingway was six years old when her grandfather, novelist Ernest Hemingway, shot and killed himself. She was forty-one in the summer of 1996, when she took her own life, by swallowing an overdose of the barbiturate phenobarbital.

Margaux was still a teenager when she burst onto the fashion scene as a model. Six feet tall and graced with strikingly good looks, she won a $1 million contract promoting Fabergé in 1975. She was photographed everywhere, enjoying a high-wire social life. She even landed a movie role. She seemed to have it all.

But behind the perfect photographs was a young woman troubled with epilepsy, alcoholism, and an eating disorder. She was treated at an Idaho psychiatric hospital for clinical depression. Her mood swings helped cost her two marriages and led to an estrangement from her younger sister, actress Mariel Hemingway. Her father and stepmother stopped talking to her for two years, calling her an angry woman who "constantly lies."

At the same time, friends thought of her as a gentle soul, full of life. Even so, she often made them uncomfortable—talking loudly in public about her sex life, for example. She went on spending sprees and fell deeply into debt. She sought spiritual healing, but had a breakdown after visiting holy sites in India.

In her final months, her life seemed to be on an upswing. She was hoping that a job hosting an outdoor adventure series would kick-start her acting career. Nonetheless, friends were worried because she didn't have her normal "up" personality. And a neighbor who passed her on the street noticed that she looked haggard and disturbed. Days later, a friend found Margaux dead in her Santa Monica, California, apartment.

For Margaux, suicide was a family legacy. Her great-grand-father, Ernest's father Clarence, who suffered from violent mood swings throughout his life, shot himself behind the right ear in 1928. Ernest's sister, Ursula, survived three cancer operations and then became depressed and took her life with a drug overdose in 1966. Ernest's brother, Leicester, shot himself in 1982.

Ernest, like his granddaughter, seemed to have it all. He had good looks, sporting skills, friends, women, and the

Nobel Prize for literature. He was in love with life but obsessed with death.

In the spring of 1936, after a disastrous breakup with a lover, Ernest was unable to sleep or write, feared that he was impotent, and contemplated killing himself. He recovered and went on to have many affairs. He was married four times.

The contradictions of his personality could be maddening. Generous to friends, he could be petty about money to his wives. Witty and cheerful, he could also be irritable and nasty.

Toward the end of his life, Ernest deteriorated, physically and psychologically. Some friends attributed it to the years of hard drinking and hard living. But A. E. Hotchner, in his book *Papa Hemingway*, paints a picture of a man who suffered from delusions and paranoia in his later years. Hotchner recalls that one night, as they passed a motel, Ernest told him somberly that the men in the window were auditors going over his accounts.

Ernest suffered from cramps, insomnia, and nightmares. He lost weight and found himself unable to write. Though he had a lifelong scorn of psychiatrists, his wife, Mary, felt that she had no choice but to admit him to the Mayo Clinic in 1960. He had electroconvulsive treatments and seemed to improve. Back at home, his mood toward his wife swung from loving to abusive. He was readmitted to Mayo in 1961.

Back at home again, Ernest felt increasingly insecure about growing old and his ability to write. Life no longer seemed worth living. So on July 2, 1961, he rose from his bed, went downstairs to a storeroom where he kept his guns, pulled out a twelve-gauge, double-barreled shotgun, walked upstairs to the foyer, and shot himself in the head.

He was one of the most influential American writers of the twentieth century.

BIPOLAR II DISORDER

Patients with bipolar II disorder have major depressive episodes and intermittent hypomania. Roughly 60 percent of bipolar patients have bipolar II illness. These patients are frequently misdiagnosed as being unipolar depressives because they ask for help only when depressed. Without a careful history and information from family members, the hypomanic features are easy to overlook. Patients will usually forget to mention them since they feel that these are their "normal" moods. Frederick Goodwin, M.D., and psychologist Kay Jamison, Ph.D., coauthors of the text *Manic-Depressive Illness*, note that bipolar disorder is underdiagnosed by a factor of two when family members are not asked about episodes of hypomania in the patient.

Bipolar II patients are frequently inappropriately treated with antidepressants alone. Antidepressants alone may cause a number of problems for bipolar II patients, including increased frequency of treatment-resistant depressions and the induction of hypomania followed by more-difficult-to-treat rapid cycling. You will recall that hypomanic episodes are characterized by increased energy, decreased need for sleep, and greater than normal self-esteem. While this may sound like a pretty good deal, hypomania can also cause a number of problems. Often the person is irritable and sometimes outright hostile when crossed. The irritability can lead to lapses in judgment that cause problems on the job or in personal relationships.

Fifty percent of patients with bipolar II illness abuse alcohol and drugs. Because these patients can be impulsive, irritable, angry, sensitive, grandiose, and arrogant at times and have trouble maintaining relationships, they are frequently misdiagnosed as personality disordered and treated with psychotherapy alone.

Bipolar II patients are predominantly female. They make more suicide attempts than do bipolar I patients and have a 15 to 19 percent probability of committing suicide. They suffer more frequently from mixed states and develop rapid cycling more often than do bipolar I patients. Bipolar II is frequently associated with eating disorders.

CHAPTER 4

MOOD DISORDERS IN CHILDREN AND ADOLESCENTS

DEPRESSION IN CHILDREN

It was once thought that children could not become depressed due to the immaturity of their psyches. Recent studies, however, show anywhere from 7 to 14 percent of children will have a major depressive episode before age fifteen. Many depressed children have a slow onset of relatively mild symptoms and tend to act badly rather than to say they feel sad. As a result, it is easy for parents to overlook the possibility that their child may be depressed.

Parents are often shocked and horrified if a mental-health professional suggests that their child may be suffering from clinical depression. They often do not want to believe it. They may need to deny the possibility because they mistakenly believe they caused the depression. It is a blow to a parent's self-image to think that their child may be ill or defective in some way. The parent may object to the diagnosis out of fear that the child will be hurt by being labeled. If medication is suggested, parents may have understandable but exaggerated concerns about side effects.

If you have been told that your child is clinically depressed, you may be tempted to ignore or dismiss the idea. If so, at least seek a second opinion. *You must carefully consider the risks of not having your child further evaluated or treated.* First and most obvious is the chance that your child will suffer needlessly. You will, too, as you are forced to manage difficult moods and behaviors. Second, depressive episodes in children last, on average, roughly an entire school year. The recurrence rate is high if the episode is not treated. Repeated bouts of depression may delay or derail a child's intellectual, psychological, and social development. Third, depression in children, if not treated, is likely to be harder to treat once the child grows into adolescence and adulthood.

Of even greater concern is that a fifth to as many as a third of children diagnosed with depression will go on to develop a bipolar illness. Psychiatric researchers Michael Strober and Hagop Akiskal have found, in separate studies, that the children most likely to have such an outcome had certain things in common: Their depressions started very quickly; they felt fatigued and slowed-down when depressed; and their family histories were loaded with relatives over several generations who had mood disorders. Psychotic episodes also predicted the development of bipolar illness. Psychotic depressions in children and adolescents recur at more than twice the rate of nonpsychotic depression, according to Strober, so early and aggressive treatment is especially important with this group of youngsters.

The most frightening risk involved with not pursuing evaluation and treatment is the risk of suicide. Although not as common in children as in adolescents, depressed children do have suicidal thoughts, make suicide attempts, and do succeed in killing themselves. There is at least one case report of a five-year-old child attempting suicide.

If you think your child may be depressed, you should first review the depression symptom list for adults given in chapter 3. More severely depressed children may have the sleep and appetite disturbances and other symptoms characteristic of adults with depression. (Rather than losing weight, however, they may fail to make expected weight gains.) Then look over the following list of symptoms, which are more characteristic of depressed children, especially those with milder depressions.

Symptoms of Depression in Children

1. They act badly or are irritable for no apparent reason. They have little frustration tolerance. They are demanding and difficult to please, and they complain about everything. Nothing makes them happy. Their attitude and behavior try the patience of adults and alienate their peers.
2. They frequently look sad, tired, or ill. They may be tearful. They do not seem to have the usual amount of childhood energy and curiosity, or they lack the sense of humor and fun that most children have.
3. They say they do not feel good, or they complain of stomachaches, headaches, or other physical ills.
4. They are easily stressed out and overwhelmed and tend to worry or have exaggerated fears.
5. They get upset when separated from their parents. They are clingy and dependent. They may regress, sucking their thumb or wetting their pants.
6. They are losing interest in activities they used to enjoy, such as club attendance or sports.
7. They are very shy or have difficulty making friends. They are nervous about interacting with or performing in front of others. They become increasingly withdrawn.
8. Their grades are declining.
9. They talk about death and dying.

Keep in mind that the presence of any one of these symptoms does not necessarily mean the child suffers from the illness of depression. Intense parental conflict or substance abuse, difficulty dealing with developmental milestones, learning disabilities, physical or sexual abuse, or other childhood psychiatric disorders can cause a child to develop poor self-esteem or other depression-like symptoms. The list is meant only to alert you to the *possibility* of clinical depression and the need to seek a professional evaluation for your child.

If you or your spouse or any of your close relatives have problems with depression and your child has any of the problems described above, you should be especially concerned your child may have a mood disorder.

If your child has been in psychotherapy for any of the problems listed above and has not gotten substantially better in three to four months, you should seek an evaluation with a child psychiatrist (a medical doctor).

DEPRESSION IN ADOLESCENTS

Picking up on a teenager's depression is particularly important because of the high rate of teen suicide. The rate of suicide among adolescents has tripled in the last thirty years. Suicide now ranks as the second leading cause of death among adolescents. Nearly 25 percent of all teen deaths are due to suicide.

Onset of depression in the teen years increases the risk for suicide attempts in later life. One study found that 25 percent of those with teenage depression attempted suicide later in life compared to only 5.4 percent of those with adult onset depression.

Parents need to be careful not to dismiss signs and symptoms of adolescent mood disorder as normal behavior for a teenager. Contrary to popular belief, most teens do not regularly have explosive outbursts or wide mood swings. Most do not engage in unruly behavior or become impossible to get along with.

Preadolescent children and teenagers are likely to develop symptoms similar to the ones described for adults in chapter 3. Adolescents who are angry and unwilling to express feelings, however, or those who have difficulty putting feelings into words, are more likely to act bad than talk about being sad.

Depression often hits teens more quickly than it does younger kids. Their symptoms and overall mood tend to shift more rapidly than those of adults, possibly because of the many physiological changes their body is undergoing.

Symptoms of Depression in Adolescents

1. They are ill-tempered, "touchy," or overreactive and difficult to get along with.
2. They are aggressive or disruptive, or engage in delinquent behavior.
3. Their grades are falling.
4. They have lost interest in clubs, athletics, spending time with friends, or other activities they were formerly interested in.
5. They are compulsive partygoers, boy or girl chasers, thrill seekers, or daredevils. Or they may be just the opposite: They can never take a break and relax. They may be compulsive exercisers or may even study excessively.
6. They have low self-esteem.
7. They have unrealistic concerns that they are unattractive or disliked by others.

CHILD AND ADOLESCENT BIPOLAR ILLNESS

It is difficult to estimate how prevalent bipolar illness is in young children and adolescents, or how early the illness can manifest itself, because of a lack of clarity concerning diagnostic signs and symptoms. It had been considered a rare illness in children until recently. There are now indications it is underdiagnosed.

The symptoms of bipolar illness in children differ from those of the typical adult manic patient in two respects. First, a child under the age of ten with bipolar illness will often first develop atypical depression symptoms (oversleeping, fatigue) and behavioral problems including sudden, long-lasting temper outbursts. The child may break things or become assaultive. Second, bipolar illness in children up to the age of ten or twelve tends to be continuous rather than episodic. It is not usually until early adolescence that episodes with clear onset and offset of symptoms become evident.

Please be aware that just as there are causes for depressed moods in children other than clinical depression, there are causes of violent temper outbursts in young children other than bipolar disorder. Continuing violent temper outbursts do not mean your child has bipolar disorder. They merely suggest that she needs to be evaluated and the diagnosis of bipolar illness considered.

Using conventional diagnostic criteria, bipolar illness has been found to occur most frequently between the ages of fifteen and nineteen. There is a second peak age of onset between ages twenty to twenty-four. Studies that have included symptoms such as violent temper outbursts as diagnostic criteria have found a much earlier age of onset.

Diagnosis before the age of ten was uncommon until recently. Cases of children as young as eight are now being reported. At least one or two groups of researchers have found evidence of bipolar illness in children under the age of five. Investigators at Massachusetts General Hospital and Harvard Medical School reported that a substantial number of children under the age of twelve referred to their study had symptoms of mania.

Older children and adolescents with bipolar illness may have a more episodic course with symptoms typical of mania, including grandiosity; pressured, difficult-to-interrupt speech; and racing thoughts. But many of them continue to have episodes with less-than-obvious manic features. Rapid cycling and mixed features, such as depressed mood, irritability, and hyperactivity, are common. Adolescents who suffer from bipolar illness may have periods of violent, destructive, and antisocial behavior.

Psychotic features are more common in adolescents suffering from mood disorders than in adults. Severe, psychotic manic-depressive illness in adolescents is frequently misdiagnosed as schizophrenia.

If a child does have bipolar illness, it will persist into adulthood. It is not something kids outgrow.

ADHD and Bipolar Illness

Attention-deficit hyperactivity disorder (ADHD) shares many symptoms and some common genetic basis with bipolar illness, so the two can be difficult to distinguish. This is especially the case for children under the age of ten, since there is more symptom overlap in that age group. Children with ADHD and bipolar illness are probably often mistaken for each other. In both disorders, the child may be irritable, hyperactive, impulsive, and distractible. The diagnosis is complicated by the fact that children can and often do suffer from *both* ADHD and bipolar disorder. The rate of ADHD in bipolar children is very high. Some researchers have suggested the symptoms of ADHD and bipolar illness overlap because they are not two separate disorders but, rather, somewhat different manifestations of the same underlying disease process.

ADHD has typically been considered to have an earlier age of onset (before age seven) than does bipolar illness. But as earlier forms of bipolar illness are diagnosed, this may no longer be a valid distinction. However, if there were no attention problems prior to the age of seven, the child cannot be diagnosed as ADHD. ADHD is four to seven times more common in boys than in girls. Bipolar illness affects equal numbers of boys and girls.

Diagnostic experts have pointed to ADHD's continuous and chronic course as opposed to the episodic or cyclic nature of the symptoms in bipolar illness as a distinguishing feature. However, early forms of bipolar illness, as noted above, typically start to follow a more episodic course, with clear onset and offset of symptoms, only when children reach ten to twelve years of age. So the course in prepubescent children may not be a useful distinguishing feature.

ADHD children do not have periods of expansive or elevated mood. But then again, young bipolar children may not, either. In fact, they tend to have chronically poor self-esteem. Although children with ADHD can be moody, the mood shifts in older bipolar children tend to be more pronounced than in children with ADHD. ADHD and bipolar children can both be irritable, but the bipolar child is more prone to violent temper outbursts. The ADHD child's behavior is frequently less focused or goal-directed than the child with bipolar illness.

Dr. Gary Spivack, a psychiatrist in Arlington, Virginia, has suggested that if the child behaves well in school but worse at home, that suggests bipolar disorder rather than ADHD. The home is more likely to be emotionally charged, which is difficult for the bipolar child to manage. The child with ADHD does better at home.

Finally, an ADHD child usually responds well to stimulant medication. Children suffering from bipolar disorder alone do not, and it may make them worse if they are not on mood-stabilizing medication.

TEEN ALCOHOL AND DRUG USE

Mood disorders sometimes prompt youngsters to turn to alcohol or drugs. Teens who are depressed may go from occasional experimentation with substances to increased use and abuse of them. If the depression is diagnosed and treated early enough, the teen *may* decrease drug or alcohol use on his own. However, the substance use should still be checked on periodically by the teen's therapist and discussed when necessary, especially if the depression is not clearing up or there are signs that the substance use is interfering with functioning. At the very least, substance abuse may be interfering with treatment for depression. It also increases the chances that the teen will have a recurrence of the depression. In some individuals, substance abuse will precipitate or hasten the onset of a developing bipolar illness. Continued use of alcohol and drugs by adolescent bipolar patients will worsen the course of bipolar disorder and may make it impossible to effectively treat the illness.

If substance use has gone on for awhile, it may have become established as a problem in its own right. It may then require specialized treatment even if it began in the context of a mood disorder.

It is critical to remember that teens can and often do develop depressive illness as a *result* of excessive alcohol or drug use. School attendance problems, disruptive behavior, temper outbursts, declining grades, and curfew violations are just as likely to be due to substance abuse as a mood disorder. Cocaine use and the subsequent crash can mimic the mood swings of bipolar disorder. When the substance abuse is the primary issue, the treatment in these cases should be geared toward stopping it. Depression and bipolar-like symptoms frequently clear up entirely once the teen is abstinent for two to four weeks. If they do not, specific treatment for those problems can then be instituted.

Not infrequently, it is difficult to sort out whether the mood disorder or substance abuse is primary or whether they are both primary disorders. It is not worth spending a lot of time trying to figure this out. It is better to just go ahead and treat both illnesses. Simultaneous treatment is especially indicated if there is a family history of mood disorder, the mood disorder clearly predates the substance abuse, there is a danger of suicide, or there have been several attempts at sobriety that have failed. In the case of the latter, it may be that the teen has an untreated mood disorder, which is making it harder to maintain sobriety.

As a parent, you need to be somewhat on guard that your teen does not get connected with a clinic or professional who is wedded to substance-abuse treatment or mental-health treatment alone.

This is becoming less of a problem as the two disciplines realize they each have something to offer the other. However, it is still possible to get referred to substance-abuse counselors who believe sobriety and twelve-step programs (such as Alcoholics Anonymous) are all that is needed. Some may be adamantly opposed to psychotherapy and the use of medication.

It is also quite possible for your teen to see a psychotherapist who will fail to adequately evaluate his alcohol or drug use or who will overlook substance abuse problems in the mistaken belief that alcohol and drug abuse will clear up on their own if therapy is successful.

The error that substance-abuse professionals make is the lesser of these two evils. It can only help if your teen stops using alcohol and drugs. However, recovery programs can be tough for depressed kids to handle. The more confrontational ones may in fact not be a good idea initially for some depressed teens. But more often these programs provide structure, stability, and support that may at least help a kid weather an undiagnosed mood-disorder episode. This may be sufficient to prevent suicide.

Undiagnosed substance abuse spells nothing but trouble, however. Nothing will get better as long as it goes unrecognized and untreated. The risk of suicide for a depressed or bipolar teen is much higher when she is abusing alcohol or drugs. Mental-health professionals who treat patients with mood disorders should also be expert in diagnosing and managing substance-abuse problems, especially if they deal with adolescents.

TREATMENT

My preference is to have children and younger adolescents see a child and adolescent psychiatrist for an evaluation. Thorough, conscientious, highly trained nonmedical therapists who are experts in childhood mood disorders and ADHD and who use a wide variety of treatment modalities do exist, but they are hard to find.

Before suggesting psychotherapy, family therapy, medication, or any other treatment, a child mental-health professional should do the following:

1. Thoroughly review (or have a physician review) the child's personal and family medical history.
2. Have the parents arrange for a physical exam and possibly a blood workup for the child.
3. Depending on the child's age, explore alcohol and drug use.
4. Get a history of the child's symptoms from the child and especially from the parents.
5. Get a thorough developmental history of the child from the parents.
6. Explore the parents' relationship and how the family functions.
7. Get a family history of any psychiatric disorders and substance abuse from the parents.
8. Get reports from the school on conduct and academic performance.

Treatment of mood disorders in children and adolescents is similar to that for adults. Milder depressions in children may be resolved with psychotherapy, changes in the child's environment, and parent counseling. Moderate to severe depression in a child or an adolescent with a family history of depression or bipolar disorder requires medication.

Antidepressants clearly have a role in the treatment of unipolar major depression in adolescents. There has been much less research on the use of antidepressants with children. An old class of antidepressant drugs called *tricyclics* has been found ineffective for childhood depression. There are a growing number of studies, however, that suggest medications such as Prozac work well in children who are depressed. Dosages used are the same as for adults.

Manic children and adolescents may require somewhat higher

doses of lithium than do adults because of the efficiency of young kidneys in removing lithium from the blood. Adolescents with bipolar symptoms that began in childhood probably require drugs called anticonvulsants. These drugs tend to be more effective in mixed and rapid-cycling bipolar illnesses, which early-onset adolescent patients are likely to have. The mood-stabilizing drugs are given at dosages that will bring the child's blood level of the drug into the same range known to be therapeutic for adults. Side effects are similar.

IF YOUR TEENAGER WILL NOT GO FOR HELP

Getting a teenager who is depressed or bipolar and who may be abusing alcohol or drugs to go for help is often difficult. Getting her to stay in treatment, take needed medications consistently, and avoid alcohol and drug use is even more so. What is a parent to do?

Start by making sure you and your spouse understand and put stock in the diagnosis your teen has been given. Get a second opinion if you have doubts. Learn about mood disorders yourself. Make sure you and your spouse are comfortable with the idea that your teen needs treatment.

Next, educate your teen about mood disorders. Let him know you believe that he may be suffering from an illness and that help is available. Give him information to read or videos on depression. If you or your spouse has suffered from a mood disorder or if your relatives have struggled with symptoms of mood disorder, let your teen know this. Explain the illness is hereditary and carries many potential problems with it. Let him know he does not have to suffer or walk around feeling angry all the time. The older he is, the more you will need to suggest to him that he get help rather than tell him he is going to get help.

Do not despair if what you say seems to go in one ear and out the other. Continue to bring it up from time to time, although not when you are angry. If your teen remains uncooperative or continues to use alcohol and drugs, seek professional advice for you and your spouse. A therapist will help you understand your teen's problem and help you rid yourself of unnecessary guilt. It is important for parents of troubled teens to learn to direct energy away from ineffective, angry attempts at control and toward efforts at education, support, and limit setting. Parents often get so enraged, scared, and guilt-ridden that they lose the ability to effectively manage their teen and her problems. A therapist will help parents get a handle on this.

The therapist can guide you on how to deal with the teen who is unrealistically gloomy or self-critical. For instance, you do not want to say "You have nothing to be depressed about" or "Don't worry so much" or "Cheer up—things will get better."

For teens who are irritable, nasty, demanding, undisciplined, abusing alcohol and drugs, or are otherwise driving you crazy, the therapist will assist you in negotiating, setting, and enforcing limits on intolerable or abusive behavior. The teen is allowed to experience the natural consequences of his own behavior (e.g., you do not talk to him if he is verbally abusive; he does not get the keys to the car if he has a substance-abuse problem he is not addressing). You want to make sure your kid gets the message that you do not sanction and will not indulge, support, or tolerate irresponsible or inappropriate behavior.

There are two main blocks parents seem to have in setting limits with kids who are acting up. One is feeling sorry for them. The other is worrying about them becoming violent or committing suicide. If you feel so sorry for your teen that you cannot set effective limits, you have to get some help both for your sake and your child's. Just think: Someone you have sacrificed for and who you are trying to help is abusing you, keeping you up all night, sick with worry, and driving you crazy. At least a part of you should feel like strangling your teen. And all you're feeling is sorry for her? You need to figure out what is so uncomfortable about feeling angry and then use your anger to set appropriate limits.

If your teen should be taking antidepressant or mood-stabilizing medication and is not, you need to educate yourself about the use of these drugs. Deal with your fears and misconceptions about medication treatment, in particular. If you and your spouse are on the same wavelength with all of this, you will have an easier time handling your teen's concerns and objections. Many times, teens become noncompliant when they discern that their parents have strong doubts about or objections to medication.

Some teens may hint at suicide or threaten violence if you attempt to set and enforce limits. These threats may be serious and *should not* be dismissed as purely manipulative. On the other hand, they may well be manipulative to some extent. If so, you cannot let yourself be held an emotional hostage. What do you do? The solution is not easy: You put your teen in the car and take him to the emergency room. If he will not get in the car, you call the police or emergency medical service and have them take your teen to the hospital. If your teen runs out the door before the police arrive, you tell them your kid is suicidal. They will try to pick up the teen. If your teen eludes the police and comes back later on, you call the police again.

When your teen is released from the hospital, you should, however, have gas in the car and be prepared for a few trips. Some teens may test you again. Do not be discouraged. Although you may not solve your teen's problems this way, at least he is alive. Your job is to protect him. You cannot live his life for him. In the worst cases, sometimes all parents can do is keep their kid alive until he grows up a bit and decides to get help for himself. Some parents have trouble getting their troubled sons and daughters out the door and on their way in life. If you do, get help.

I cannot, of course, guarantee that your teen or young adult child will not hurt herself if you set and enforce limits on behavior. But the chances are good that she will respond to this straightforward approach. The alternative, letting yourself be manipulated, will only give your teen permission to escalate out-of-control behavior.

CHAPTER 5

OTHER PSYCHIATRIC DISORDERS OFTEN FOUND TOGETHER WITH MOOD DISORDERS

Depression and especially bipolar disorder rarely occur alone. They typically are accompanied by at least one other psychiatric illness. Sometimes depressive illness is secondary to another psychiatric illness, such as panic disorder. When two or more psychiatric disorders occur together, they are said to be comorbid. Following are brief summaries of illnesses frequently comorbid with depression.

SUBSTANCE ABUSE

Mood disorders and substance abuse go hand in hand. Someone seeking help for either one should always be evaluated for the other. One study showed a group of women who were depressed were twice as likely to develop alcohol abuse as those without depression. Abuse of alcohol often leads to depression, as well, especially among men.

Alcohol and drug abuse are particularly common among patients with bipolar disorder. Manic individuals usually increase their use of alcohol and stimulant drugs such as cocaine during the manic phase of their illness. This could be because alcohol relieves the agitation the manic feels. Cocaine sustains or enhances euphoria. It is also likely that substance abuse is simply a result of poor judgment and the increased risk-taking characteristic of the manic phase of bipolar disorder. Men are somewhat more likely than women to drink excessively when in the manic phase of manic-depressive illness.

Having a bipolar illness puts an individual at ten times the risk of having a substance abuse problem compared to someone without the illness. Up to 60 percent of manic-depressive patients may have an alcohol problem. Two-thirds of those will need treatment for alcohol dependence. Nearly 50 percent of patients with bipolar II disorder have an alcohol problem.

If you have some form of bipolar illness and abuse alcohol or drugs, your chances of recovery from the bipolar disorder are slim if you continue your substance abuse. Alcohol and drugs adversely affect the same neurotransmitter systems implicated in mood disorders. They act as kindling agents—substances that trigger episodes of illness. Drug use can worsen the severity of the illness by precipitating psychotic episodes and may induce rapid cycling.

Just as there is a greater incidence of alcohol and drug abuse among those with mood disorders than among the general population, alcohol and substance abusers have higher rates of mood disorders than does the general population. Five to 6 percent of the population suffers from some form of bipolar illness, for instance, while up to 30 percent of cocaine abusers may have the disorder.

Alcoholics and drug abusers with mood disorders—especially those with dysthymia and cyclothymia—frequently go unrecognized and untreated in substance abuse treatment settings. Substance abusers can spend a lot of time working on their most troublesome "character defects" (angry, irritable behavior probably being the primary one) without realizing that these are symptoms of a mood disorder.

When they first come to treatment, a very large percentage of alcoholics have symptoms of depression. After a month of sobriety, however, many of them will no longer feel depressed. Mental health professionals must be careful not to treat symptoms of depression as the primary problem in patients with severe alcohol abuse or dependence.

However, alcoholics or substance abusers who meet diagnostic criteria for major depression (rather than just having depressed mood and a few other symptoms of depression), those with family histories of depression, and those who report clear episodes of depressive illness in childhood or during extended periods of abstinence should be considered for immediate treatment with antidepressants. Some doctors are now recommending treatment for depression in such cases, even if the patient is not abstinent. They have found that the depressive illness will respond to treatment and it may even help the alcohol abuse to some extent.

Finally, alcoholics and substance abusers who have frequent relapses should be reevaluated for the possibility that they have an undiagnosed mood disorder. In one study, 40 percent of 6,355 alcoholics had a diagnosis of major depression at some point in their lives. Depression was a common self-reported cause of relapse by the participants in this study.

EATING DISORDERS

Eating disorders include *anorexia nervosa, bulimia,* and *binge-eating disorder.*

In anorexia nervosa a person, typically a young woman, becomes preoccupied with food, fears becoming fat, greatly restricts the amount and kind of food she eats, loses a great deal of weight, and yet still believes she is too heavy. In middle to advanced stages of the illness, women patients will frequently stop menstruating. Although the illness leads to death in 10 percent of patients, many patients resist treatment.

In bulimia, the patient loses control of eating. Usually, there is a rapid intake of a large quantity of food, which is later purged. The food is purged by self-induced vomiting, enemas, and the abuse of laxatives. Some bulimic individuals use diuretic medications to promote the excretion of urine. Bulimia is roughly four times as common as anorexia. The weight of the evidence strongly suggests that bulimia is related somehow to major depression. Often patients start out being depressed and later become anorexic and then anorexic and bulimic. About 80 percent of bulimic patients in one study had experienced at least one episode of major depression or bipolar illness in their lives. Bulimic patients frequently have other impulse-control problems, as well. Studies have reported, for instance, from 12 to 65 percent of patients with bulimia are compulsive shoplifters.

The same patient may have symptoms of anorexia and bulimia, either simultaneously or at different times. Patients may be compulsive exercisers as well.

In binge-eating disorder, the patient consumes large quantities of food, especially sweets and carbohydrate-rich foods, without purging.

ANXIETY DISORDER AND PANIC DISORDER

Anxiety-disordered patients complain that they feel constantly anxious, tense, nervous, wound up, worried, or uptight. They will usually complain that they have difficulty controlling the anxiety, worry, or tension. They are usually easily fatigued and often report trouble sleeping. They may report a number of physical symptoms such as trembling, twitching, dry mouth, sweating, nausea, diarrhea, or a sensation of a lump in the throat. Patients who seek help for problems with anxiety virtually always have some form of mood disorder. It is unusual for a patient to have long-standing problems with anxiety alone, in the absence of a diagnosis of depression or other mood disorder. Some clinicians have suggested that this may be because anxiety is an early symptom of depression. Roughly 60 percent of depressed patients have symptoms of anxiety.

In panic disorder, a patient will repeatedly experience, often for no apparent reason, a sudden wave of frightening physical sensations and emotional symptoms: a thumping, racing heartbeat, shaking, sweaty palms, a heaviness or pain in the chest, lightheadedness, numbness or tingling sensations, or shortness of breath. An intense dread or sense of doom overtakes the patient. The patient frequently thinks she may be dying, having a heart attack, or going crazy and losing control. Panic-attack patients frequently wind up in hospital emergency rooms for what they believe may be a heart attack. Sometimes panic-disorder patients have the difficult-to-describe experience that nothing is real (*derealization*) or that they are somehow detached from themselves (*depersonalization*). All these feelings tend to peak rapidly and then fade away fairly quickly. The person may feel shaken for several hours after the acute symptoms, however.

Patients can have panic disorder alone, in the absence of any other diagnosis, but such patients are in the minority. For instance, 20 percent of families affected by bipolar disorder are also affected by panic disorder. Only 2 percent of families in the general population are affected by panic disorder. Fifteen to 30 percent of depressed patients have panic disorder. In about a third of these patients, the depression comes before the panic disorder.

After several panic attacks, it is common for a person to try to avoid situations where the attacks have occurred: stores, bridges, tunnels, subways, elevators, and traffic jams, for instance. Patients often express the fear that they will not be able to get out of or away from these places when they have an attack. Just the idea that they may have a panic attack while out somewhere provokes anxiety. This is referred to as *anticipatory anxiety*.

Some patients are so incapacitated by the combination of panic attacks, anticipatory anxiety, and the avoidance of places associated with the attacks that they rarely leave home. This is referred to as *agoraphobia*.

Perhaps as many as half of adult panic-disorder patients, most of whom are women, were, as children, especially fearful of leaving their mothers to go to school. This is referred to as *separation anxiety.*

OBSESSIVE COMPULSIVE DISORDER

Obsessions are persistent thoughts that involuntarily preoccupy the mind. They are frequently, but not always, considered by the person experiencing them as intrusive, senseless, and unpleasant. Compulsions are impulses to perform irrational, repetitive acts or behaviors. Not performing the compulsion leads to increasing anxiety.

This category includes not only OCD proper (intrusive hostile thoughts, hand-washing compulsions, etc.) but also a very wide variety of problems that frequently coexist with and may be related to mood disorders. Those who suffer from OCD often have a high rate of depression. OCD and mood-disorder patients have in common a number of so-called biological markers of their illnesses. Following are some of the problems that overlap mood disorders and OCD-related disorders.

Obsessive Personality Psychoanalysts have long pointed out how depressed individuals frequently have obsessive personalities. Kraepelin noted that depressed individuals often have anxious, indecisive, and ruminative tendencies. Rumination means continuously and repetitively thinking about some aspect of a subject or issue without coming to a productive solution.

Body Dysmorphic Disorder This is a disorder in which the patient is convinced that he has a very noticeable body defect that is not actually there or is minor.

Hypochondriasis This refers to a tendency to be preoccupied with illness. Hypochondriacs often feel compelled to get diagnostic evaluations and reassurance from others that no illness exists.

Sexual Compulsions and Perversions Compulsive desire for sex, masturbation, or perverse sexual stimulation or gratification (voyeurism, exhibitionism, pedophilia).

Impulse-Control Problems Compulsive shoplifting, compulsive spending, fire-setting, self-mutilation, or explosive temper. Disorders of impulse control can be found together with unipolar and bipolar disorders or may be the only obvious problems a patient has.

Obsessive Romantic Preoccupation The preoccupation is often with someone who is unable or unwilling to make a commitment to a relationship.

Pathological Jealousy Obsessive, unpleasant, and intrusive thoughts of jealousy combined with compulsions to check on a partner's fidelity.

CHAPTER 6

MOOD DISORDERS AND MARITAL PROBLEMS

L ike any other illness, depression affects not only patients' lives but the lives of family members. We will examine the strains depression puts on a marriage and how husbands and wives typically deal with the symptoms before a diagnosis is made. Suggestions on productive ways of handling a loved one's depression will be offered, including how to deal with the threat of suicide. The thorny problem of what to do when a depressed person is resisting or refusing help will be covered as well.

MAJOR DEPRESSION AND MARRIAGE

Fred is a forty-year-old married father of three children. He is known as a soft-spoken and caring person by his friends and family. He is a supervisor in a government agency. Six weeks ago, he had to deal with a major setback in his career. He was passed over for a management position he had thought would be offered to him. He was counting on the promotion and the substantial pay raise it would bring to qualify for a mortgage. For the first few weeks after the bad news, Fred was understandably distraught. He felt down in the dumps and had trouble falling asleep. He had no symptoms of clinical depression, however. His family and friends were sympathetic. They knew how much the promotion meant to Fred. He appreciated their support. It made him feel better, at least for awhile.

After about two weeks, however, Fred was still feeling very down. Now it seemed as if nothing anyone said really made him feel better. He felt bad about this and started to pretend that he felt comforted. He did not want to make anyone feel unappreciated.

He had been feeling tired for the past few weeks. He looked forward to going to bed. This puzzled his wife, since Fred had never been one to rush off to bed. Fred fell asleep without difficulty but began to find himself waking up at night and not feeling rested in the morning. He began to dwell on mistakes he had made on the job. He began to doubt himself. He was getting irritable and critical.

His family and friends, who all loved Fred for his willingness to help others, managed to remain patient with him. They reassured him that he would do fine in the future. But Fred continued to ruminate about mistakes he had made, how terrible his job was, and how bleak the future looked. He began to wonder if he just was not cut out for his job. His wife began to get impatient with Fred's gloominess. She did not express this directly—a part of her still felt sorry for him and could see he was in pain. As much as they cared for him, Fred's friends were starting to feel uncomfortable being around him, since nothing seemed to cheer him up. Everyone was beginning to wonder why Fred kept torturing himself.

As the illness progresses, family members begin to tire of the depressed person's unceasing gloom, irritability, and negativity. None of the measures taken by friends or family may help. This creates feelings of helplessness and frustration for them. Family and friends grow annoyed and impatient. They experience the depressed person as a bother. This may create quite a conflict for them, since another part of them wants to be helpful.

Some people act on their impatience and annoyance by withdrawing from the person. Others go to the opposite extreme and wind up spending too much of their time listening to and attempting to help the depressed person. Some begin to let the irritation out in disguised ways.

The tone of Fred's wife's voice began to change when she talked to Fred about his problems. A degree of impatience became noticeable. She began to urge him "to put the past behind you," "move ahead with your life," and "to feel grateful you have a job at all." Fred felt hurt, angry, and misunderstood. Friends who used to inquire how Fred was feeling about the setback now began to sidestep the issue.

Fred was becoming more reluctant to be around his family and friends. He no longer had the patience or energy to pretend he was feeling okay. No one seemed to understand or really care about his problem. And he really did not want to be a burden. It was easier for everyone if he just kept to himself.

At work, Fred was becoming less productive. His immediate superior, who had thought Fred had lost the manager's position on the basis of politics, had been sympathetic until recently. He took Fred aside one day and told him to "snap out of it." His supervisor told Fred that his work was backing up and it would do no good for him to walk around with a chip on his shoulder. Fred felt devastated. He went home and told his wife, who got scared that he might lose his job. She thought that Fred had not seemed happy lately unless he was making everyone else miserable. She also felt some sympathy for Fred's supervisor, since Fred had not been doing much around the house or with the kids lately.

The depressed person and his family can get caught in a downward spiral at this point. The depressed person feels torn between guilt for being such a burden and resentment that no one understands. He may begin to think others would be better off without him.

As a person becomes more deeply depressed, the advice people give can become tinged with irritation. The advice is an indirect way of saying, "Shut up. I have had enough." This spiral can be reversed if the family can learn that the depressed person cannot simply put his troubles out of his mind. He is not deliberately making himself or others unhappy. He may be expressing his anger in indirect ways, but this is an effect of the illness.

Eventually, when a person gets severely depressed, it will occur to all involved that something is wrong. When medical help is sought in these cases, the family is told that the depressed person is ill. If this is accepted, the patient and family can begin healing. Being ill allows the patient to relinquish some or most of his responsibilities and gives him permission to not be himself for a while. As long as the illness does not last too long and the patient is struggling to get better, the family will return to a greater degree of tolerance. They may be doubtful that what the doctor tells them is true, but at least for a while they will try to be more patient. Significant resentment and tension will start to build only if the illness lasts too long, or if the depressed person is not following medical advice and seems to be making little effort to get well.

BIPOLAR I ILLNESS AND MARRIAGE

Bipolar illness has an especially destructive effect on marriage. One study done in the days before lithium became available showed the divorce rate was seven times higher for manic patients than it was for depressed patients. The manic phase of manic-depressive illness makes people demanding, critical, and complaining. It makes them say and do hurtful things. Manic-depressive illness causes patients to spend money their family cannot afford to spend, causes lapses in judgment that can lead to the loss of a job, alcohol and drug abuse, sexual indiscretions, and problems with the law. Then, when they come back down to earth, they may collapse into a helpless depression, forcing spouses and family members to care for them and pick up the pieces. All of this creates a great deal of resentment. It is hard to maintain your cool and want to help someone who is making life miserable. To make matters worse, the manic patient will often complain that his spouse does not show she cares about him.

Spouses in this situation often wind up feeling like they are being driven crazy. They typically feel angry yet guilt-ridden for being cold and distant. They often have the feeling they are walking on eggshells, trying to avoid saying or doing anything to provoke an outburst in the manic patient. But no matter what they do or do not do, there are outbursts. If they stay in the marriage, they may develop what is referred to as learned helplessness. They get beaten down, passive, and withdrawn. They become very unassertive. They may develop symptoms of depression.

The manic patient and the spouse who stay married often become involved in an overly entwined relationship where they lose some individual identity. The spouse of the manic patient does not feel free to have her own life. Doing so threatens the manic spouse. It causes separation anxiety and a reactive rage to the threat of abandonment. Sometimes the manic-depressive patient will become threatening or suicidal. The spouse feels so worried about these possibilities or so responsible for maintaining the manic patient's stability that she becomes trapped in the relationship. The spouse may well be trapped if she has children, no money, and nowhere to go with them. Although the relationship seems to become a one-way relationship, the spouse of the manic patient may derive some gratification from having someone depend on her. It also allows her to deny and avoid her own dependency needs and, if she has depressive tendencies, may fulfill unconscious needs for criticism and punishment.

A spouse of a manic patient should be in treatment along with the patient. It will help the patient and the spouse as well.

Some important goals of the treatment for the spouse include:

1. Learning about bipolar illness and its symptoms. Psychoeducation is important for the spouse and relatives of the bipolar patient. Understanding that the patient's manic or depressed behavior may not be willful can reduce tension

in the family. The ability to get some emotional distance from the patient's problems will help the family manage them better. The problems may be more easily tackled if they are not seen as personal attacks or willful misconduct.

2. Learning how to assert yourself, protect yourself, and set limits on the manic's behavior without generating a lot of emotional turmoil. Just because you understand that the manic's behavior is not necessarily consciously chosen does not mean you have to tolerate it.

   Many spouses and relatives seem to know only two options for dealing with the manic: They either walk on eggshells, saying nothing and tolerating inappropriate behavior in order to keep the peace, or they get drawn into a fight. It is important to learn how to take a stand without either defending yourself or trying to convince the manic patient he is wrong. For instance, when a spouse feels she is the victim of her manic husband's undue irritability or criticism, she needs to simply end the discussion. She can say she will not tolerate the person's behavior. She may need to walk away or leave the house. This is preferable to explaining oneself, blowing up in anger, or getting into countercriticism and put-downs.

3. Developing a support system for yourself. You are going to be torn by many conflicting feelings—rage, guilt for wanting to flee, helplessness, fear, and concern. You will need the understanding and help of others who have gone through the emotional turmoil you are going through.

4. Learning how to recognize and deal with a spouse's manic or depressive episode. Know the signs of your spouse's illness. Have a plan in place to deal with the episodes. It will help you function better at a moment of crisis.

5. Developing other sources of satisfaction. It will be important for you to insist on your right to have a life outside of

your marriage. If you do not, the resentment you feel will further erode your relationship.

MILDER MOOD DISORDERS AND MARRIAGE

Things sometimes take a much different course when a spouse has mild, chronic depression, or a mild bipolar illness. Here it may never become apparent that the spouse is ill. The afflicted husband or wife may be a chronic complainer. He or she may be rather moody, irritable, and critical. The spouse and family either learn to be careful about what they say and do so as not to provoke the person, or the entire family may become involved in successive rounds of criticism and countercriticism. There are frequent fights and possibly domestic violence. Spouses who have learned to walk on eggshells may become mildly depressed themselves.

If the depressed spouse suffers an acute episode of more severe depression or bipolar illness, his irritability and complaining may get worse. Feelings of being stressed out or overwhelmed with responsibilities may grow. The patient may grow increasingly obsessive and complain about inconsequential problems: a dish left on the counter, for instance. But unless the patient becomes dysfunctional, it may still not be clear he is ill. Symptoms like undue irritability are overly intense forms of normal emotions. That is, the symptoms are different in degree from normal experiences, not different in kind. Such exacerbations of chronic mood problems often prompt couples to seek counseling.

How the marriage weathers the ill spouse's irritability, stress intolerance, and gloominess depends as much on the emotional health of the well spouse as it does on the course of the mood disorder. A husband, for instance, who is sensitive and easily provoked to anger will have a harder time managing his depressed wife's irritability than will one who is more secure and patient. The spouse of a depressed person may have a hard time taking responsibility for how his response to her illness contributes to their problems together. Often, the well spouse may talk about feeling compelled to get into an argument; indeed, he may be quite convinced that there is no alternative. A therapist has to help the well spouse take responsibility for his behavior and consider alternative means of coping with his frustrations.

Jill's mother had problems with depression. Jill's father, to whom she was very close, died about two years ago. Jill has been growing increasingly moody, irritable, and tearful over the last several months. She has been demanding a lot from her husband, Bob.

Bob has always been sensitive to criticism. His self-esteem is shaky, and he is overly dependent on getting positive feedback from others. This hasn't been much of a problem for the past several years, because he and his wife have had a good, supportive relationship.

But with her growing increasingly depressed, his own problems have begun to emerge. He feels guilt-ridden, angry, and above all, confused. He reacts to his wife's criticisms as if he really had something to feel terrible about. He begins to wonder, "Am I really as rotten a person as my wife makes me out to be?" Because of his own emotional limitations, Bob is having a hard time discerning his part in the couple's growing problems. Bob increasingly gets drawn into defending himself, counterattacking with complaints or put-downs of his own, and withdrawing into angry silence. He bounces back and forth between thinking that his wife is being unreasonable and that he is being uncaring.

Sorting out problems like this is complicated by the fact that the complaints of the ill spouse often contain an element of truth.

For instance, if a husband is by nature less affectionate and attentive than his wife would like, she may manage this reasonably well if she is not depressed. She may initiate constructive problem-solving discussions. She might ask her husband to work on changing his behavior. Or she could use humor and sarcasm to express her feelings.

She might find herself feeling reasonably accepting of him, given his other, more desirable, traits. As a depressive illness takes hold, however, she will likely find herself growing increasingly hurt and frustrated by her husband. Dependency needs and irritability increase in depression, and tolerance decreases. She may begin to press her husband to modify his behavior. She may think, "If only he were more loving, caring, or considerate, then I would not feel so depressed or so irritated." The husband may fail to maintain perspective. Rather than weighing her complaints, judging them himself, and talking all this over, he acts out his own frustration.

The reader may object that marital problems can cause depression and that treating a spouse for depression when the other spouse's behavior is contributing to the problem is like blaming the victim of a crime. There is some validity to this objection. It is important to remember that there is a complex and circular interaction between clinical depression and relationship problems. Often it is easy to discern how life events are adversely affecting a person's mood. What is very often not taken into account by patients and therapists alike is how a person's mood or mood disorder insidiously affects a marriage. Once a depressive episode has started, it will often become autonomous and make worse what may already be a troubled relationship.

Those with a feminist perspective may balk at the biological perspective, since many more women than men are depressed. Diagnosing a wife as depressed can certainly be used as a weapon to put her in a one-down position. However, it may still be that she is depressed and needs treatment. Often, it is best for the therapist to discuss the diagnosis with the wife alone. If she reveals this information to her husband and he misuses it by dismissing all of their problems as being due to her illness, the therapist must assist the patient in putting a stop to this.

Some might suggest the difference in power between men and women in our society is in fact the cause of depression. Undoubtedly, power differences do contribute to depression. However, keep in mind that depression can become autonomous and need treatment regardless of what caused it. Changing the environment is often important for facilitating recovery, but it may well not be sufficient. In addition, there is no clear evidence to suggest that the patriarchal structure of our society is the *main* causative element in depression.

Moreover, it is frequently overlooked that men who physically abuse their wives or terrorize them with temper outbursts often have some sort of mood disorder. Treatment programs for batterers tend to look upon the abuser's violence as a choice. This may not be true in many cases. Concern about the male batterer not taking responsibility for his behavior is understandable but can be dealt with. First of all, medication is unlikely to be the sole solution to a batterer's problem. Medication will merely increase the man's control over his temper. Even if adequately treated with medication, these men will still need group and individual therapy to help them relinquish psychological defenses, which are geared toward shifting responsibility for their behavior to others. Regardless of the cause, the man can and should be held responsible for his behavior and for doing something about it. Understanding an important source of the abuser's lack of control is not the same as justifying or tolerating it.

Marital problems are further compounded when both spouses have chronic, low-grade mood disorders. It is actually not uncommon for two people with mood disorders to get married. This is referred to as "assortative mating."

For instance: A wife has a chronic retarded depression with a great deal of guilt and shame about her poor functioning. The husband has an agitated depression or mild bipolar illness that drives him to work constantly. These men can be quite rigid, demanding, critical, and complaining. Since depressed people often blame themselves for everything that goes wrong, it may be hard for the wife to realize that her husband is too demanding. Given the cognitive distortions that are so common in depression, the depressed spouse who is being attacked is likely to accept the spouse's nastiness as justified and reasonable.

When patients call complaining of marital problems or requesting marital counseling, a therapist should always consider the possibility that one or both of the spouses is suffering from a mood disorder.

A therapist working with a patient who repeatedly complains about his spouse should not necessarily side with the patient and urge him to press his complaints. If the complaints seem to be about trivial matters or are accompanied by excessive irritation, they may be fueled by a mood disorder. Advising the patient to be more open about his feelings in this case can make matters worse.

HOW FAMILY MEMBERS CAN HELP

Educate yourself about depression and its symptoms. Try to limit the amount of advice you give the depressed person. Stay with how the depressed person feels. Do not try to talk the person out of depression, especially if the depression is moderate to severe. This will not work and may contribute to a worsening of the depression. The depressed person will begin to feel guilty and ashamed about being unable to be consoled.

After sympathizing with the pain he is in, begin to educate the person about the illness of depression. Expect to get a defensive reaction. People usually do not like to hear that they may be clinically depressed. Drop it for the moment, but do not apologize. Bring up the subject again at an appropriate time. Encourage the person to do some reading on mood disorders. Unless it is an emergency, do not push him to get help until he has begun to come around to the idea that he may have a mood disorder.

When first attempting to get a person to go for help, focus on how treatment will bring him relief from his misery. Do not stress that he has to go for help because he is making you miserable. For instance, talk about how he would feel less depressed, anxious, or agitated if he got help and not about how unpleasant his irritability is for you. If this does not work, then you may need to confront the person with how his illness is hurting you and others. Always strive to separate the problems the illness is causing from the person himself. That is, make the illness the enemy, not the person or his personality.

If the person is in therapy and you get the sense that the therapist is not aware of the depressive illness, suggest to him that he bring it up to his therapist. Suggest getting a second opinion. Continually express confidence that the illness will improve with correct diagnosis and proper treatment.

Once a family member is in treatment, you can help by keeping an eye out for signs of deterioration in his mood and functioning. Point out when you believe the patient's mood or behavior is being influenced by the mood disorder. The depressed person is going to need to learn that he cannot entirely trust his feelings. Of course, no one likes to hear that his perceptions or feelings may be distorted, so this is an issue likely to lead to some conflict. There is also the real danger that family members may misinterpret a patient's normal feelings or reactions as a sign of illness. Family members must be careful to consider the possibility that a patient's feelings, reactions, and perceptions may be appropriate, at least to some degree.

If Your Spouse or Relative Refuses Help

Even if you know a person has a depressive illness and is unable to "snap out of it," and even if you follow the suggestions listed above, you may still get burned out. Check yourself to see if you have not slipped into trying to rescue the depressed person. This will only serve to compound your frustration.

You may get especially frustrated if the depressed person you are trying to help refuses to seek professional assistance and does not seem to be doing anything to get well. There may come a point where you need to set limits. You cannot listen indefinitely to the depressed person's pain and tales of woe. If you try, the resentment you build up will destroy the relationship. If you worry about hurting the person's feelings, remember it may be worse not to set limits. You may find yourself withdrawing or avoiding the person. This will hurt the depressed person more. In extreme cases, friends and family members can begin to have fantasies or wishes that the person would commit suicide and end everyone's misery. The guilt these kinds of fantasies provoke sometimes leads family members to set even fewer limits. Family members who are obviously being driven crazy may say that they feel sorry for the person. The anger they feel toward the patient is buried. Setting limits by refusing to listen to the same problems repeatedly may help the depressed person see the need to get professional help.

Threats of Suicide

If you *suspect* that the depressed person is in danger of taking her life or hurting someone else, you should urge the person to go to the emergency room of a hospital for an evaluation. If the person is drunk or high, the risk of something bad happening is greatly increased. If you think the person will cooperate, offer to drive her to the emergency room. Alert her doctor or therapist. You should not try to determine on your own whether or not the person is in immediate danger or what kind of help is needed. Your personal involvement and lack of training make it very unwise to put yourself in such a role.

If the person refuses to go with you to the emergency room, you should call the police, fire department, local ambulance service, or crisis team to intervene. You may worry that you will anger or alienate the person. In the long run, the person will probably thank you. But so what if she is angry? At least she is alive. You can sleep that night.

If the person is released from the hospital immediately, try not to feel bad. You did not have to determine whether the person should be hospitalized or not. That was up to the doctors. You did what you had to do. Do not hesitate to have the person taken back to the emergency room that very same day if she starts talking about suicide again! As hard as it is, consistent limit setting is critical.

CHAPTER 7

PSYCHOTHERAPY FOR DEPRESSION

Before beginning to discuss *how* depression is treated, we should first consider *where* it should be treated. The majority of patients with mood disorders can be treated on an outpatient basis. Hospitalization is necessary when a patient is an immediate danger to herself or others—that is, if the patient is at serious risk of committing suicide or self-harm, or physically assaulting others. Usually, the patient's family, doctor, or therapist are able to convince the patient of the need for hospitalization. The patient then voluntarily admits herself to the psychiatric unit of a general hospital or to a hospital specializing in psychiatric treatment.

On occasion, when a patient cannot recognize the danger she is in or control her destructive impulses, she may need to be hospitalized involuntarily. This is not easy to do in most states. Nor should it be.

If a patient is brought to an emergency room for psychiatric problems, it usually requires the authorization of at least one physician, and in many states two, to have the person admitted involuntarily. The person may be held for evaluation only for a short period of time (generally two to three days at most). If the person is to be held beyond that time, there must be additional evaluations and legal proceedings to determine the need for and legality of continued confinement.

It is sometimes desirable for a patient to be admitted to the hospital even if there is no imminent danger of harm. If a patient is not eating or not sleeping, if she is terribly distraught, has a substance abuse or medical problem, or if outpatient treatment is not going well, it may come as a great relief to a patient and her family if she is admitted. In addition, doctors can be much more aggressive with treatment in the hospital, since the patient can be closely monitored.

Patients often have very mixed feelings about going into the hospital for psychiatric illness. Since the depressed person can feel quite indecisive and frightened in the first place, it is often a gut-wrenching decision. On the one hand, the patient is often scared and ashamed to be admitted. The patient mistakenly believes admission to a hospital implies he is crazy and weak. Of course, it does not, but it is hard to feel otherwise at the moment.

On the other hand, depressed patients sometimes *want* to go into the hospital. First of all, a depressed patient often feels overwhelmed and unable to cope. Second, dependency needs intensify in depression, particularly if there are significant unmet emotional needs from childhood. Depressed people want to be taken care of. But it is hard for them to acknowledge this. It stirs up all sorts of anxieties. Patients often need help to feel it is okay to be taken care of for a while.

WIDELY PRACTICED TYPES OF PSYCHOTHERAPY FOR DEPRESSION

Psychoanalytic Psychotherapy for Depression (PPD)

This psychotherapy, derived from Sigmund Freud's work and developed by his followers, is founded on the idea that depression is based on the childhood disappointment of wishes for parental affection and affirmation, and the child's failure to fix a parent's unhappiness. This leads to:

1. Low self-esteem, guilt, and shame based on the belief developed in childhood that personal inadequacy is the reason why parents were not affectionate or were unhappy. A

failure to please important people or to fulfill an ideal or goal that might bring approval from others can then precipitate depression in adulthood.

2. A sense of emptiness and a search—doomed to failure—of someone or something to fill the emptiness. The person also feels ashamed of his intense neediness.

3. Rage regarding the unmet needs, directed at the image of the parent who has been internalized, which leads to unrealistic expectations, repeated disappointment in current relationships, and conflicts over expressing rage to important others.

The psychoanalytic therapist will not and should not start out by trying to explore these issues with the patient. Acutely and severely depressed people spend enough time as it is tortured by painful memories; and they are often very guilt-ridden about the anger they feel. A therapist who urges depressed patients to discuss their past or who pushes them to become aware of their anger will cause more harm than good. The analytic therapist will adopt a supportive approach at first until the worst of the depression is past. The analytic therapist tends to give less direct advice than other therapists. However, she will probably, like most other therapists, focus initially on bolstering self-esteem, reducing undue guilt, and helping the patient cope with day-to-day problems.

Later, when the patient is feeling somewhat better, the psychoanalytic therapist will begin to explore more painful issues. The therapist may encourage the patient to remember feelings of loss, emptiness, inadequacy, and rage for the love and affirmation they did not receive. She will help the patient modify psychological defenses so that the patient can become more aware of fantasies and feelings. She will help the patient begin to grieve and let go of the childlike wish for someone who will be perfectly caring and understanding.

Advice-giving is avoided in later stages of analytic therapy with depressed patients. The patient is generally given free reign over the material he wishes to discuss. In fact, patients are advised to say whatever comes to mind and not to censor what they say. In contrast, therapists from the other schools of therapy described later encourage their patients to focus on certain topics or areas.

The analytic therapist looks for ways in which the patient recreates early relationship patterns with the therapist. Some analytic therapists believe that helping the patient become aware of and resolve problems in the therapy relationship is the best way to help the patient get better. Although short-term or time-limited psychoanalytic therapies do exist, psychoanalytic therapy has historically been open-ended.

Analytic therapists have traditionally had a bias against the use of medication. This has slowly changed, especially among medically trained analysts. It would be unusual to find an analytic therapist who would advocate treating a moderately to severely depressed patient with psychotherapy alone.

Cognitive-Behavioral Therapy (CBT)

The basic tenet of CBT is that depression is a result of automatic and unquestioned assumptions or thoughts about oneself, others, and the future. If a person believes, for example, that she is a failure because of a failure to get a promotion, she will be prone to depression.

The CBT therapist attempts to get the person to discover distorted thinking and cognitive errors and subject them to rational analysis. What is the evidence for and against the thought? How does failing at something, such as a relationship, make you a failure as a person overall? If you can never be as happy with someone else (itself a questionable assumption), does that mean you are doomed to complete misery?

The cognitive therapist also has the patient try behavioral experiments to get her to change behaviors linked to depression. For instance, the therapist might have the patient, who is in a retarded depression and who believes nothing can give her pleasure, make a schedule of daily activities. The patient has to agree to follow the schedule even if she does not feel like it. Generally, patients will find that they gain some measure of satisfaction from the activities once started. These techniques may be useful for individuals who are more severely depressed and unable to correct irrational thoughts through thinking alone.

Cognitive therapy is focused on here-and-now issues. At more advanced stages of therapy, therapists will, however, try to help patients understand and modify long-standing assumptions about themselves and the world. Cognitive therapy is a highly structured therapy. That is, patient and therapist follow a fairly set agenda for each session. Patients are expected to do a considerable amount of homework.

Interpersonal Therapy (IPT)

This approach emphasizes the role that disturbed interpersonal relationships play in depression. Patients are helped to solve interpersonal problems. Interpersonal therapists view four problem areas as key to helping patients with depression: loss and grief, negotiating expectations in relationships, coping with difficult life transitions, and social-skills deficits.

Interpersonal therapists adhere to the view that depression is a medical or biological illness. In initial sessions, they focus on educating the patient about depressive illness and providing hope for recovery. They try to help the patient reduce undue self-criticism and shame by pointing out that her problems are caused not by weakness of character but by the illness of depression.

Interpersonal therapists do not assert that interpersonal problems are the cause of depression. However, the research studies they have conducted indicate that helping people solve interpersonal problems can alleviate depression. The therapist focuses on here-and-now interpersonal issues of emotional importance to the client. There is little emphasis placed on understanding childhood experiences, the conflicts these experiences may have generated, or the relationship between the therapist and the patient.

Interpersonal therapists usually focus on helping patients in one or two of the following areas: (1) expressing and resolving grief over the death of a loved one; (2) altering relationships that are abusive, lack intimacy, or are otherwise unsatisfying; (3) managing life transitions such as divorce or retirement; and (4) resolving difficulties that keep socially isolated patients from forming or maintaining relationships.

Therapists help patients decide what they want and do not want in a relationship and how to alter the relationship in a way that is mutually acceptable to both parties. Special emphasis is placed on helping patients become aware of and more comfortable with anger and using the anger to fuel appropriate assertiveness. While cognitive therapists assert that feelings are a result of thoughts, interpersonal therapists view feelings as more central to the work of therapy. They do not believe that thoughts are a primary cause of psychological distress.

Interpersonal therapists make extensive use of role-play. Patients are encouraged to act out various roles with the therapist in order to practice new interpersonal skills. Interpersonal therapists actively and strongly encourage the patient to put into practice what he learns during sessions with the therapist. However, they tend to assign much less in the way of formal homework than do cognitive-behavioral therapists. Although the focus on current interpersonal issues makes this therapy more structured than psychoanalytic therapy, interpersonal therapy sessions are less structured than cognitive therapy sessions.

Interpersonal therapy, like cognitive therapy, was designed to be short-term. Patients are sometimes seen twice a week for the first two weeks and then once per week thereafter for a total of twelve to sixteen weeks of therapy. Patients are usually offered and encouraged to make use of once-a-month "booster" sessions after this initial period of work.

Interpersonal therapists feel that their therapy is quite compatible with the use of antidepressant medication.

Biologically Informed Psychotherapy of Depression (BIPD)

Adherents to this approach view depression as a biologically based, genetically transmitted medical illness. Abnormal brain biochemistry leads to vulnerability to depression triggered initially by psychosocial stress. Barring specific, treatable medical problems contributing to the depression, medication (or other biological approaches, such as bright-light treatment) combined with patient and family education about the illness are cornerstones of the treatment.

In this model, patients and family members are taught a new and more helpful perspective on the symptoms and manifestations of depression. Patients are helped to understand, for instance, that their difficulty tolerating stress is not a personal weakness for which they need to be ashamed. They are helped to see that being easily overwhelmed and stressed out is as much a symptom of the illness of depression as a fever is of pneumonia.

Therapists of this group make use of a wide variety of therapeutic techniques from the cognitive-behavioral, interpersonal, and psychoanalytic models. However, the cognitive and psychoanalytic explanations for depression are discarded.

Cognitive distortions are viewed as a symptom of depressive illness in BIPD rather than as its cause, as in cognitive therapy.

Psychoanalytic clinicians have noted that depressed individuals typically have an intense longing or need to be admired, loved, and cared for. They have an equally intense sensitivity to criticism or rejection. In short, their self-esteem is too closely tied to what others think of them. Therapists and often patients believe that this is because the patient's parents were cold, critical, or abusive.

But it is very likely that abusive parents had some sort of mood disorder themselves and that the child inherited depressive tendencies from them. This genetic vulnerability to depression was then triggered by the stress of growing up with abusive parents. The parents' failings may well have been among the first triggers for the onset of depression.

BIPD therapists also point out that just as depression damages people's view of themselves and their future—unrealistically lowering self-esteem and causing undue pessimism—it distorts their view of the past. Childhood experiences viewed through the lens of depression often cause anguish and anger that dissipates when the depression is treated with medication. Many patients report that they are no longer as preoccupied or angered by the past when they recover from depression.

BIPD therapists have found the work done in any form of therapy is considerably easier for the patient if she is adequately treated with medication. For some patients, progress may be possible only if they are first treated with medication. It is hard for many of us who have not suffered from depression to believe it, but patients in the throes of depression may, for instance, find it nearly impossible to bring an unsatisfying or clearly destructive relationship to an end. Doing so might seem to be a simple matter of will-power for most of us, but the fact is that the anxiety and anguish that comes with these bold steps is often too much for a depressed person to bear. Patients often feel ashamed of themselves for this supposed character weakness. The BIPD therapist tries to help the patient decrease this shame by pointing out that fear of bold steps is a symptom of depression. Avoidance of risk goes with depression like the inability to walk goes with a broken leg.

ART BUCHWALD

*Pulitzer Prize-winning humorist Art Buchwald may be one of the
last people you would think of as having battled depressive illness for
much of his life. In spite of his suffering, he has been able to earn a
living by making others chuckle.*

*His life story reveals how both genetic factors and early trauma
combine to produce depressive illness. It also reminds us that success
and fame do not prevent or cure depression.*

For those who may have cursed fate for saddling them with depression, Buchwald offers some solace: "Out of the suffering caused by depressive illness can come personal growth and a new sense of self."

Art Buchwald never knew his mother. Chronically depressed,
she was committed to a mental institution when he was three
months old. Art and his three older sisters told friends their
mother was dead. In his memoir, *Leaving Home*, he writes that
he never visited her because he preferred the mother he had
invented to the real one in the hospital.

Art's father, Joseph, sent his infant son, who had rickets,
first to a foundling home and then to a boardinghouse for ailing children. Unable to support his children, he put them in a
foster home when Art was five. By the time he was fifteen, Art
had lived in six homes. In 1942, he joined the marines—after
bribing a derelict with a bottle of whiskey to sign his parental-consent papers. He welcomed the discipline of the marines,
calling the corps "the best foster home I ever had."

After the war, he went to Paris and began writing a tongue-in-cheek column for the *Herald Tribune*. He married and
adopted three children, and his column became increasingly
popular. In 1963, he moved back to the United States and
started writing his Washington column and made his mark as
a political satirist. Despite his professional success, he sank

into a depression so deep that he felt ready to kill himself. He was hospitalized for a month.

In 1987, he suffered another depression so severe that he was hospitalized again. He managed to continue writing, with the help of psychoanalysis and lithium.

In a 1994 interview with the magazine *Psychology Today*, Buchwald talked about his depressions. He said he didn't care what caused depression. "But I do feel that if you can just get through the experience, you come out of it a better person. You just have to hang on. And this isn't an original idea of mine. It was told to me when I was in the middle of it. My doctor kept telling me, 'Arty, hold on, hold on.'"

He also talked about how he grew personally as a result of his depressions. "What happened to me was, there was no pill. I had these terrible depressions; they lasted four months or six months, no more than six months. And out of it, I got relieved of tremendous amounts of hang-ups. I got relieved of guilt.

"I had therapy with it. I had a lot of therapy. So I'm grateful how it came out for me, and I'm also grateful with—you see, the biggest danger obviously of a humorist is when he goes into a depression is he'll never be funny again, and that causes more depression. But I personally give credit to my depressions for making me a better writer and a better person."

CAN PSYCHOTHERAPY ALLEVIATE DEPRESSION? HOW DOES IT COMPARE TO MEDICATION?

Since the early 1980s, researchers have been studying the effectiveness of cognitive and interpersonal therapy in the treatment of major depressive episodes. Researchers have also done studies comparing the effectiveness of these therapies to each other and to antidepressant medication. What do the results tell us about how well psychotherapy works, especially when compared to medication?

Unfortunately, the answer is not straightforward and often depends on how the outcome data are analyzed. For instance, the National Institute of Mental Health (NIMH) sponsored a study comparing the effectiveness of cognitive therapy, interpersonal therapy, an antidepressant medication called imipramine, and a sugar pill (placebo) combined with reassuring contacts with a doctor in the treatment of major depressive episodes. Initial analysis indicated that the cognitive therapy, interpersonal therapy, and the medication were about equally effective.

Then Donald Klein, M.D., a psychiatrist and psychopharmacology researcher, reanalyzed the data and found the following: Medication provided faster relief and greater overall benefit than both psychotherapies and placebo for patients who were severely depressed. Interpersonal therapy was somewhat better than placebo for this group. Cognitive therapy was no better than placebo. For mildly depressed patients, Klein's analysis indicated that the psychotherapies and the medication were equally effective. This might lead the reader to think that they should opt for psychotherapy if they suffer from mild depression. But placebo treatment turned out to be as effective as the psychotherapies in mild depression. This suggests that someone who is mildly depressed should not even bother seeking help!

But then Klein did another analysis of the data. He excluded from the analysis those patients who had so-called atypical symptoms of depression (about 30 percent of the patients had atypical symptoms). Why? Most patients with atypical symptoms do not respond well to imipramine—the medication used in the NIMH study (although they often have an excellent response to an entirely different class of medication called MAO inhibitors). The patients with the atypical depression drastically lowered the apparent response rate to medication. When these patients were excluded from the analysis, a clear ordering of treatment response was found. Medication was superior to both placebo and the psychotherapies even in those patients with mild depression!

Cognitive therapy, you may recall, is based on the premise that errors in thinking lead to clinical depression. That depressed people have cognitive distortions is a matter of fact. But this does not prove cognitive distortions *cause* depression. Since there is no evidence that cognitive distortions precede depressive episodes, it is more likely that they are an *effect* of depression. Evidence for this can be seen in the majority of patients treated with medication. When medication is effective, cognitive distortions decrease. In addition, interpersonal therapy does not systematically address cognitive distortions and yet works as well with depression as does cognitive therapy.

Contrary to the cognitive theory of depression, there is increasing evidence that intense human emotions are not mediated by conscious thoughts and beliefs. The processing of emotional information occurs in a structure of the brain removed from the centers of conscious rational thought. Moreover, there are more robust connections running from the brain structures involved in emotion to those involved in rational thought than the other way around. The emotional part of our brains may speak with a clearer and louder voice than the rational part.

In a 1995 review of outcome studies on cognitive therapy of depression, a British researcher noted that studies of CBT's effectiveness have critical methodological problems, which call results of the studies into question. He concluded that CBT's benefits in acute depression have not been proven.

Psychotherapy for Dysthymia

Cognitive and interpersonal therapy were originally tested on people with discrete episodes of major depression. But a substantial number of patients who seek psychiatric help (at least a third) suffer from dysthymia—mild, yet chronic, and in many cases, lifelong depression. The evidence that these therapies alone can alleviate dysthymia is sparse. What little evidence there is may favor interpersonal therapy.

If interpersonal therapy is not effective in three to four months, however, medication should be considered. As of now, research studies support the use of medication as the treatment of choice for dysthymia. Medication can often produce dramatic and life-transforming changes in the 50 to 60 percent of dysthymic patients who respond to it (see chap. 8).

Are Cognitive Therapy and Interpersonal Therapy Superior to Less-Focused, Supportive Therapy?

Many people tend to take for granted that the modern psychotherapies designed specifically for depression are an improvement over old-fashioned supportive therapy. The argument is based on the appealing notion that focusing on problems associated specifically with the illness of depression (automatic thoughts or interpersonal problems) is more efficient and effective than providing support, education, and reassurance. In fact, it is not at all clear that this is true. Psychotherapy research has generally shown that therapies based on very different theories tend to produce roughly the same clinical results. There must be common elements in all forms of psychotherapy that account for this—elements that have nothing to do with theory or specific technique.

KEY ELEMENTS OF ANY PSYCHOTHERAPY FOR DEPRESSION

One of the key "active ingredients" in any form of therapy is the therapist's nurturing and support of the patient. Having someone who is kind, calm, encouraging, and confident by your side can obviously be very reassuring. Not surprisingly, research has shown that therapists who are warm, accepting, genuine, and able to communicate their understanding of another person's emotional pain are the most helpful. It is hard to imagine how even the most technically skilled cognitive, analytic, or interpersonal therapist could be helpful if he were consistently nasty, critical, or lacked empathy, or if he communicated a sense of hopelessness.

Another key element, which requires a solid bond between therapist and patient, is the therapist's ability to help the patient make specific behavioral changes. Simply put, the therapist has to help the patient do things the patient is afraid of (grieve, stand up for herself, go in the subway, or look for a new job) and stop doing things that are destructive or that perpetuate a problem (washing her hands, losing her temper, or doing drugs). Changing behavior probably causes semipermanent changes in brain function and perhaps even brain structure.

However, therapists need to be careful about expecting too much early in treatment from moderately to severely depressed patients. These patients often do not have the energy or confidence necessary to attempt changes that may help alleviate their depression. Pushing these patients to change when they cannot is counterproductive. The depressed patient will not say, "Heh, doctor, you should ease up. I am clinically depressed. Don't you know that one of the problems associated with depressive illness is that it's very hard for people to make changes that might help them? You're expecting way too much too soon." Instead, the patient will blame himself and be left feeling incompetent and inadequate. The therapist has to know when to back off and not push for change. She should give the patient permission to lay low and not work too hard at first.

A therapist should provide information on depressive illness that may help reduce a patient's undue guilt and shame. For instance, the therapist could point out that difficulty coping with everyday stress is a result of depressive illness and not a weakness of character. John Markowitz, M.D., tells patients that they have been trying to fight with one hand tied behind their backs. The therapist can reassure the patient that when he begins to feel better, he will find himself more able to tackle problems. In addition, the therapist can comment on how the patient has managed to keep functioning in some areas in spite of the depression.

Exploration of painful issues from the past should be avoided early on. A depressed patient tends to be tortured by thoughts and feelings from the past. The therapist should try to help the patient bolster defenses against the awareness of these issues and feelings. Patients can be encouraged, for instance, to distract themselves in various ways when they find themselves dwelling on the past.

The therapist should be flexible enough to make use of a wide range of psychotherapeutic techniques. I happen to believe, however, that a basically biological orientation, combined with an appreciation of psychodynamics (a psychoanalytic perspective on the forces and feelings governing human behavior and relationships), should form the foundation of treatment. A therapist treating depressed patients will be better able to help the patient understand the subtleties of his feelings and relationship patterns if the therapist understands psychodynamics.

Ideally, the therapist treating depressed patients should know the following: Basic information on the brain biochemistry of mood disorders, psychopharmacology, medical mimics of mood disorders, and some knowledge of the significance of physical exam and lab results. An appreciation of the subtle manifestations of mood disorders, a familiarity with all major psychotherapeutic models, and an understanding of family dynamics in mood disorders are also important. She should have expertise in the diagnosis and treatment of alcohol and drug abuse.

Since depressive illness can make a person unmercifully self-critical, it is helpful for a therapist to point out ways in which he continues to function, in spite of the illness.

The therapist should be able to take criticism and anger without retaliating and should be able to admit mistakes. The therapist will have to sense when a patient is angry with him and help the patient discuss it. The therapist will make this much easier for the patient if he remains humble and willing to learn about his own emotional shortcomings and difficulties. The therapist is in an excellent position to be able to help the depressed patient realize that anger is not something to be feared. The patient needs to see that anger will not destroy a relationship.

In later stages of therapy, a therapist has to help a patient understand how he has had a hand in his interpersonal problems. Certainly, a depressed patient often needs an ally to help him realize he is not at fault for everything. Depressed people often feel overly responsible for anything that does not go well in their life. However, becoming too closely allied with the patient's point of view will ultimately do him a disservice. It can greatly harm his interpersonal relationships.

Marriages are especially vulnerable. A therapist who consistently goes along with making a patient's spouse the enemy is going to hurt the patient more than help him. Many times, a patient will interpret his spouse's behavior in very negative ways. The depressed patient may, for instance, view a spouse's temporary withdrawal or indifference as a sign of lack of love, caring, or commitment to the relationship. It may have a different meaning, however. Although by no means justified, it may be the spouse's way of expressing resentment she does not feel free to express directly. Except when a spouse has an addiction, is abusive, obviously manipulative, controlling, or neglectful, helping a patient see how his own behavior is connected to a spouse's behavior may help reduce conflict.

The danger is that a depressed individual will take what the therapist is saying and turn it into yet another reason to beat up on himself. This may be an unconscious defense, which the therapist needs to discuss. Or the patient may simply need to be helped to see that understanding someone else's behavior is not the same as justifying or excusing it and that, ultimately, a spouse is responsible for her own behavior. In spite of this danger, the patient may need help seeing that just as he is not all bad, his spouse is not all bad either.

A therapist must become emotionally involved with his patient and yet should maintain a degree of emotional distance as well. Failure to do so will make it difficult for the therapist to do his job. A therapist has a professional obligation to deal with the feelings aroused in him by the work in a special way. They are to be used in the service of understanding and helping the patient. They should not be acted upon. For instance, if a therapist feels irritated, he should not allow himself to get nasty with the patient. Instead, the therapist should try to understand what is going on in the relationship with the patient. This insight can then be used to help the patient understand and change similar problems in other relationships.

In a patient's darkest moments, particularly if his depression has not been responding to treatment, the therapist has to help the patient see that there is still hope for recovery. This requires that the therapist have a handle on his own depressive tendencies. This may be hard for some therapists, since many struggle with depressive feelings and ways of thinking of their own.

A therapist has to be able to accept limits on his ability to help. One motive therapists sometimes have for choosing their line of work is the need to symbolically rescue or change the mother or father they failed to save. This is perfectly fine up to a point. But if the therapist feels bad about himself for being unable to fix a patient's pain, just as he felt when he could not help Mom or Dad, he will ultimately end up burdening the patient.

A patient should not have to deal with the therapist's need to have him get better. When a therapist can calmly share a patient's despair, it gives the patient a message that pain can be tolerated and endured. A patient needs to sense that he can come in depressed time and time again and the therapist, while sympathetic, will not feel overwhelmed or in a panic.

In order to protect his own self-esteem, a therapist may unwittingly start to blame a patient if that patient is not improving. This unconscious defensive strategy, designed to help the therapist prop up his own mental health, can have a devastating impact on the patient. A depressed patient is all too often ready to accept blame he does not deserve.

A depressed patient is used to seeking warmth and affection

from others by pleasing them, often at his own expense. A depressed person may feel a need to act as if he has improved when in fact he has not. The person hopes that by making the therapist feel good, he can win the therapist's affection and approval.

In addition, it seems many a depressed person grew up feeling she should not burden Mom or Dad with her problems or feelings. She felt that she had to be the good girl whose job it was to keep the depressed parent happy. She felt compelled to do this to earn the attention and love she wanted. A therapist has to be careful that this dynamic does not re-create itself in psychotherapy.

A therapist should be reasonably consistent in maintaining a set day and time for a patient's appointment. A patient has to know the therapist is someone he can rely on. A therapist should give the patient his full, undivided attention during the session and not interrupt it to take phone calls or deal with other matters.

A therapist should keep revelations about his personal life to a minimum and should never burden a patient with his own problems. The therapist should not get involved in dual roles with a patient. For instance, a therapist should not treat a patient and do business with the patient either while the patient is in therapy or afterward. Avoiding dual roles ensures the patient's needs remain paramount.

As discussed in chapter 1, the therapist should not treat and should not accept a referral from the patient to treat other members of the patient's family or his friends or work associates. To do so invites a great deal of trouble, even if everyone agrees to the arrangement. It brings up possible problems with confidentiality and privacy and may impair the patient's sense that the therapist has his interests alone in mind. Members of the patient's family can and should be included in the treatment process, however, in terms of education, guidance, and support.

All of this is certainly a tall order. While no one therapist will be able to master everything there is to know, every therapist has an ethical responsibility to continually strive to do so.

CHAPTER 8

MEDICATION FOR DEPRESSION

M any people, when first told by their therapist or doctor that they are suffering from depression, react with shock and disbelief. The diagnosis comes as something of a blow to their ego. To then be told that their condition would likely respond to treatment with antidepressants is even more disconcerting. Many people still feel that the use of medication is shameful. They should not have to feel that way, given the biological nature of their illness. Nevertheless, many people still equate being depressed and using medication with being weak or crazy.

Before the 1970s, many people had similar reactions to the idea of seeing a psychotherapist. It was not something people spoke about openly. Now, in some parts of the country at least, few people think it odd if someone mentions he is in therapy. People even talk openly about what their therapist has told them.

By the start of the second or third decade of the twenty-first century, there will no longer be a stigma attached to taking medication for depression. People already discuss their antidepressant medication at parties. Prozac has been discussed on TV and in major publications. But for now, the fear about using these medications is based on misconception and misinformation. Let's approach this topic by looking at the kind of concerns and questions people often have about depression and the use of medication.

*I didn't think I was in such bad shape
that I needed medication. I can function.*

If a doctor or therapist suggests that you might benefit from medication, this does *not* mean you are in "bad shape." The suggestion does not imply anything about the severity of your illness. It does not mean you are crazy or out of control. It is a myth that only people who are severely depressed and cannot function should take medication. The fact is, less severe depressions respond just as well to medication. If you have a less severe depression, you may not *need* medication, but it will probably improve your life. Once you feel better, you may decide you were crazy for not trying it sooner.

*But I've always felt this way.
It's just the way I am.*

People often do not realize that they have always been mildly depressed and that they do not have to live with gloom, irritability, or anxiety. It may not be your personality. The modern antidepressants may be especially useful for chronic, mild depression (dysthymia). Some patients with chronic depression experience profound changes in their quality of life when properly treated.

Many of the presumed "character traits" of those with dysthymia may melt away when medication works well. Successfully treated dysthymic patients often report that they feel more energetic and motivated, more able to take on life's problems, more confident, less shy, and less afraid of anger and self-assertion within four to eight weeks of beginning medication. What were once thought to be traits—personal characteristics of the patient—turn out to be manifestations of a long-term state of mild depression.

*So how do you tell the difference between
a lousy mood and depressive illness?*

There are a number of areas your therapist or doctor explores to tell the difference. For one thing, depressive illness includes a number of symptoms other than depressed mood. If you have enough of these symptoms, then you may have a depressive illness even if you have good reasons to be feeling down. In addition to your current symptoms, however, your therapist or doctor will ask about a past history of similar symptoms and family history.

The intensity of your mood problem, how long it has lasted (more than three or four weeks and it's probably depression), and how pervasively it affects your quality of life and your functioning are key factors. Your therapist or doctor will try to discern whether the kind and intensity of symptoms you are having are in keeping with the nature of the stress or trigger. Your therapist may ask to see your spouse or a family member to determine if he or she has noticed changes in your mood. The therapist may want to know, for instance, if your spouse perceives that you have been unduly irritable lately. Repeated interpersonal conflicts in several different settings suggest a mood disorder.

But aren't medications for
depression just happy pills?

No. They will not make someone who is not clinically depressed feel happy. They will not get you high. They will not even make someone who is sad or grieving feel better, since these are normal mood states.

Isn't it better to go through some
pain in psychotherapy to get at the
root of my depression? I don't want
to just cover things up.

This concern is based on two erroneous assumptions: first, that your symptoms are largely due to deep-rooted problems of which you are not conscious and, second, that antidepressants cover up the emotional roots of problems. Neither of these assumptions is true. There is no credible scientific evidence linking past problems to the specific symptoms of depression. So there is nothing to cover. Moreover, the antidepressants correct, at least temporarily, the underlying biochemical problems that cause the depression symptoms.

Research has demonstrated that antidepressants do not interfere with learning new ways of thinking, behaving, and dealing with feelings in therapy or on your own. In fact, by alleviating undue psychic pain, they often make learning possible.

So I will just walk around feeling like
everything is okay? I want to change my life,
not just make believe it's fine.

This concern is based on the assumption that your depression is caused solely by your life circumstances. If only they would change, you figure the depression would go away. Although life stresses and relationship problems are major triggers for depression, they are not its root cause. Many people remain depressed for years after an event that set off the depression, even if things start going their way. Many people who experience profound traumas in their lives do not get depressed. You may find this hard to believe, but it is a fact: If you treat the depression, things in your life could stay the same and you will still feel better. Those treated for depression nearly always report that they feel much more comfortable handling pressure, criticism, and stress. They generally lose the feeling of being emotionally overwhelmed and physically exhausted.

Finally, treating the depression will not make you apathetic and less likely to change your life. Quite the contrary, banishing your depression will help make you feel as if you want to and can change your life.

I'm worried I'll not be myself or not
feel normal on medication. I don't
want to walk around like a zombie.

Antidepressants will not transform you into a zombie. They may cause some sleepiness, but this usually wears off once your body gets used to the medication. Feelings of being sedated or overmedicated usually pass as well.

On occasion, some patients complain of being absentminded, forgetful, or "foggy." These are undesirable side effects and not the goal of antidepressant therapy. Bring these problems to your doctor's attention. She will either adjust the dosage of your medication or switch you to another antidepressant. When effectively treated, you will feel perfectly normal and like yourself. Most people actually report they feel more like themselves.

But I want to learn how to deal with
my problems on my own, without medication.
Medication is just a crutch.

Nothing could be further from the truth. This belief is based on the assumption that you could pull yourself out of the pits emotionally if only you had the guts or the right tools or if you could figure out what is "really" bothering you. You probably have more guts than the average person! If you did not, you would not have been able to expend the extra effort to drag yourself through life. People with depression who keep functioning in their usual roles as worker, parent, or partner (although not functioning as well or as efficiently as they would like) are like people who keep going all day even though they have pneumonia and a fever of 103 degrees. The right tools can help you manage your depression, but they will not fix it. And if you are severely depressed, trying to fix your depression with psychological tools may leave you feeling frustrated and upset with yourself. You will get angry at yourself for not being able to do something you thought you should be able to do. The result may be that you get more depressed. Once you understand the nature of depression, it will seem odd that you would blame yourself for being weak and unable to snap out of it.

So what do medications do exactly?
How do they work?

Various research studies have demonstrated that depressive illness is an inherited, biologically based vulnerability to stress. The brain of the depressed person has difficulty buffering itself against adverse life events. Loss of an important relationship, for instance, or the fear of that loss, adversely affects brain biochemistry responsible for the maintenance of mood and self-esteem. Antidepressants work by correcting imbalances in brain chemistry responsible for depressed mood, low self-esteem, difficulty thinking clearly, and disturbances in sleep and appetite.

But my father had a bad temper. I could
never please him and he really did
not seem too interested in being a dad.
My mother was always irritable and impatient.
Wouldn't anyone grow up to be depressed under
those circumstances?

The available evidence suggests early environment is certainly important but that it alone cannot explain why some people get depressed. Chaotic family life is an early stress on a brain that is at an especially vulnerable stage of development. Many subtle or low-grade depressions probably start in childhood for this reason.

In addition, just because you feel terrible about the way you grew up does not mean growing up in a harsh environment is the main reason why you now feel terrible. When someone is properly treated for a depressive illness, she often finds that feelings of bitterness and sadness about the past decrease. She finds it easier to temporarily forget the past or at least easier to put it in proper perspective. That is because depressive illness makes it hard to forget. Most people have the ability to put bad things out of their minds for a while. Not so the depressed person. The past can torture her.

But in my case there's nothing wrong with
my life. I have nothing to be depressed about.
I feel guilty and ashamed for being depressed.

But this is the whole point about clinical depression. You do not need to have something wrong with your life to get clinically depressed. Often life events trigger depression, especially the early episodes. People who have had several previous episodes of depression and are not taking medication are likely to have another bout even without any stress.

If I decide to try medication, how long
will it take before I begin to feel better?

Once you decide to go ahead with medication, you will probably feel it is taking too long! It is natural to want to feel better as soon as possible. But antidepressants take time to work. Before you begin to feel better, you may notice that you are sleeping more soundly. Others may notice subtle differences in your mood before you do. They will typically say that you seem calmer or a bit less stressed by things. Many patients will gradually begin to feel better in two to four weeks. Others feel nothing for two to four weeks and then suddenly feel better. It is not uncommon to notice small improvements for up to twelve or sixteen weeks after starting the medication.

The important thing is to remind yourself that it takes time and to try not to get too discouraged about the long-term prospects for recovery based on how you are feeling after a couple of weeks on the medication. Hopelessness and impatience are frequent symptoms of depression, so this can be hard to do. It will help if you read about depression and its treatment, turn to your doctor or therapist for support and encouragement, or join a support group. Your family should also learn about depression and what to expect from treatment so that they can help provide encouragement during the early weeks of treatment.

You will also need to keep in mind that it is normal for recovery from depression to be uneven. You may not feel steadily better over time. Especially in the early weeks of treatment, you may feel better and then slip back. There are many reasons why this may happen, but two are most common. Your doctor will start you on a low dose of medication to reduce the risk of unpleasant side effects. Once your brain adapts to the low starting dose, you may lose any initial therapeutic response. When the dosage is raised, you will almost certainly feel better again.

Patients may also slip back early on in treatment if they frequently get embroiled in angry exchanges with their husband, wife, family, or others with whom they are close. A lack of warmth and caring between the patient and significant others is a problem as well. In the early stages of treatment, the biochemical pathways implicated in the symptoms of depression and bipolar disorder remain extremely vulnerable to emotional stress. It may not take much to set off a relapse, since stress disrupts the biochemistry that medication is attempting to correct.

Couple or family therapy geared toward helping the patient and significant others understand mood disorders and to reduce the amount of negative emotion expressed is often helpful and sometimes critical to the patient's recovery. The patient may have to work especially hard at controlling irritation and anger.

Can I stop the medication as soon as I feel better?

No. It is virtually certain that your symptoms will return within a few days to a few weeks, depending on what medication you have been taking. You may even feel worse than before you started if you stop the medication prematurely, especially if you have been depressed for a long time. It is harder in some ways to feel good for a while and then feel rotten again than it is to never have felt good.

So how long do I have to take it for? Do I have to take it for the rest of my life?

If this is your first episode of major depression, you have not had any symptoms of chronic mild depression prior to this episode, and if you have had an excellent response to medication, you should stay on it for roughly six to nine months and taper off under your doctor's supervision. Unfortunately, depression is a recurrent illness. You will need to monitor yourself carefully and get back on medication if symptoms recur.

If you have had chronic mild depression (dysthymia), repeated bouts of depression, or less than a complete response to the medications you have tried, you will have to carefully weigh the risks and benefits, in consultation with your doctor and therapist, of trying to go off the medication. It may certainly be worth a try if you have been completely well for several years and there are no major stresses in your life that could trigger a relapse. The dosage of the medication should be tapered off very slowly (over the course of several months) while you and your doctor watch for the reemergence of symptoms. If symptoms do return, it would be in your best interests to strongly consider staying on the medication for life.

This can be a discouraging thought for some people. Exactly why is an interesting question. Certainly no one *likes* the idea of having to take medication every day for the rest of their life. But it does not mean what a lot of people think it means. It is not so horrible if it dramatically improves the quality of your life. I always suggest to people that they wait to see how they feel on the medication before making any decisions. If you are feeling good on it and you remember how lousy you used to feel, you may not want to give it up. Feeling less self-critical and ashamed will put you in a better position to make a good decision.

Some doctors are starting to make decisions about discontinuing medication on the basis of laboratory values of critical biological markers of depression. For instance, if a urine screen reveals the level of a metabolite of the neurotransmitter norepinephrine is still low after nine months on an antidepressant meant to correct norepinephrine functioning, the doctor may decide to keep you on the medication even if you are feeling well. Use of laboratory testing of this kind is not yet widespread.

What are the side effects? What about unknown long-term side effects? Can antidepressants cause cancer or other long-term problems?

The side effects of widely used antidepressants such as Prozac, Zoloft, and Paxil are usually mild and diminish as your body adapts to the medication. However, you must be prepared to deal with side effects before you start feeling better. It can be hard to tolerate side effects when you feel the medication is not doing anything for you.

Check a drug reference manual and you will notice that the list of possible side effects for your particular antidepressant is quite long. However, people often have few or none of these side effects. This is especially the case if you and your doctor follow the rule "Start low and go slow." That is, start with a low dose, allow time for your body to adapt, and increase the dosage slowly. Rapidly increasing the dosage in an attempt to feel better more quickly often backfires: You will get unpleasant side effects, stop the medication, and feel discouraged.

For a discussion of specific side effects you may have when first using Prozac and other drugs, please see the section below on types of antidepressants.

As for long-term side effects, the best we can say at this point is that the medications are probably safe. The older antidepressants, which affect many neurotransmitters, have been around for forty years and have created no serious problems in patients over the long term. There was one report from a Canadian researcher that tumor growth was *stimulated* by Prozac and an older antidepressant, Elavil, in laboratory rats and mice who were *injected* with tumor cells. The antidepressants did not *cause* the tumors, however. There is no evidence that they stimulate tumor growth in humans. You should also be aware of conflicting evidence suggesting that antidepressants in high doses may suppress the growth of tumors. Antidepressants have also been used in the treatment of prostate cancer. Still, there can be no guarantee that some rare and potentially fatal side effect will not occur.

You also need to weigh the chance of unlikely long-term effects against the known long-term side effects of *not* treating your mood disorder. It is not just a matter of feeling better. Success in your career, marriage, or other long-term relationships may be at stake. In addition, we know that untreated mood disorders can lead to other medical problems due to the biological and psychological stress placed on the body. The fact is, people with untreated depression do not live as long as the rest of the population. Heart disease is more likely to kill you if you are clinically depressed, for instance.

There is also the very real possibility of subtle damage to the brain over time if your mood disorder is not treated. This is especially the case in bipolar disorder.

Okay, but I still don't like taking anything unnatural.
I don't even take an aspirin if I have a headache.

This objection probably has as much to do with the purpose for which you are taking something unnatural as it does with concerns about an unnatural substance in your body. The proof of this is seen in people who use alcohol, drugs, and cigarettes and who raise the question. They may have taken large quantities of harmful or illicit substances for years and may still not be comfortable with the idea of using medication for a mood disorder. Why? Because they mistakenly believe that they are weak if they cannot fix themselves.

You never drink, smoke, or use drugs? Well, consider this: Do you eat meat, drink soda, eat processed and prepared foods, junk food, or supermarket produce grown in fields treated with chemical fertilizers, pesticides, and herbicides? Do you wear antiperspirant or dye your hair? Do you breathe when you mop your floor or clean your windows with chemical cleaners? Do you inhale when you cut your lawn with a gas-powered mower or drive on the highway? Of course you do. *So you are putting unnatural substances into your body every day.* The real issue is this: It is uncomfortable to think that you have to put something unnatural into your body to fix that which you mistakenly believe should be under your control.

Won't I get hooked on these
antidepressants if they make me feel good?

Not at all. They are not addicting. You cannot buy antidepressants or mood stabilizers on the street. The reason is that if someone without a mood disorder takes them, they do not feel anything (except perhaps for some minor side effects).

My spouse or family does not
think I need antidepressants.

Spouses often have many of the same concerns and misconceptions as do patients about medications for depression. These frequently lead family members to give inaccurate and potentially dangerous medical and psychiatric advice for which they have absolutely no qualifications. Often patients express their relatives' concerns as a way of expressing their own misgivings.

Can I drink?

As you might imagine, the official word is to avoid using alcohol if you are on antidepressants, especially when you are first starting them. Alcohol may increase any sleepiness or mental impairment you may have for a while from the antidepressant. With any of the newer antidepressants (Prozac, Zoloft, and Paxil), once your body is used to it, however, occasional social use (up to two drinks per day for men, one for women) will *probably* not be a problem. The modern antidepressants are quite safe in combination with alcohol. The use of alcohol and older antidepressants is not a good idea at all.

If you are not responding to an antidepressant or not as well as hoped, you should not drink at all until you and your doctor figure out what is going on and what to do about it. Alcohol can interfere with the therapeutic effect of antidepressants and can worsen your mood disorder.

Of course, if you have ever had a drinking problem, you should not drink for that reason alone. And you should never drink more than the amount mentioned above in any case, just for general good health.

Doctors will sometimes prescribe tranquilizing or sleep medication in the first week or two of antidepressant treatment to diminish anxiety and insomnia. These may be symptoms of depression or they may be side effects of the medication. In either case, using alcohol and tranquilizers in combination is something you should not do. They are both respiratory-system depressants and could be quite dangerous when taken together.

Can I take antidepressants with other medications?

That depends on the antidepressant and the other medication. Generally, the SSRIs are safe in combination with most other medications. However, there are some interactions that you and your doctor need to be on the lookout for. Coumadin blood levels, for instance, can be increased when using sertraline/Zoloft. YOU SHOULD ALWAYS CHECK WITH YOUR DOCTOR AND PHARMACIST BEFORE MIXING ANY MEDICATIONS, INCLUDING OVER-THE-COUNTER MEDICATIONS, WITH ANTIDEPRESSANTS. THE SAME IS TRUE FOR HERBS AND NUTRITIONAL SUPPLEMENTS.

How often do I have to take medication?

The nice thing about many modern antidepressants is that they are convenient to take. Often it amounts to taking one or two pills once in the morning with breakfast. Some antidepressants require more frequent dosing because the active ingredients do not last long in your body. This does get to be a bit of a hassle. You will have to work out a system for yourself so that you don't forget a dose. This is especially critical if you have to take a medication three times a day. Pharmaceutical manufacturers realize the need for divided dosing makes their antidepressant less attractive in a highly competitive marketplace. For this reason, companies have developed or are developing extended- or sustained-release formulations of their medications requiring more than once per day dosing (Wellbutrin and Effexor, for instance).

Whom should I tell and not tell about
my illness and my use of medications?

It is unfortunate that patients feel the need to hide their illness and the type of treatment they are receiving. Would anyone think of keeping their bronchitis and antibiotic use a secret? The more open you are about your mood disorder and your use of medication, the more you will help yourself heal the needless embarrassment and shame you feel.

On the other hand, it is a reality that there is still a stigma attached to having a mood disorder and to using medications. Others may hold it against you. They are ignorant of the facts, but still, you need to be careful.

Job applicants often wonder whether they should reveal their diagnosis or their medication use to prospective employers. In the first place, it is illegal for employers to request this information. Second, if your depression or bipolar illness has been under control for some time and you are able to function, there would seem to be little reason to reveal it.

If you have been out of work for some time or have been hospitalized, you may be asked to explain gaps in your work history. Be honest but keep it simple. Say you were depressed but that now you are well and eager to return to work.

On the other hand, if your mood disorder is not well controlled and you anticipate that there may be times when you will not perform to capacity, or may need to take time off work, then you might consider telling your employer this after you have been on the job a few weeks. If your mood disorder is not well controlled and you have been employed with a company for a while, you may also want to consider having a discussion with your boss about your condition, its course, and its treatment. You can let your employer know that you are under a doctor's care and treating your illness aggressively and that you take your work responsibilities seriously, but there may be times when you may not be able to function as well as you would like. The advantage of having this type of discussion is that the next time you have a recurrence of symptoms and your productivity drops off, your employer will not conclude that you are not a good employee.

You may be able to gain protection under the federal Americans with Disabilities Act, a law enacted in the mid-1990s to protect workers with physical, psychiatric, and chemical-dependency problems. Under the law, an employer has to grant a person with a disability certain reasonable accommodations. This might include a reduced work load at times or reduced productivity requirements. You should check with an attorney who has special interest and knowledge in this area.

You have to weigh the decision to reveal your illness carefully, however, since any employer might react negatively to your announcement. In fifteen to twenty years, it probably will not matter much. Depression will no longer be called a mental illness. Everyone will understand that it is a brain illness.

I have heard about a number of antidepressants lately. Which is the best one?

There is no one best antidepressant. All antidepressants, old and new, are roughly equal in efficacy. They all cause minor side effects for a short time for many people. One antidepressant may work better for you than another, or your body may tolerate one antidepressant better than another. Depending on the nature of your symptoms, your doctor may choose to start you out on one kind of antidepressant as opposed to another. Certain clusters of symptoms respond to particular classes of antidepressants. Atypical depression, for instance, responds better to MAOIs than to tricyclics. Atypical depression also responds better to bupropion/Wellbutrin and SSRIs than to tricyclics. Severe depression may respond better to tricyclics, Effexor, or Remeron.

My doctor has suggested an increase in dosage. I really do not feel that my depression is serious enough to warrant an increased dose.

This objection is based on the mistaken assumption that dose and severity of illness are related. This is not true. Therapeutic dosage depends more on the symptoms being treated and how an individual's body metabolizes a drug than on the severity of an illness. For instance, the typical therapeutic dose for Prozac for depression is 20 milligrams. However, some people respond to 10 milligrams. Others may require 40 milligrams. Obsessive-compulsive symptoms, bulimia, and various impulse-control problems typically require 60 to 80 milligrams. There have been case reports of Prozac being used in excess of 100 milligrams. in individuals who tolerate the drug well.

My doctor just switched me from Prozac to Effexor. He had me on 20 milligrams of Prozac but wants to start me on 75 milligrams of Effexor. That seems like a lot. Isn't that a little too strong to start off with?

The drugs are not equivalent. There is no one set dosage that is right for every drug. Your doctor will prescribe the dose appropriate for the drug chosen.

What if I forget to take a dose
of my medication?

This depends in part on the type of medication and the frequency with which you take it. You should check with your doctor. Generally, however, you do not want to double up on any dose if the previous one has been missed. If it is early enough in the day or soon enough after the time you should have taken the last dose, it may be okay to go ahead and take it. You should not worry about missing a dose here and there, especially with something like Prozac, which lasts a long time in your body. If you keep forgetting doses, you should ask yourself if you are reluctant to take the medication for any reason. Discuss these issues with your doctor and therapist.

What if the medications
do not work?

Most people respond well to the first medication tried. If the first medication you try is not working, the first thing to do is to make sure you have been on enough of it for a long enough time and that you have been taking it as prescribed. If it is only partially effective after an adequate trial at an appropriate dose, you and your doctor may try augmenting it with another drug or switching to another antidepressant. Do not settle for simply feeling better. Let your doctor know if you still do not feel your best. Getting well is the goal of treatment. Fully recovering from depression makes it less likely that you will have a relapse in the future.

Undiagnosed medical illness should always be considered if you have not responded to several medications. In the unlikely event that no medication or combination of medications works for you, there are effective alternative treatments, such as ECT (electroconvulsive therapy) for severe, refractory mood disorders, and other possibilities discussed below for more mild depressions. (For more information on this subject, see the section on Alternative Treatments.

*If I do decide to use medication, what are
my chances for making a full recovery?*

This depends on a number of factors. A little bit of luck helps: If
life is kind and relatively stress-free, you will probably make a
quicker and more satisfying recovery. Having a stable, satisfying
job you are good at and an understanding, supportive spouse will
go a long way. If you have a stormy relationship or an unsatisfying
job or family problems, this will keep the pot boiling and make it
harder, but not impossible, to make a complete recovery. In these
cases, the support and guidance of a therapist is helpful. Once you
are feeling substantially better, your therapist should help you do
something that is a bit painful: look at yourself and understand how
your illness and your personality contributed to some of your problems in the first place (such as your irritability contributing to marital problems). Changing your ways of dealing with yourself, your
feelings, and your loved ones is important for helping you stay well.

TYPES OF ANTIDEPRESSANTS

CAUTION: Descriptions of common interactions between antidepressants and other drugs are discussed below. These descriptions *do
not* include all possible interactions. Always check with your doctor
and pharmacist before taking any medication—*including over-the-
counter drugs*—in combination with *any* other medication, nutritional supplement, or dietary supplement.

WARNING: As mentioned in chapters 1 and 3, antidepressant
medications can cause a number of problems when given to people
who have bipolar as opposed to unipolar depression. Be sure your
doctor has considered the possibility that you may have a bipolar
depression before you agree to take an antidepressant. The most
critical diagnostic task facing a therapist or doctor is determining
whether your symptoms of depression are part of a unipolar or

bipolar disorder. Please see chapter 1 for information on distinguishing unipolar from bipolar depression, chapter 2 for information on cyclothymia (a mild form of bipolar illness), and chapter 3 for information on bipolar II disorder (major depressive episodes with at least one episode of hypomania).

Monoamine Oxidase Inhibitors (MAOIs)

This class of drug derives its name from how the drugs function. MAOIs inhibit (actually destroy) an enzyme called monoamine oxidase. (There are two types of monoamine oxidase, type A and type B.) Monoamine oxidase metabolizes or breaks down chemicals called neurotransmitters in the brain believed to be responsible for regulating mood and other body functions. By destroying monoamine oxidase, these drugs supposedly alleviate depression by increasing the amount of neurotransmitters such as serotonin and norepinephrine.

This is one of the first class of antidepressant medications to be discovered. They were discovered by accident in the 1950s. Researchers were looking for treatments for tuberculosis and discovered that these drugs elevated the moods of the patients they were tested on. The first MAOI was used to treat depression in 1957.

These medications fell into disfavor in the United States with the advent of another class of antidepressants called the tricyclics. One reason that MAOIs were not used much is that they prevent the breakdown of a substance called tyramine. If a person ingests enough tyramine while on MAOIs, he can experience a sudden and dangerous increase in blood pressure. This problem can be dealt with by having a patient restrict his intake of foods high in tyramine (mostly aged cheeses). The person can also carry a drug called nifedipine. If he develops the characteristic pounding headache at the back of the head typical of a high-blood-pressure (hypertensive) crisis, he takes the nifedipine and his blood pressure will fall immediately.

Other common side effects include drowsiness, dry mouth, constipation, and drops in blood pressure if the person stands up quickly (orthostatic hypotension). The latter may lead to a brief period of dizziness or momentary dulling or loss of consciousness. These effects sometimes wear off as the body gets used to the medication. If not, they can be easily remedied. For instance, the orthostatic hypotension can be gotten around by getting up slowly and sitting before standing if you have been lying down.

The hassle of the diet, the dangers involved in the use of the drug, and especially the development of the newer antidepressants have caused most patients and psychiatrists in this country to avoid the use of MAOIs. You would be hard pressed to find more than a few recent graduates of psychiatric residency programs who have prescribed MAOIs.

Nevertheless, these are excellent antidepressant drugs. They help many people who do not respond to other medications, especially those with atypical depression and bipolar depression. They can also be useful in helping relieve panic attacks, social phobia, and posttraumatic stress disorder. The response rate in atypical depression is about 70 to 85 percent. You will recall atypical depression is characterized by oversleeping, overeating, lethargy, mood reactivity, and rejection sensitivity.

There is a newer generation of MAOIs referred to as RIMAs (reversible inhibitors of monoamine oxidase type A) that do not wipe out the body's supply of monoamine oxidase. Therefore, they do not have the dietary restrictions of the older MAOIs and cannot cause a hypertensive crisis. Moclobimide is a RIMA available in Canada but will probably never be officially approved for use in the United States. Its patent has expired, and no pharmaceutical company will spend the money it takes to get the drug approved if it cannot make a good profit on it. Fortunately, some pharmaceutical companies are developing their own brand of RIMAs. These may become available in the United States in the near future.

Clinicians have found, however, that some people who respond to older MAOIs do not respond to moclobimide. This may be because the moclobimide is not being given in high enough doses or because it does not inhibit monoamine oxidase type B. It may be that a full antidepressant effect requires the inhibition of both type A and type B monoamine oxidase. If you have been effectively treated with one of the older MAOIs, you may not want to switch when the RIMAs become available. It may be, however, that a RIMA can be combined with another readily available drug that inhibits monoamine oxidase type B (the drug is called Selegiline/Eldepryl or Deprenyl) to produce a full effect.

Eldepryl has also been found useful when used alone for depression. Some patients who have not responded to any other medications do quite well on Eldepryl.

Common drug interactions: MAOI drugs can cause extreme low blood sugar when used in combination with antidiabetic agents. Use of narcotic analgesics is not recommended while on MAOIs. The combination can sometimes be fatal. MAOI and tricyclic combinations are generally avoided. If they are used together, a tricyclic should not be given to a person already on an MAOI. The MAOI can be added if a person is on a tricyclic, however, or the two can be started at the same time at lower dosages. Drugs such as Prozac, Zoloft, and Paxil should not be combined with MAOIs. *Various over-the-counter cold and allergy medications should not be used if you are on an MAOI.*

Tricyclics

This is the other class of medication first used to treat depression. They, too, were discovered by accident in the late 1950s. A Swiss psychiatrist reported that the drug imipramine, tested on roughly three-hundred patients with various psychiatric problems, had helped those with retarded depression. The drug class derives its name from the chemical structures of the antidepressants. They have three rings. There are over twenty-five tricyclic and related monocyclic (one ring), bicyclic (two rings), and tetracyclic (four rings) antidepressants available in the world. They are believed to work by inhibiting the absorption (reuptake) of neurotransmitters back into the cells that produced them.

These compounds differ mainly in side-effect profiles. For instance, some are generally sedating and therefore of use in agitated, sleepless patients while others are activating and therefore useful in patients who lack energy and are slowed down. They all have roughly equal efficacy (about 65 to 70 percent of patients respond to them) in the treatment of major depression.

Some patients, however, may respond well to one but not to another. This may be due to the different degree to which each one inhibits the reuptake of either serotonin or norepinephrine. Some tricyclics are more potent serotonin reuptake inhibitors, some more potent norepinephrine reuptake inhibitors, and some are balanced reuptake inhibitors. Many doctors check blood levels of the tricyclic antidepressants to guide dosage adjustments. There are known therapeutic ranges for many of the drugs.

Common side effects of the tricyclics include dry mouth, blurry vision, orthostatic hypotension, and sexual dysfunction (decreased interest in sex, problems with erection, and lack of orgasm in both women and men). Perhaps of greatest concern to depressed women is the tendency of the tricyclics to contribute to weight gain. Except perhaps for the sexual dysfunction, all these side effects are easily managed. Everyone, but especially people with cardiovascular disease, should have an EKG (a recording of the electrical activity of the heart) prior to beginning treatment with a tricyclic. The tricyclics can affect heart rhythm. For this reason, they are rather dangerous if taken in an overdose.

Some tricyclics are useful in the treatment of chronic pain, bulimia, and panic disorder. They are generally avoided in bipolar depressions because they can precipitate hypomanic and manic episodes.

Tricyclics are no longer typically chosen as the first drug in the treatment of depression. Most psychiatrists will start with one of the newer antidepressants like sertraline/Zoloft. The tricyclics are certainly no less effective, on average, than the newer antidepressants. (Although some patients who do not respond to tricyclics respond to the newer antidepressants, the reverse is also true.) There is also some evidence that tricyclics—particularly those that inhibit the reuptake of both serotonin and norepinephrine—may be *more* effective in severely depressed or hospitalized patients than drugs like Zoloft, which inhibit only the uptake of serotonin.

The explanation usually given for why the newer drugs are prescribed more often than the tricyclics is that patients tolerate them better and have fewer side effects. The new drugs are certainly safer for patients with cardiovascular disease, and they are much harder to overdose on. They only infrequently cause dry mouth, blurry vision, or weight gain. But with only a few exceptions, they cause the same kinds of sexual dysfunction seen with the tricyclics. They can also frequently cause their own unique set of troublesome side effects, such as agitation and anxiety, gastrointestinal discomfort, nausea, and loose stools (these tend to ease with time).

Some modern antidepressants, such as venlafaxine/Effexor and mirtazapine/Remeron, inhibit the reuptake of both serotonin and norepinephrine. They may be useful for severe depression without having the side-effect profile of the tricyclics.

Common drug interactions: Tricyclics may lower the effectiveness of antiseizure drugs. Dosage of the antiseizure drug may need to be adjusted. Tricyclics, however, may increase the blood level of the antiseizure drug phenytoin/Dilantin. Taking blood-thinning drugs such as warfarin/Coumadin together with tricyclics increases the risk of internal bleeding. Use of tricyclics and narcotic analgesics can be dangerous and even fatal. You should not use alcohol while you are on tricyclics. Tricyclic and MAOI combinations are generally avoided. If they are used together, the tricyclic should not be given to a person already on an MAOI. The MAOI can be added if a person is on a tricyclic, however, or the two can be started at the same time at lower dosages. Tricyclics and drugs such as Prozac, Zoloft, Luvox, and Paxil can be used together with caution. Blood concentration of the tricyclics can climb to unsafe levels when combined with these drugs. Blood levels of tricyclics need to be carefully monitored when combined with Prozac, Zoloft, Luvox, or Paxil.

Selective Serotonin Reuptake Inhibitors (SSRIs)

This class of drugs derives its name from the hypothesized method of antidepressant action. The drugs block the absorption of the neurotransmitter serotonin back into the cells that produced it. They do this virtually without any action on other neurotransmitters, such as norepinephrine.

Fluoxetine/Prozac came on the market in 1987. It is probably the most famous and misunderstood of all antidepressants. (Sertraline/Zoloft, paroxetine/Paxil, and fluvoxamine/Luvox are the other SSRIs you may have heard of.) More than 20 million patients have used it. Lest you think doctors are handing out too much of the stuff, you should keep in mind that only a minority of people with depression are correctly diagnosed and adequately treated with medications such as Prozac.

PRINCESS DIANA

People with depressive illness sometimes think they would not be depressed if only they were more attractive, had more money, a better place to live, were well-known, or were widely admired. Then why had Princess Diana taken antidepressant medication? Well, you might say, her marriage fell apart. Who would not be depressed?

Keep in mind that feeling depressed is not the same as having depressive illness. Most people whose marriages break up feel *depressed but they do not develop a depressive illness. Nor do they engage in self-mutilation or suicide gestures as Diana had done. Those usually result when, through no fault of their own, a patient's brain becomes depleted of the neurotransmitter serotonin.*

Diana had been in psychotherapy long before she started taking an antidepressant. But being treated with an antidepressant was a major factor in helping her become well.

Diana Spencer was born July 1, 1961, into an aristocratic British household. Although her parents were delighted with their new baby, they had been hoping for a male heir to carry on the family name and hadn't even considered girls' names. And just eighteen months earlier, Lady Althorp, Diana's mother, had borne a son, John, who survived only ten hours.

Diana grew up knowing that her parents had desperately wanted a boy. Three years later, her brother Charles was born. They both developed a fascination with graveyards and frequently visited their dead brother's grave in a Sandringham churchyard. When Diana was six, her parents' marriage broke up. She has told friends that it was an extremely painful time; she remembers her mother's tears and her father's silences.

Diana's mother lost the custody fight, and the children remained with their father. Though he loved them and indulged them with expensive toys, he relied on nannies to help raise them. The children resented the nannies, taunting them mercilessly. Despite her privileged surroundings, she felt lonely and isolated.

When she met and fell in love with Prince Charles, Diana was still a teenager. She felt at sea in Buckingham Palace and was confused by Charles's relationship with Camilla Parker Bowles. During her engagement to Charles, she developed bulimia. Palace staffers recall her raiding the refrigerator late at night and eating huge amounts of food, even while she was rapidly losing weight. Diana later admitted that she was making herself sick four or five times a day. She even considered calling off the wedding at the last minute but felt she couldn't.

After her marriage, the public quickly embraced Diana. She soon outshone Charles and led what seemed to be a fairy-tale life, with a royal yacht, several palaces, private jets at her disposal, and millions in jewelry and designer clothing. Though she handled her official duties with grace, Diana felt anxious and unhappy much of the time and had violent arguments with her husband. During one argument, while she was pregnant with her first son, William, she threatened to kill herself. Charles didn't take her seriously and prepared to go out riding. She then threw herself down a wooden staircase. Though she wasn't seriously hurt, her belly was bruised.

That was one of several attempts to hurt herself or commit suicide. One time, she slashed her wrists with a razor blade; another time, she cut herself with a lemon slicer. Then there was the time she threw herself against a glass display case. And during one argument with Charles, she cut her chest and thighs with a penknife, according to her biographer, Andrew Morton.

After William was born, Diana sank into a severe postpartum depression, she told interviewers. She would cling to Charles, begging him not to leave and telling him that she could not eat while he was away. She sought help from various psychologists for her depression but found no relief.

A close friend, concerned about her bulimia, learned that chronic deprivation of vital minerals, such as zinc and potassium, can lead to depression and tiredness. She threatened Diana with going public about her disease unless she sought help. Diana did.

The doctor who treated her convinced her that bulimia was associated with her depression and that she needed help for both. Within six months she improved, although stressful situations could still trigger bulimic episodes.

As her own marriage broke down in public, various press

reports speculated about her erratic behavior and mental state. In 1994, a tabloid reported that she had made over three-hundred harassing phone calls to millionaire art expert Oliver Hoare, who had been a friend to both Charles and Diana. Though Diana has denied making all the calls, the tabloid said police had traced calls to Kensington Palace and to her mobile phone. And relatives said that she had a tendency to "embroider" the truth, according to *People* magazine.

Before Diana died in a car crash in 1997, she had been taking Prozac and seeing a therapist regularly.

Prozac has gotten a lot of bad press. Patients are often concerned that its use might precipitate violent or suicidal behavior. The risks of this are vastly overblown. You may be surprised to learn that Prozac is effectively used to treat temper outbursts and irritability. The evidence is clear: The vast majority of individuals with unipolar depression who use the medication become more peaceful, not more aggressive.

As previously noted, patients who suffer from bipolar depression need to be careful about using any antidepressant. Among the risks of using antidepressants for patients with bipolar depression is the possibility of precipitating an irritable or even violent mania. It is likely that some of the reports that Prozac made people angry or violent were due to the induction of mania in patients misdiagnosed as suffering from unipolar depression. Many doctors are now recommending that patients with bipolar depression be treated first with a class of medications referred to as mood stabilizers (see chap. 9) rather than with antidepressants.

What about the connection between suicide and Prozac? There have been several case reports in the professional literature linking the use of Prozac to the emergence of suicidal thoughts in patients treated for depression. However, these reports do not present convincing evidence that Prozac *caused* the increase in suicidal thinking. A correlation between two events does not imply one caused the other. (Increasing amounts of light in the Northern Hemisphere after December 21 correlates, for instance, with increasing snowfall amounts through the months of January and February in the New York City area. But the increase in light does not cause it to snow more in the Big Apple after the first of the year.) Rigorous scientific studies of Prozac, Paxil, and Luvox have shown all these SSRI drugs reduce suicidal thoughts and protect patients from their emergence. Prozac has been used to successfully treat millions of suicidally de-pressed individuals and has undoubtedly helped save many lives. Nevertheless, we cannot say the risk of a paradoxical reaction is nonexistent. You, your therapist, and your doctor should *always* work together to keep an eye out for side effects. If you do this, you do not need to spend any more time worrying than it takes to read this sentence. If your doctor recommends a trial of Prozac for your depression and you are still not comfortable trying it, simply talk to him about trying Zoloft or Paxil instead.

The SSRIs may be more effective than a placebo in treating atypical depression but perhaps not as effective as originally hoped for. Since they are a lot easier to use than the MAOIs, most doctors start treating atypical depression patients with one of the SSRIs. On one hand, Prozac may be the SSRI most likely to work for atypical depression. On the other, some doctors suggest patients with atypical symptoms are best started on Zoloft or Paxil first and not Prozac. The reason is that if Zoloft or Paxil do not work, you can begin using an MAOI in as little as two weeks after discontinu-ing them. Prozac lasts so long in your body that you have to wait five or six weeks before you can switch to the MAOI. If your symp-toms of atypical depression are not responding to an SSRI, some doctors will augment the SSRI with stimulant medication rather than switching immediately to an MAOI.

Prozac is sometimes chosen over other SSRIs if the patient has a retarded depression. It is considered to be more stimulating than the other SSRIs. For anxious or agitated depression, Paxil and Luvox are preferred.

The SSRIs are effective in bipolar depression, but Prozac, in particular, may be more likely to precipitate a hypomanic or manic attack than the other SSRIs.

The SSRIs effectively treat not only depression but a number of other conditions as well: obsessive-compulsive disorder, panic attacks, bulimia, posttraumatic stress disorder, and many impulse-control disorders such as temper outbursts and sexual perversions. Prozac and Luvox are the preferred drugs for obsessive-compulsive disorder. The doses used to treat obsessive-compulsive disorder are generally higher than those used to treat depression. All the SSRIs treat panic attacks effectively, although Paxil and Luvox may be the best choices. Your doctor may start you off on as little as 5 milligrams or even 2.5 milligrams of Prozac (20 milligrams is the typical starting dose) if he chooses that medication to treat your panic. Starting off with more than 10 milligrams may induce edginess, restlessness, anxiety, and even panic.

Part of the reason for the popularity of the SSRIs is that they are convenient to use. They need to be taken only once a day. Patients are advised to take the SSRIs with meals to minimize gastrointestinal problems. (Some patients, however, have reported that they are less prone to nausea if they take Zoloft on an empty stomach.) With the exception of Luvox, the SSRIs are generally taken in the morning to minimize the chances of insomnia. Luvox is taken at bedtime since it is usually sedating. These are not hard-and-fast rules. Luvox can cause insomnia, so it may be best for some people to take it in the morning. The other SSRIs can cause sedation (especially Paxil), so some individuals may prefer to take them at night.

Prozac is available in 10-milligram tablets, 20-milligram capsules, and in a liquid form. Twenty milligrams is a common starting dose, although your doctor may start you on much less if you have panic attacks. Most people with depression respond to 20 to 40 milligrams a day. If you have not improved at all or have only minimal improvement on 20 milligrams by six weeks, however, you are unlikely to respond to 40 milligrams. If you are partially improved or have improved but then slipped back substantially, you will probably respond nicely to 40 milligrams.

Prozac is also approved by the federal Food and Drug Administration (FDA) for use with obsessive-compulsive disorder and bulimia.

Zoloft is available in 50- and 100-milligram tablets. The tablets are scored so that they can easily be broken in half. The usual starting dose is 50 milligrams per day, and most family physicians and internists start their patients on that dose. It seems, however, that more psychiatrists are starting their patients on 25 milligrams for four to seven days before going to 50 milligrams. This may decrease the incidence of side effects. (This should probably be standard practice for elderly patients.) Thereafter, the dose should not be increased more frequently than every five to seven days. You may have to wait up to two weeks or more before considering a dose increase if side effects are hanging on awhile. Zoloft is FDA approved for panic disorder obsessive-compulsive disorder, social phobia, and post-traumatic stress disorders.

Paxil is available in 20- and 30-milligram tablets. The usual starting dose is 20 milligrams. Most patients respond to somewhere between 30 and 50 milligrams per day. The manufacturer recently came out with a controlled release formulation that dissolves in the intestines instead of the stomach. This may lower the incidence of nausea. Paxil appears to have a relatively low rate of inducing mania, so it is probably a reasonable choice for bipolar depression if mood stabilizers are not effective in treating depression. Paxil may be especially useful if you are anxious, agitated, and unable to get to sleep. It is approved for use in panic disorder, obsessive-compulsive disorders, and social phobia.

Luvox is available in 50- and 100-milligram scored tablets. The usual starting dose is 50 milligrams per day at bedtime. Maximum dose is 300 milligrams. Luvox is only approved for use with obsessive-compulsive disorder in the United States. It may soon be approved for use in depression in the United States. It is used in over forty countries as an antidepressant.

The latest SSRI drug to be introduced to the U.S. market is citalopram/Celexa. It was approved by the FDA in July 1998. Although a newcomer in the United States, it has been used extensively in Europe and elsewhere for many years. The usual starting dose is 20 milligrams per day. The dosage can be increased to 40 or 60 milligrams per day if the patient does not respond to 20 milligrams. A few studies have indicated that Celexa may be better tolerated and have a more rapid and robust antidepressant effect than Zoloft or Prozac. It may cause less sexual dysfunction (decreased libido, delayed ejaculation, difficulty attaining orgasm) than other SSRI drugs.

Although some labs are now offering blood-level measurements of the SSRIs, it is rare for a doctor to order such a test. There is no data available to suggest what blood levels correspond to clinical improvement.

All SSRIs need to be used cautiously in patients with a history of seizures and may need to be discontinued if a patient develops seizures.

Common side effects of all the SSRIs include nausea and other gastrointestinal discomfort, diarrhea, and sleepiness or insomnia. Some patients report problems with short-term memory, especially on Prozac. Although infrequent, SSRIs may precipitate so-called movement disorders: tremor, restlessness and inability to sit still, muscle spasms and twitches, and involuntary movements of the face, limbs, and trunk.

Another side effect common to all SSRIs—with the possible exception of Luvox—is sexual dysfunction. Men and women may notice a decrease in sexual desire. Women may have trouble achieving orgasm. Men can experience a decrease or change in physical sensation in the penis. Ejaculation may be delayed or difficult to achieve. The forcefulness of ejaculation may decrease or the sensations associated with ejaculation may change.

The incidence of sexual problems can be reduced by starting at a low dose of the SSRI and increasing it slowly. If sexual problems appear, they may fade over time. Lowering the dosage of the medication may be effective in some cases. A patient can be switched to Wellbutrin or Serzone, which both have a much lower incidence of sexual side effects. Wellbutrin, stimulants, and several other drugs can be given along with the SSRI to counteract sexual dysfunction. Gingko biloba may also be effective.

There are two other discouraging but manageable problems common to the SSRIs. First, a number of people who have had a good sustained response to a given dose may lose the antidepressant effect over time. This goes by the technical name of "Prozac poop-out" (although it happens with Zoloft and the others, too).

Poop-out is an odd thing if you stop to think about it. What has happened is that your neurotransmitter systems have slowly worked to get themselves back to their former state of disrepair. Why would they do such a dumb thing? Well, because that's the way the boss wants it. The boss is your genetic code, which gives a lot of the orders about how various chemical balances are to be maintained. If there is an error in your genetic code, which instructs the serotonin system to maintain a certain chemical (im)balance, well, so be it. It just follows orders. You and your doctor come along and try to change the balance to suit yourselves. The boss comes in one day and notices all this extra serotonin lying around. The boss tells his employees to get busy and clean things up. He wants things back the way they were. Never mind that it was screwed up to begin with. Often a dosage increase is all that is needed to take care of this problem. (Dump enough serotonin reuptake inhibitors around and the serotonin really piles up. No matter how much the boss yells at them, the employees cannot get rid of it fast enough.)

The other problem that occurs at times is a gradual loss of zest, energy, or motivation. A feeling of apathy settles in. This is believed to be due to indirect effects of the SSRIs on the dopamine neurotransmitter system. (The boss is telling the dopamine system what to do but the employees are not listening—they are drunk and not in the mood for working.) This can usually be easily remedied by adding stimulant medication or the antidepressant Wellbutrin to the SSRI.

Common drug interactions for the SSRIs: Caution is needed in the use of blood-thinning agents (warfarin/Coumadin) with SSRIs. SSRIs may be used with tricyclics and antiseizure drugs, but caution is needed since SSRIs can increase the blood levels of both. Tricyclics especially can show dramatic increases in blood concentration (a two- to tenfold increase in imipramine is possible, for instance). Blood levels for the tricyclics should be done periodically. SSRIs and MAOIs should not be combined. At least five weeks should elapse between the discontinuation of Prozac and the start of an MAOI. Two weeks is adequate for Zoloft and Paxil. Blood levels of antiarrythmia drugs may be increased by SSRIs. Zoloft may be less of a problem in this regard than is Prozac.

Novel Antidepressants

Venlafaxine/Effexor   This drug is similar to some of the older tricyclics in its actions. It may be especially useful for more severe depressions, lethargic depression, and depressions that have not responded to SSRIs. This may be because Effexor blocks reuptake of norepinephrine as well as serotonin. (It is thus referred to as an SNRI or serotonin-norepinephrine reuptake inhibitor.) Effexor was recently approved for use in generalized anxiety disorder.

The side effects for Effexor are fairly similar to the SSRIs, although it may cause somewhat more dry mouth and constipation. Unlike SSRIs, however, Effexor has caused an increase in blood pressure in more than 5 percent of patients taking over 200 milligrams per day. Blood pressure should be monitored while taking Effexor. Drug interaction precautions are the same as for the SSRIs.

With the SSRIs, there is conflicting evidence about whether higher doses produce greater therapeutic effects for most depressed patients. In other words, it is not clear whether 200 milligrams of Zoloft does a lot more than 50 milligrams when you look at a large number of patients (although it is clear that any one patient may require higher doses than another). Effexor, on the other hand, seems to work better at higher doses. Most patients seem to need at least 225 milligrams per day. Dosages up to 375 milligrams per day in three divided doses can be used. The usual starting dose is 37.5 milligrams twice a day. Effexor is available in a number of dosages: 18.75 milligrams, 37.5 milligrams, 50 milligrams, 75 milligrams, and higher. It is also available in extended or slow release form.

Common drug interactions: Roughly the same as the SSRIs. Check with your doctor and pharmacist.

Bupropion/Wellbutrin How Wellbutrin works is even more of a mystery than how other antidepressants work. Initially, it was thought that it worked mainly on the dopamine neurotransmitter system. Other researchers believe its main action is on the norepinephrine system. In any case, it is a clinically useful antidepressant. It has a low incidence of sexual side effects, usually does not cause weight gain, and does not cause dry mouth. Its chemical structure resembles that of the stimulant drug diethylpropion/Tenuate, so it can have stimulantlike effects (it has been used to treat attention deficit–hyperactivity disorder). On the one hand, this may make it useful for patients with atypical depression who are lethargic and tend to overeat. On the other hand, Wellbutrin can lead to restlessness, agitation, and insomnia in some patients. It supposedly has less risk of inducing hypomania and so is a preferred antidepressant for bipolar depression.

It is available in 75- and 100-milligram tablets. The usual starting dose is 75 milligrams per day or 75 milligrams twice a day. The effective dose is generally somewhere between 225 and 300 milligrams per day divided into two or three doses.

The manufacturer indicates that the following precautions should be taken to prevent the possibility of seizure (which appears to be higher in Wellbutrin than with other antidepressants): (1) No one dose should be greater than 150 milligrams, (2) dosage adjustments should be made very slowly, and (3) the total daily dose should not exceed 450 milligrams.

In 1996, Wellbutrin became available in a sustained-release formulation. This decreases the need for divided doses and may have lowered the risk of seizures.

Wellbutrin should not be used by eating-disordered patients, patients with a history of head trauma, or those with a brain tumor, since they may be at higher risk for seizures with Wellbutrin. It is considered ineffective in panic disorder and is not a good drug for those depressed patients who are anxious.

Common drug interactions: Metabolism and effectiveness may be altered by coadministration with antiseizure drugs. Concurrent use of L-dopa should be done cautiously. Coadministration with drugs which lower seizure threshold should be avoided. If benzodiazepine drugs are used with Wellbutrin and then discontinued, the benzodiazepine should be tapered off slowly. Rapid tapering could reduce seizure threshold. Alcohol should be avoided. MAOIs should not be used in combination with Wellbutrin.

Nefazadone/Serzone   Like SSRIs, Serzone blocks the reuptake of serotonin back into the cells that originally released the serotonin. But it also exerts antidepressant effects by altering or blocking the functioning of subtypes of serotonin receptors (places where the neurotransmitter serotonin binds after being released from a nerve ending).

It causes little in the way of sexual side effects. It is useful in depressed patients with prominent anxiety and sleep problems. It may be particularly helpful in getting patients to spend more time in the deepest, most restorative phase of sleep. The most common side effects are light-headedness, dizziness, and daytime drowsiness. These side effects tend to wear off in about two weeks.

Serzone might be useful for patients with fibromyalgia, a syndrome characterized by muscle pain and stiffness, and migraine headache.

Serzone is supplied in 100-, 150-, 200-, and 250 milligram tablets. The usual starting dose is 100 milligrams twice a day. Older patients should be started on 50 milligrams twice a day. Serzone is another drug that requires doses well above starting doses to be effective. The minimum effective dose is probably around 300 milligrams per day. Doses of 500 to 600 milligrams per day are needed for some patients. One small study showed that Serzone given once a day at bedtime reduced daytime drowsiness without decreasing antidepressant effect in a group of male patients.

Common drug interactions: Use of Serzone with some tranquilizing drugs (triazolam/Halcion and alprazolam/Xanax) can increase the blood level of the tranquilizer and adversely affect mental and physical performance. Dose reductions in the tranquilizers are necessary when they are combined with Serzone. Combined use of Serzone and the antiallergy drugs terfenadine/Seldane and astemizole/Hismanal is not recommended. Use with cisapride/Propulsid, a medication used for gastrointestinal problems, is also not advised. Blood levels of digoxin/Lanoxin or Cardoxin should be monitored when coadministered with Serzone. Serzone can increase the blood levels of digoxin.

Mirtazapine/Remeron Remeron was approved for use in the United States in mid-1996. Although it affects serotonin and norepinephrine neurotransmission, it does so in unique ways. It gets nerve cells to release more serotonin and norepinephrine by blocking sensors that tell the cell to stop producing the neurotransmitters. It is analogous to getting your home furnace to continue producing heat by somehow blocking the thermostat's ability to register how warm it is in the house.

It does not have some of the side effects of the SSRIs and appears to be especially useful for anxiety and insomnia. It may be useful if a patient does not respond to an SSRI, has severe depression, or cannot tolerate SSRI side effects. Studies have indicated that the most common side effects are dry mouth, daytime sleepiness (for a week or two), possibly increased appetite, and weight gain. In rare cases, it may cause a decrease in a certain kind of white blood cell, which fights infection. The decrease apparently reverses if the medication is stopped. Patients who develop a sore throat, fever, or inflammation of the mucous membranes of the mouth should contact their physician immediately.

Dosages range from 15 milligrams per day when the medication is first started to 45 milligrams per day when necessary.

Common drug interactions: Check with your doctor and pharmacist.

So how does the doctor know which
of all these medications to prescribe?
How does he know what dose to use?

Generally, psychiatrists will choose a medication on the basis of *clinical* predictors of response to specific medications. If you have been on a specific antidepressant before with minimal side effects and have had a good response, your doctor will probably put you back on the same medication. If someone in your immediate family has responded to a specific antidepressant, your doctor will probably start you on that antidepressant.

Following are drugs typically used in specific conditions:

- *Severe depression:* Some doctors will start you on a tricyclic, especially if you are in the hospital. Others might choose Effexor or one of the SSRIs.
- *Bipolar depression:* Wellbutrin, an SSRI, an MAOI, or lithium.
- *Atypical depression:* An SSRI or an MAOI.
- *Psychotic depression:* Antipsychotic medication in combination with an antidepressant. The tricyclic antidepressant Ascendin

might also be prescribed, since it has antipsychotic properties.
- *Depression with pronounced obsessive-compulsive features:* Luvox or Prozac.
- *Depression with anxiety and insomnia:* Paxil or Serzone. You might also be given any other antidepressant at a low dose (with the exception of Wellbutrin) or in combination with a tranquilizing drug.
- *Depression with panic attacks:* Any of the SSRIs might be prescribed, although you will be started off on a low dose so as not to set off a panic attack. Xanax might also be prescribed for a short period of time.
- *Seasonal affective disorder:* Wellbutrin or Prozac. Bright-light therapy might be tried first, however.

The dose of the medication prescribed will be increased slowly until you have a response. If you have side effects you do not want to put up with, your doctor will switch you to another drug. If you reach maximum dosage of a medication without a response or only a partial response, your doctor will either add a second medication or switch you to a different class of antidepressant (see below).

If you are given a tricyclic, blood levels of the drug may be monitored to determine the correct dose.

Most patients treated on an outpatient basis who have typical, moderate symptoms of a unipolar depression or dysthymia will be started on an SSRI.

What do doctors do if the first medication they try does not work or if it works for a while but the depression comes back?

If you have tried medication for depression and it has not been effective or is only partially effective, do not give up hope! Your therapist and doctor will work with you to find another medication or medications that will be effective. Depending on your doctor, you may have to push for this. Do not sit around waiting for the doctor to suggest something else. Educate yourself about the available alternatives and discuss them with your doctor. If your doctor balks at the idea of trying other strategies, get a second opinion.

Following are the steps your doctor will likely take when the first antidepressant drug you try does not seem to be working or has brought only partial relief.

- *Check to make sure the medication is being taken regularly.* Occasionally, patients forget to take their medication. This tends not to be much of a problem with the SSRIs, since they are taken only once a day. It is more of a problem with the older antidepressants and Effexor, Wellbutrin, and Serzone, which need to be taken two or three times a day. Some patients do not tell their doctor and therapist that they have stopped taking the medication or are taking it only sporadically. This is partly because they are afraid the doctor will disapprove or be disappointed. Also, the doctor or therapist may have temporarily convinced the patient to try a medication without exploring and discussing the patient's reservations about the use of medication.
- *Check to make sure the patient has been treated for a sufficient length of time on the highest dose possible.* Some patients respond very slowly to antidepressant medication. If a patient is not severely or suicidally depressed and there has been some improvement by four to six weeks, it is sometimes best to let more time pass before drawing any conclusions about the drug's efficacy. Obsessive-compulsive symptoms and dysthymia can take sixteen weeks to respond fully to SSRI medications.

  Insufficient doses of the antidepressants are frequently responsible for nonresponse. You and your doctor should discuss the possibility of increasing the dosage of your medication after the first two or three weeks if there has been little or no response. Family doctors in particular tend to underdose when treating depression. In the absence of troubling side effects or medical problems, your doctor will probably gradually increase your dosage to the maximum suggested by the manufacturer (200 milligrams a day for Zoloft, for instance). He may want to keep you on the maximum dose for up to four to six weeks before concluding the medication is ineffective. With the tricyclics and MAOIs, up to a point, higher doses are clearly more effective than are lower doses.

There is some controversy about this for the SSRI antidepressants. On the one hand, studies of a large number of patients indicate that doses higher than 50 milligrams for Zoloft (the usual starting dose), for instance, do not produce substantially better outcomes. On the other hand, case reports clearly show that some patients respond to higher doses of the SSRIs.

Other medications, such as Effexor and Serzone, clearly work better for most patients at higher doses.

Blood levels of some medications, especially the tricyclic antidepressants, can often help determine if the patient is on an adequate dosage.

* *Check on alcohol and drug use.* Alcohol and illicit drug use can cause the patient to forget doses, will directly interfere with the effectiveness of medication, and will cause the patient interpersonal, vocational, and legal problems. These problems will create added stress, which will, in turn, exacerbate mood disorders.

* *Reconsider the diagnosis.* The doctor will ask himself: Does the patient have atypical depressive features I have missed? Could he have a subtle bipolar or psychotic depression, which I have overlooked? A patient with atypical features may respond best to MAOIs. Subtle bipolar depressions seem to respond less well to standard treatments for depression, such as SSRIs and tricyclics. They often require a mood stabilizer in addition to or instead of an antidepressant. Subtle psychotic depressions

are common and often difficult to detect. One study indicated that as many as half of depressed patients may have psychotic depression. This form of depression responds poorly to antidepressants alone.

Your doctor may also consider whether you have a primary obsessive-compulsive illness or eating disorder to which the depression is secondary. If so, it would make sense to first treat the obsessive-compulsive or eating disorder.

- *Consider the possibility of undiagnosed medical illness, especially thyroid illness.* Undiagnosed medical illnesses are not rare. If you fail to respond to standard treatments for depression, your doctor should intensify the search for an underlying medical illness.

Nonmedical therapists may never think of this or may assume the psychiatrist will pick up on any medical problems. Once a patient has had a physical exam and blood workup, the possibility of medical problems causing the mood problems is often forgotten about by all concerned.

- *Check for stressful interpersonal, vocational, financial, or legal problems. For women patients, be particularly alert for signs that the patient may be a victim of domestic violence.* Depression and manic-depressive illness may not respond well to medication if the patient has an unsupportive, critical, or violent spouse or a chaotic family environment. Job loss or career setbacks can also retard recovery, especially for men, who often base much of their self-esteem on how well they do at work. All these stresses perturb brain biochemistry. It is as if a patient with a broken leg tried to resume walking, running, and going up and down stairs the day she got a cast on her leg.

Therapists will need to provide as much support and realistic encouragement as possible to help a patient resolve or weather these problems. A depressed patient often overlooks her positive qualities and focuses exclusively on mistakes and shortcomings. It is especially helpful, therefore, for a therapist to point out a patient's strengths or good points. Helping a patient recall how she has solved problems in the past or getting her to think of potential solutions on her own can help boost self-esteem.

Your therapist should not just view you as a passive victim of stress, however. Very often, a patient's mood disorder causes havoc in her life that then worsens her mood problems. Irritability and demandingness, for example, can drive others away, leaving the patient bereft of support and wounded by the loss of those most important to her. Therapists should help their patients restrain their complaints, criticisms, and demands on others, especially those directed toward their spouses. It can be very destructive for a therapist to encourage a moody, irritable patient to "let the anger out."

• *If there has been an incomplete response to the first medication, try augmentation strategies before switching to another drug.* While no one likes the idea of prescribing more than one medication at a time for a mood disorder, it is perfectly reasonable to do so. Combinations of medications are the rule rather than the exception in treating many illnesses. Two or more drugs are often prescribed for controlling high blood pressure or treating AIDS and cancer, for instance.

• *Switch to a medication from a different class of antidepressants.* Some doctors prefer to switch drugs rather than augment if there has been no response to the first antidepressant tried. With the possible exception of the tricyclics and SSRIs, this should be a medication from a class different than the ineffective medication. Research indicates a patient is most likely to respond to a second medication if this principle is followed.

As mentioned above, different tricyclic drugs work on different neurotransmitter systems. So switching from a tricyclic that affects mainly norepinephrine, for instance, to one that affects both norepinephrine and serotonin may make some sense.

There are also indications a patient may respond to, say,

Zoloft, even if he has not responded to Prozac. The reverse is also true.

If two SSRIs have been tried without success, the next option would be to switch to tricyclics, the traditional MAOIs (after two to five weeks of being off the SSRI), or any of the other drugs listed above.

Venlafaxine/Effexor has been reported to be an especially useful drug when used alone for treatment-resistant depression, possibly because it works on both the serotonin and norepinephrine systems.

PATTY DUKE

Patty Duke's story demonstrates how often even doctors can overlook the presence of a mood disorder. Many patients see several therapists and doctors before being accurately diagnosed. Patty's depressions should have been a clue to the nature of her illness: The early onset, her periods of immobility, and explosive rage were all signs of a bipolar depression.

One of Patty Duke's earliest memories, she says in her autobiography, *Call Me Anna*, is of going through her father's duffel bag and finding a wooden soap dish. A few feet away, her parents were having a violent argument, so bad that her father suddenly picked up the bag and left. Little Patty clung to that soap dish, until a little while later, her mother still in a fury, threw it out.

Everyone in her family had a temper. Patty remembers times when her mother would fly into a rage and try to hurt herself. Once she actually broke her nose when she threw herself against a wall. And when her mother was depressed, there was crying, crying so relentless it would last for days. Patty's mother was hospitalized three times for depression.

After her father left for good, Patty's mother took her to a couple who coached child actors, John and Ethel Ross. They changed her name from Anna Marie to Patty and changed her hair, clothes, and voice. Eventually, she moved in with them. They constantly criticized her and gradually became abusive toward her. She felt that nothing about her was right. But thanks to her own talent and drive, the acting jobs started to come.

At eighteen, she married an older man, Harry Falk. The next year, her wildly popular TV series, *The Patty Duke Show*, folded. Though she felt relieved, she went into a major depression. Just shopping for groceries would be four or five hours in the planning. When she finally mustered the strength to go out, she would think, "Do they know? Can they see?"

She developed anorexia, and her weight dropped to 76 pounds. Much of the time, she was virtually catatonic, refusing to speak. Her distraught husband finally admitted her to a psychiatric hospital. After treatment, she was stable for awhile.

But within two years, the strains in her marriage were too much, and the couple divorced. Patty became manic, what she calls "Moby Wife." She bombarded Harry with phone calls, sent him pizzas he hadn't ordered, and showed up at places where she knew he'd be. Her pain became so overwhelming that she attempted suicide by swallowing a bottle of tranquilizers. A friend saved her life.

In 1970, at the age of twenty-three, she dated seventeen-year-old Desi Arnaz, Jr. That same year, she won an Emmy for *My Sweet Charlie*. She gave a disjointed, rambling acceptance speech to a stunned audience. Many people assumed that she was on drugs. She was not. She was overwhelmed by career pressures and the fact that Desi's mother, Lucille Ball, disapproved of their relationship and ultimately forced them to end it. And Patty still did not know that she suffered from the disease of manic depression.

While shooting a TV series, *It Takes Two*, Patty developed

laryngitis. A doctor gave her a shot of cortisone to relieve it. That set off a manic attack. She became edgy, spoke quickly, had insomnia, and spent money wildly. That was followed by a depressive state, in which she felt "zonked out." She managed to continue acting in spurts but had two more failed marriages.

Finally, a psychiatrist diagnosed her disease and treated her with lithium. In her book, she says that she feels the drug has enhanced her creativity. She is able to get up in the morning and not feel afraid. And for the first time, Patty says, she has a feeling of self-control in her life. The pain her disease has caused lingers. She feels worse about the pain it has caused her two sons.

One night around midnight, she heard a noise in her older son Sean's room. She got up to investigate and saw an intruder climbing in the window. She screamed and then realized the intruder was Sean's friend. At that moment, her other son, Mackenzie, was up the hallway, sobbing and howling. "I turned to him and said, 'It's okay. It's okay. I thought it was a burglar.' And he said, 'A burglar? Oh, thank God! I thought you forgot to take your lithium.'"

What drugs do doctors give in addition to an antidepressant when the first antidepressant does not work or work as well as hoped?

- *Lithium.* This is the best studied and most widely used drug for treatment-resistant depression. It has been studied most extensively as an augmentation drug for tricyclics. Thirty to 50 percent of treatment-resistant patients will have a good response to the addition of lithium to their antidepressant. This is the case even in strictly unipolar depression. There have been reports that some patients have improved in as little as two to three days on low doses of lithium (600 milligrams).

This may be unusual, however. Lithium should be tried for at least a month at higher doses before deciding on its effectiveness. For more information on lithium, see chapter 9.

- *Thyroid supplements.* Even in cases where your blood work indicates that your thyroid is functioning normally, the addition of thyroid supplements can be useful. Standard blood tests are not able to detect the most subtle forms of low thyroid function (referred to as subclinical hypothyroidism). There are two kinds of thyroid supplements: triiodothyronine (T3)/Cytomel and thyroxine (T4)/Synthroid. Some doctors prefer to give one supplement or the other, and others prefer to give the patient a combination of the two.
- *Tricyclic antidepressants.* Adding a tricyclic to an SSRI may produce a result within three weeks in treatment-resistant patients. Whether this combination is more effective than switching to a tricyclic alone is not clear. Your doctor will want to carefully monitor the blood level of the tricyclic, since an SSRI can dramatically increase its concentration in the blood.
- *Psychostimulants.* Drugs such as dextroamphetamine/Dexidrine, methylphenidate/Ritalin, and magnesium pemoline/Cylert may produce rapid antidepressant effects in treatment-resistant depression. Unfortunately, some patients may not maintain their response over the long run. Nonresponse to an SSRI may be due to attention-deficit hyperactivity disorder (ADHD), in which case treatment with stimulants in addition to the SSRI would clearly be indicated (stimulants are the treatment of choice for ADHD). Switching to Effexor or Wellbutrin alone would also be reasonable, since these antidepressants are effective with ADHD, as well as depression.

  Psychostimulants must be used with caution, since they can be abused. Patients with a history of substance abuse must be especially careful and should perhaps avoid the stimulants altogether.
- *Estrogen.* Estrogen replacement is commonly prescribed for

postmenopausal women as protection against cardiovascular disease and loss of bone mass. Estrogen also has antidepressant effects for menopausal women when used in combination with antidepressant medication.

In addition, very high doses of estrogen may help some depressed women who have not responded to other methods of treatment.

Novel or Experimental Strategies

- *B vitamins*. See chapter 11 on self-help.
- *Ketoconazole/Nizoral, metyrapone/Metopirone.* These drugs reduce the level of naturally occurring steroid hormones such as cortisol. These hormones increase in response to stress and are elevated in some types of depression, especially severe and psychotic depression. Whether the increased hormone levels cause depression or are a result of it is not clear, but reducing their concentration in the blood appears to be therapeutic. There are case reports of dramatic improvement in patients who have not responded to the usual antidepressant drugs. These drugs have been useful in depression when administered alone or in combination with antidepressants.

  Some physicians and nontraditionally trained healers maintain a candida (yeast) infection can cause depression. Nizoral is an anticandida drug that these clinicians claim has been useful in treating depression. Although they claim the drug works by eliminating the yeast infection, it is equally likely it works by lowering steroid hormone levels.

  Nizoral and similar drugs are generally given for depression in research settings only. Patients using them require close medical supervision and blood monitoring because of the potential for liver damage and other adverse side effects.

- *Buspirone/Buspar, pindolol/Visken, trazadone/Desyrel.* These drugs enhance serotonin neurotransmission in more selective ways than do the SSRI antidepressants.

Buspar is an antianxiety drug or minor tranquilizer with little abuse potential. Twenty to 90 milligrams per day for two to four weeks appears to be very effective in augmenting SSRI drugs. This drug may be especially useful early in the treatment of the large percentage of depressed patients suffering from anxiety as well. Buspar is well tolerated by most patients.

Visken, an antihypertensive drug, has been used successfully in treatment-resistant depression at doses of 2.5 milligrams three times a day.

Desyrel, an antidepressant most often prescribed as a sleep aid in combination with a primary antidepressant, may also be useful as an augmenting agent. Some doctors hesitate to prescribe it for men, since there is a small chance it can cause a painful, prolonged erection requiring emergency surgery to correct.

- *Fenfluramine/Pondimin and phentermine/Ionamin.* These are antiobesity drugs. There have been some case reports of their use in treatment-resistant depression. Patients with depression and obesity may do quite well on a combination of an antidepressant and one of these drugs.

    Some doctors are reluctant to prescribe these drugs except in severe cases of obesity because of the possibility of a fatal side effect: high blood pressure in the blood vessels of the lungs.

- *Pergolide/Permax, bromocriptine/Parlodel, amantadine/Symmetrel.* These drugs enhance the functioning of the dopamine neurotransmitter system. There are case reports of them being useful but no controlled studies have been done.

- *Bupropion/Wellbutrin.* Typically given to SSRI-treated patients for side effects such as sexual dysfunction or apathy, Wellbutrin may also be useful as an augmenting agent in patients only partially responsive to an SSRI.

- *Moclobimide.* Unlike other MAOIs, it can be used in conjunction with an SSRI.

- *Buphrenophine/Buprenex.* This is a narcotic or opiate drug. It and a number of other opiates have been found to be quite effective in some treatment-resistant patients. The human brain has a natural opiate neurotransmitter system. Giving patients opiates may work by correcting dysfunctions in this system. Depressed patients responding to opiate drugs typically do not get high or crave increased dosages of the medication.
- *Mifepristone.* A medication used in an illness called *Cushings Syndrome*, this drug has been used to rapidly reverse psychotic major depression.

Aerobic exercise may be useful in depression by increasing the level of the brain's natural opiates (called endorphins). See chapter 11 for more information on exercise and depression.

Keep in mind that bright-light therapy, sleep deprivation, phase advance, and psychotherapy can all be added to antidepressants in cases of treatment-resistant depression. Naturally occurring supplements, especially the amino acids tryptophan and tyrosine, may be helpful. See chapter 10.

This is an admittedly bewildering variety of drugs and augmentation strategies. You certainly should not try to guess which one might be right for you. Discuss these options with your doctor first.

If you are on a combination of medications, be sure to discuss any troubling side effects with your doctor. Work with him, even if you have to push yourself to be assertive. Similarly, do not just stop medications without talking to your doctor.

Can I use antidepressants while attempting to conceive or while pregnant?

This is a decision you need to make in consultation with your psychiatrist and obstetrician after weighing risks and benefits. If you have or have had only mild major depression or dysthymia, you may want to consider not using antidepressants until after you give birth. On the other hand, if you have had serious, recurrent, or life-threatening major depressions, psychotic depressions, or previous postpartum depression episodes, the risks to you and your baby associated with *not* treating or *not* continuing to treat your depression may be substantial.

Tricyclic antidepressants appear to be relatively safe to use while you are pregnant in terms of the risk of causing deformities. Babies sometimes show symptoms of tricyclic withdrawal after birth (irritability, jitteriness, convulsions). There have been no long-term effects found on babies' development from the use of tricyclics during pregnancy. Studies have revealed behavioral and neurochemical changes in offspring of *animals* given tricyclics, but the implications of these findings for humans are not clear.

In general, SSRIs also appear to be safe to use during pregnancy. There have been no reported long-term effects on babies whose mothers used Prozac while pregnant. However, since Prozac and its metabolites last a long time in the body, many doctors advise against its use while pregnant or at least near the time of the baby's birth.

In one study of MAOIs, the babies of mothers using these antidepressants were born with a higher-than-normal rate of congenital malformations.

Data on other antidepressants is minimal or absent. As a result, if you do need to take an antidepressant while pregnant, you should probably consider tricyclics, Zoloft, or Paxil (both of which are SSRIs).

The safest treatment for severely depressed or suicidal women who are pregnant is electroconvulsive therapy (ECT) or shock therapy. See chapter 10.

What about breast-feeding and antidepressants?

Here again, the decision to use antidepressants (or not to breast-feed) must be made on an individual basis after weighing risks and benefits. Tricyclics and SSRIs are excreted into breast milk, but their concentration in the milk is generally much lower than that in the mother's bloodstream. Measurable levels of the tricyclics amitriptyline/Elavil and nortriptyline/Pamelor (among others) and the SSRI sertraline/Zoloft cannot be detected in babies who are breast-fed. No adverse effects have been reported in these babies. These are, therefore, the medications of choice for depressed women who are breast-feeding.

Prozac should probably not be used by nursing mothers. It has been associated with some adverse effects on babies (cholic and high blood levels of Prozac in the baby).

CHAPTER 9

TREATMENT OF
BIPOLAR DISORDERS

Just as the border between North Carolina and South Carolina separates two states that are both part of a larger union, modern psychiatry has drawn a border between the unipolar and bipolar illnesses and declared them to be part of a larger group, the mood disorders. Given the belief that depression and bipolar I disorder (full-blown manic-depression) are conceived of as at least related parts of a greater whole, it is odd that there should be such controversy raging about the treatment of depression and so little disagreement regarding the treatment of manic-depressive illness.

It is as if it were late autumn and raining with gale force winds in North Carolina and immediately across the border in South Carolina it was a sunny spring day with a pleasant breeze. No one advocates treating bipolar I and II patients with psychotherapy or natural alternatives *alone*. Even in the milder spectrum of bipolar illnesses, the emerging consensus is that these disorders require treatment with mood-stabilizing agents.

It is true that there have been a few clouds in the bipolar sky of late. Lithium used to be the standard pharmacologic treatment for bipolar illnesses. There has been some controversy about which groups of bipolar I and II patients should receive the time-honored lithium treatment and which should initially receive treatment with divalproex/Depakote (the only drug since lithium to be approved for use in mania) or other anticonvulsant drugs. There has also been controversy about which medications to use when treating a bipolar patient in a depressive episode. Nevertheless, there has been fairly consistent agreement regarding the treatment of the manic phase of bipolar illnesses.

MEDICATIONS TYPICALLY USED FOR THE TREATMENT OF BIPOLAR ILLNESSES

Lithium

Lithium has been the standard treatment for many years. Lithium is an element—a simple substance, which cannot be broken down into simpler components by chemical means. It was discovered in 1817, and is in the same chemical family as the elements sodium (found in table salt) and potassium. Danish doctors used it in the treatment of mood disorders as early as the late 1800s, but their work was ignored. It was not until the late 1940s that an Australian psychiatrist, John Cade, accidentally discovered the calming effects of the substance in guinea pigs. He took doses himself to check on its safety and then administered it to ten manic patients, all of whom dramatically improved.

Lithium was not approved for use in the United States until 1970 due to exaggerated concern about its potential toxicity. When the blood concentration of lithium is monitored and kept below a certain level, it is safe.

Severely ill hospitalized patients are generally treated with 900 to 1,800 milligrams of lithium per day. The dosage is increased gradually until a therapeutic blood level is achieved seven to ten days later. This is generally between 0.8 and 1.2 milliequivalents—one-thousandth of a gram—per liter of blood.

The dosage would probably be decreased after the patient starts to respond. Acutely manic patients can take large doses of lithium and achieve only moderate blood levels. Blood levels may increase to toxic levels once the mania subsides.

For less severely ill outpatients, proper blood levels are typically achieved with doses between 900 and 1,200 milligrams of lithium per day. Some physicians prescribe a full day's dose at night. This is not only convenient for the patient, but it may also reduce problems with kidney function.

Lithium is also used to prevent the occurrence of depressive episodes in bipolar patients and to reduce the risk of suicide.

Lithium is generally prescribed in 300-milligram capsules. A controlled-release formulation is available that minimizes variations in blood levels of lithium between doses. This may decrease side effects in some individuals. In addition, it permits less frequent dosing for those who do not take all their lithium at night.

Patients preparing to take lithium will be asked by their doctor to get a preliminary blood workup in order to obtain baseline measurements of thyroid, kidney, and other body functions that lithium may affect. These measurements will be rechecked periodically, along with blood levels of lithium, to help your doctor decide on dosage adjustments. Some people mistakenly believe that these blood tests help a doctor diagnose bipolar illness. They do not. They are done only to check the amount of lithium in someone's bloodstream (from the lithium prescribed by the doctor—there is normally no detectable lithium in human blood) and the functioning of organs that lithium can affect.

Checks of lithium levels should be done twelve hours after the final dose of the day. If you take lithium at 10:30 P.M., for instance, you would go to the lab to have your blood drawn at 10:30 A.M. the next morning.

It is probably a good idea for all patients taking lithium to take megadoses of the B-complex vitamins, since lithium can interfere with the absorption of these vitamins.

Lithium's most common side effects include excessive thirst, increased urination, a slight shaking in your hands, and weight gain. Some patients complain of mental slowness, emotional blunting, memory problems, and a lack of motivation. These side effects may be more pronounced in older adults. Keep in mind that many patients do not experience these side effects. Alterations in kidney and thyroid function are possible, which are not hard to manage. As long as lithium levels and kidney functioning are monitored with regular blood tests, there is no long-term risk to health.

Lithium should never be discontinued without carefully weighing with your doctor the problems associated with doing so. In addition to the high probability of relapse and all its attendant problems (especially if you stop the drug suddenly), there are other problems. One psychiatric researcher, Robert Post, has found that some patients who stop lithium do not respond to it if it is restarted. In a few cases, patients *did not respond to any other treatments once the lithium had been stopped.*

Strenuous physical exercise or illness with vomiting, fever, and dehydration can raise the concentration of lithium in the blood, sometimes to toxic levels. If you drink plenty of water this will not be a problem. Also be sure to maintain adequate salt intake. You do not need to take salt tablets, but a low-sodium diet is not advised, since this may increase lithium levels.

All patients taking lithium and their families should be aware of the signs of lithium toxicity. At moderately toxic blood levels, patients may appear drunk. They may be giddy or drowsy, with slurred speech and an unsteady gait. They may seem confused or disoriented. They may be nauseous, and at higher blood levels may vomit. The patient's doctor should be called immediately.

You will probably not be able to use lithium if you have kidney problems or have recently had a heart attack.

Common drug interactions: As with all drugs, speak to your doctor or pharmacist before taking lithium with other prescriptions or over-the-counter medications. You must be particularly careful about taking lithium if you are using thiazide diuretics (water pills). These diuretics can reduce your body's ability to excrete lithium and can raise the blood level of lithium to dangerous levels. High-blood-pressure medications may increase lithium levels, and lithium may decrease the effectiveness of the high-blood-pressure medication. Over-the-counter anti-inflammatory medications (ibuprofen, naproxen) may also increase lithium levels.

Divalproex/Depakote

Depakote has been used since the 1960s as an anticonvulsant (anti-seizure) drug. It was first tried with manic patients in 1981. It enhances the action of GABA, a neurotransmitter suspected of being in short supply in manic patients. Depakote may work by substituting for some of the natural and essential fatty acids that are crucial for the proper functioning of brain cells. See chapter 11 for more information on the importance of essential fatty acids in mental health and chapter 10 on the use of fatty acids in the treatment of bipolar illness. It has been used with increasing frequency since the early 1990s as an alternative or adjunct to lithium. The manufacturer, Abbott Laboratories, has been heavily promoting its use. Its use for manic-depressive illness was approved by the FDA in 1995. It is the first drug since lithium to gain such approval. Depakote may have antidepressant properties and might help prevent future depressive episodes in bipolar patients to some degree. However, it is less effective than lithium in this regard.

Depakote is a very well tolerated drug. It usually does not cause the kind of mental fogginess or memory problems seen with lithium. Some patients, however, have reported confusion and other symptoms of cognitive impairment. If this is a problem, doctors will sometimes order a blood test to see how much ammonia is in your blood. Depakote can cause increased ammonia levels in the blood, which can be one source of cognitive impairment. Such cases, however, are unusual.

Depakote usually has no adverse effects on the thyroid or on kidney functioning. It is much less toxic at high doses than lithium. Like lithium, it may cause weight gain. It can cause stomach and intestinal distress. This is reduced if it is taken after a meal or with a lot of water. In the first few weeks of treatment, Depakote may cause drowsiness. Depakote can adversely affect liver functioning. Cases of fatal liver problems induced by Depakote have been reported, but this seems to be confined to seriously epileptic children on several anticonvulsants.

Signs of Depakote toxicity should be kept in mind. These include malaise, weakness, lethargy, loss of appetite, and vomiting.

Depakote may cause hair loss. Taking the minerals zinc and selenium may help reduce this side effect. Take the minerals either two hours before or two hours after taking Depakote.

Depakote is available in 125-milligram, 250-milligram, and 500-milligram tablets.

The usual starting dose is 750 milligrams for adults in divided doses. Like lithium, however, Depakote can often be taken in one dose at bedtime. The manufacturer may soon market a sustained-release form of Depakote.

Before starting you on Depakote, your doctor may ask you to get a blood workup to check on liver function. Your liver function, along with blood levels of the Depakote, will be checked periodically thereafter. The usual therapeutic range is 50 to 125 micrograms (millionths of a gram) per milliliter of blood. The vast majority of patients take between 1,000 milligrams and 2,500 milligrams per day to reach this blood level. A small percentage take up to 4,500 milligrams per day. You may not be able to use Depakote if you have liver disease.

Common drug interactions: The main drug interactions to watch for if you are taking Depakote are the interactions with other anticonvulsants, particularly Tegretol. (These drugs are sometimes combined for tough cases of bipolar disorder.) Carbamazepine/ Tegretol makes your body excrete divalproex more rapidly. A Tegretol and Depakote combination can also increase the blood levels of a metabolite of Tegretol. You should not drink alcohol while using Depakote.

Carbamazepine/Tegretol

This is another antiseizure drug with acute antimanic and prophylactic effects in bipolar disorder. It has gotten a lot less press than Depakote because its patent expired in 1990 (meaning any pharmaceutical house can sell a generic version).

Tegretol is generally prescribed in 200-milligram tablets. The usual starting dose is 200 milligrams twice a day with meals, but if you are on lithium, it may be started at a much lower dose. The usual dose range is from 800 to 1,200 milligrams per day. Some patients have been treated with as much as 1,600 milligrams per day. Tegretol became available in an extended release formula in 1997. This made it possible to take the drug only twice a day as opposed to three or four times per day. Blood levels should be between 4 and 12 micrograms per milliliter. Tests to check white-cell count, platelets (a clotting agent in the blood), liver function, and a number of other functions should be done prior to beginning treatment and at periodic intervals. Blood levels of Tegretol need to be taken periodically as well. Tegretol can prompt the liver to accelerate metabolism of the drug, with a resulting decrease in blood levels and a loss of efficacy over time.

Tegretol can cause a number of blood disorders and liver problems. These are rare, however, and when properly monitored, the drug is safe. Your doctor probably will not use Tegretol if you have any liver, kidney, or heart problems. Signs of toxicity include impaired consciousness, muscle twitches, tremor, fever, sore throat, easy bruising, and a rash.

Common side effects upon initiating treatment include dizziness, drowsiness, unsteadiness, and nausea. Tegretol is somewhat less likely to cause weight gain than are lithium or Depakote.

Common drug interactions: Some antibiotics and verapamil/Calan (used for angina and heart arrhythmias) can increase blood levels of Tegretol and lead to toxic reactions. Other anticonvulsant drugs can lead to increases in the blood level of Tegretol as well.

Tegretol can decrease the effectiveness of theophylline/Theo-dur (used in asthma and emphysema) and warfarin/Coumadin (a blood-thinning drug). You should not take Tegretol for at least fourteen days after stopping an MAOI antidepressant. You should not consume alcohol while taking Tegretol. The combination can cause extreme drowsiness.

Major Tranquilizers (Antipsychotics)

Drugs such as thiothixene/Navane have frequently been used in the initial phases of treatment for agitated and psychotic bipolar patients. It is not clear if they have mood-stabilizing effects or are effective simply because they sedate the patient and treat psychosis. Manic-depressive patients may be at greater risk of developing serious neurological problems than are schizophrenics on these medications. Doctors, therefore, tend to use low doses for as brief a period as possible.

Selected Minor Tranquilizers

Some physicians have found it possible to treat acutely ill and agitated manics with minor tranquilizers instead of antipsychotic medication. The tranquilizer clonazepam/Klonopin, at doses of 4 to 16 milligrams a day, effectively reduces agitation and other symptoms in acute manic episodes. This is partially due to its sedative effects, but the drug also has anticonvulsant properties. It is also used as an adjunct to other partially effective mood-stabilizing medications and in patients with anxiety and insomnia. Klonopin should not be used by patients with glaucoma.

Lorazepam/Ativan, when given as an injection, is another minor tranquilizer effective in calming manic patients.

The advantage of these drugs is that they do not require the blood testing needed with the other mood stabilizers. The main side effects include sedation and impairment of cognitive and motor skills, especially early in treatment. A small percentage of patients have a paradoxical reaction to tranquilizing drugs and become irritable and explosive. Minor tranquilizers should be used with great caution in patients with a history of alcohol or drug abuse. Patients should not drink alcohol while on these medications.

THE USUAL COURSE OF TREATMENT

Once considered a magic bullet for the treatment of manic-depressive illness, doctors have come to realize that lithium works best as an acute treatment in the first episode or two of euphoric manic-depressive illness. Some manic-depressives begin their illness with a manic episode and some with a depression. Those who begin with a manic episode respond more frequently to lithium treatment than do those whose illnesses start with a depression.

Lithium can be used alone in patients with milder symptoms (hypomania and stage 1 mania) or in combination with sedating drugs to improve sleep. Severely ill manic patients admitted to the hospital may initially be treated with a combination of antipsychotic medication and lithium. Lithium can take up to fourteen days to work, so the antipsychotic is used to calm the patient and, of course, to treat any hallucinations or delusions the patient may be experiencing. To avoid side effects from the combination of lithium and antipsychotics, both the antipsychotic medication and lithium are generally used in lower doses than usual. Once the patient has been stable for awhile on an outpatient basis, the antipsychotic medication can be tapered off.

Although the indications for the use of lithium have narrowed over the past several years, it still has an important role in the treatment of bipolar illness. Its use has consistently been shown to reduce the risk of suicide, for instance.

Some doctors are now trying different initial strategies for the treatment of severe euphoric mania. Since Depakote may have an earlier onset of action and because it is a well-tolerated drug that does not cause some troublesome side effects common to the antipsychotics, many doctors are using it alone (or with minor tranquilizers) in large doses when patients are first hospitalized. Some patients respond in as little as one to three days with this "loading strategy." If this does not work, they will use a combination of lithium and Depakote.

Certain patients with bipolar illness are now generally started on anticonvulsant drugs alone or various combinations of lithium and anticonvulsants. These include patients with pronounced mixtures of depression, irritability, and euphoria; those with rapid cycling between depression and mania; and those who are psychotic, or who have had more than three episodes of mania, or who are alcohol and drug abusers. Some doctors have expressed concern about putting a patient with a history of alcohol or drug abuse on anticonvulsants. Alcohol and drugs have toxic effects on the liver. Depakote and Tegretol can have such effects too. However, if liver function is carefully monitored, substance-abusing patients can generally be safely maintained on anticonvulsants.

In some cases of treatment-resistant bipolar illness, patients may be given lithium, Depakote, and Tegretol. It is becoming more common to see bipolar patients on multiple drugs. This may worry the patient, but it is accepted practice and can bring much better results than one drug alone.

Depakote is now commonly used in outpatient practice with patients who have milder forms of bipolar disorder, such as bipolar II and cyclothymia. Outpatients with irritability, impulsive aggression, or temper outbursts who do not respond to antidepressants often respond to Depakote. This may be due to the fact that some of these patients, while not having obvious signs or symptoms of neurological disorders such as epilepsy, do have mild neurological dysfunctions that are revealed only on careful neurological examination. Tegretol may be particularly useful in combination with lithium for patients with rapid-cycling bipolar disorder. It is also quite effective in the treatment of impulsive aggression.

How long should a patient who has had his or her first episode of bipolar I illness stay on mood-stabilizing and anticonvulsant medications?

Since the vast majority of bipolar patients have multiple episodes, even the patient with just one episode should not be too anxious to discontinue medication that has been effective. The average time between the onset of the first and second episodes is somewhat more than four years, so stopping medication in the interim could be an error. This would especially be the case if a patient has some residual symptoms after the first episode or if there is a family history of multiple episodes of bipolar illness. Patients need to keep in mind that each episode increases the likelihood of having another. The time between episodes tends to decrease as well.

If you do decide you would like to go off lithium or mood-stabilizing medication, be sure to do so under your doctor's supervision. *A patient with bipolar illness should never stop medication on his own.* Premature or rapid discontinuation makes it very likely that you will have a relapse.

A bipolar I patient who has had two manic episodes should stay on mood stabilizing medications indefinitely.

OTHER TREATMENT STRATEGIES

If various combinations of lithium, antipsychotics, and anticonvulsants do not adequately control acute manic episodes or prevent relapse, a number of other strategies can be tried once interfering factors such as noncompliance, substance abuse, and medical problems have been ruled out.

New Anticonvulsant Drugs

Lamotrigine/Lamictal, gabapentin/Neurontin, topiramate/Topamax, and tiagabine/Gabitril are among a new generation of anticonvulsant drugs that are being used with increasing frequency among patients who do not respond to or do not tolerate more traditional treatments. They are sometimes used alone, but more commonly as adjuncts to other mood stabilizing drugs.

In 1998, a well-conducted study showed that Lamictal was effective in treating the depressed phase of bipolar illness. This study was the first of its kind. No other medications have been shown to be specifically effective for bipolar depression.

Topamax has the unique advantage of causing weight loss. Most mood-stabilizing drugs cause weight gain. Topamax contributes to kidney stone formation in about 1 percent of patients who take it.

Common side effects of Neurontin include sedation, dizziness, and gastrointestinal distress. Combining Lamictal and Depakote may not be a good idea because of the possible increased risk of a rash.

New Antipsychotic Drugs

Recently developed antipsychotic drugs such as clozapine/Clozaril and risperidone/Risperdal appear to have specific mood-stabilizing effects in acutely ill manic patients and patients not responsive to other treatments. They have less of the side-effect risks typical of the older antipsychotics. Although developed and approved for use in treatment-resistant schizophrenics, Clozaril has been found in at least one study to be more effective for bipolar disorder than for schizophrenia. It appears to be most effective in the treatment of psychotic and mixed manic episodes as well as in rapid cycling and schizoaffective patients. However, it is generally not the first drug used. It often works well when used alone for patients who have not responded to mood stabilizers.

It may be best not to use Risperdal alone for patients with bipolar disorder since some studies indicate it may cause agitation or a worsening of manic symptoms. When combined with mood stabilizers, however, it is safe and effective.

These new antipsychotic drugs appear to be useful not only for the initial treatment of patients with bipolar illness but also to help prevent relapse.

Side effects of Clozaril include sedation, weight gain, and the small risk of developing a potentially fatal white-blood-cell disorder. The latter is not of great concern as long as regular blood tests are done. Clozaril should not be used in combination with Tegretol.

The newest antipsychotic medications, such as olanzapine/ Zyprexa and sertindole/Serlect, may have benefits similar to Clozaril in the treatment of bipolar disorder without some of Clozaril's side effects.

Calcium Channel Blockers

The human body uses calcium for, among other things, the transmission of nerve impulses. Calcium channel blockers such as verapamil/Calan regulate the amount of calcium available for nerve transmission. Calan has turned out to be rather disappointing when used alone in bipolar disorder. This may be because it does not get into the brain easily. It may have a role in helping prevent relapse when used in conjunction with lithium.

Nimodipine/Nimotop is another calcium channel blocker under

study. It has more potential than Calan in the treatment of bipolar illness since it works on the central nervous system.

Thyroid Hormone

Raising a manic patient's thyroid hormone level to above normal can have antimanic effects. This may be an especially useful strategy for patients with rapid-cycling bipolar disorder. Most patients have trouble handling high doses of thyroid hormone, however. Patients who can tolerate the treatment often do quite well.

Clonidine/Catapres

This is a high-blood-pressure medication. Some open trials have suggested it may be a useful antimanic agent, but double-blind studies do not provide clear evidence of efficacy.

Pramipexole

This is a new medication under investigation for the treatment of bipolar depression. It is thought to have a very low risk of inducing mania.

Tamoxifen

This anticancer drug has been found to have rapid-onset antimanic properties.

Protirelin (TRH)

This compound was found to have substantial antidepressant properties for bipolar depressed patients.

TREATMENT OF BIPOLAR DEPRESSION

There is increasing concern among psychiatrists that the use of antidepressants alone in any type of bipolar patient may adversely affect the course of the illness. Clinicians have noted several patterns. Even after successful treatment of a depressive episode, antidepressants may increase the frequency of future depressive episodes. Future depressive episodes may then become resistant to antidepressant treatment. As a result, the patient's illness may take on a chronic rather than episodic course. This chronic state may have mixed features rather than purely depressive ones: impatience, irritability, anxiety, and increased sexual tension may be prominent. Antidepressants may induce hypomania, which is then followed by rapid cycling between depression and hypomania.

These changes in the course of an illness can occur in patients who are mistakenly diagnosed as unipolar but who actually have a history of hypomanic symptoms (bipolar II and cyclothymic disorder) not detected at evaluation.

Increasingly, psychiatrists are choosing to treat a depressive episode in a bipolar patient with mood stabilizers first. If the depression is severe or psychotic, ECT is often the first choice.

If antidepressants are required, Wellbutrin may be the drug of choice. It may induce hypomania less frequently than do other drugs. Paxil and MAOIs are also less likely to cause mania. Tricyclic antidepressants are avoided since they are associated with a high rate of induced hypomania in vulnerable individuals.

Patients with bipolar depression should be aware that the treatment of this condition is more complicated and time-consuming than the treatment of unipolar depression. It often requires some trial and error and in the end, more than one medication to stabilize the condition.

TREATMENT OF MANIC AND DEPRESSIVE EPISODES IN PATIENTS ALREADY ON MEDICATIONS

Lethargy, lack of motivation, and difficulty functioning are common symptoms of breakthrough depression in bipolar I patients already on mood stabilizing medication. If these symptoms appear, factors that might be interfering with treatment should be considered: alcohol and drug use, failure to take medication as prescribed, life stress, and suppressed thyroid function if the patient is on lithium.

If none of these are relevant, the first step in treating a breakthrough depression in a bipolar I patient would be to add lithium or, if the patient is already on it, to increase the dosage. Some doctors might add an anticonvulsant drug if lithium side effects are a problem or give the patient supplemental thyroid hormone.

If these strategies do not work, only then would the patient be considered for an antidepressant. Except in cases of severe depression, antidepressants should be avoided if at all possible in bipolar I patients, since they may worsen the course of the illness. An SSRI, MAOI or Wellbutrin are the antidepressants of choice. Bright light therapy for winter depression, sleep deprivation, and ECT could also be considered in place of antidepressants.

What if a bipolar patient who is already on antidepressants becomes depressed? Psychiatrists are finding that many patients with bipolar disorder who remain depressed or who continue to cycle into periods of depression in spite of being on antidepressant medication often do better when the antidepressants are discontinued.

Breakthrough manic episodes would be treated by increasing doses of the mood stabilizing medication the patient is already on, or by adding a second or third mood stabilizer. A patient on lithium who has a sudden manic episode would probably be treated immediately with an anticonvulsant drug or an antipsychotic drug. Psychotic symptoms would be treated with an antipsychotic. Any antidepressant the patient is on might be stopped. If none of these strategies work, then any of the alternative medications, natural compounds, or procedures previously mentioned in this chapter might be tried.

MOOD-STABILIZING DRUGS, PREGNANCY, AND BREAST-FEEDING

The use of lithium and mood stabilizers in patients who are pregnant or breast-feeding is somewhat more problematic than the use of antidepressants with these patients. Decisions about continuing or discontinuing these drugs or adjusting their dosage are complicated and should certainly not be made on the general information that is to follow. Treatment decisions should be done only in close consultation with your physicians.

Fetuses exposed to lithium in the first trimester have a significantly higher risk of cardiovascular malformations than do those who are not, although the absolute risk is still relatively low. If a woman who is stable on lithium has a history of severe or psychotic bipolar disorder, the risks of discontinuing the lithium to herself and her baby may well outweigh the risks of staying on it. There is some indication that women who are pregnant are not as likely to have a new episode of bipolar illness as women who are not. Therefore, women with less severe bipolar disorders or long episodes of normal mood between episodes may be able to slowly taper off their lithium prior to conception. Unfortunately, the risk of having a new episode after the baby is born is eight to ten times that of normal. And as previously noted, lithium may not be as effective or may not work at all if it is stopped and then restarted. ECT or Klonopin could also be considered, since they are considered safe to use in bipolar women who are pregnant.

Women with bipolar disorder who use anticonvulsants during pregnancy are more likely to have babies with structural defects in their skull or spinal column. The risk may be reduced by the use of B-vitamin supplements and the use of the lowest dose possible.

Lithium concentrations in breast milk are about 40 percent of the concentration in the mother's blood. Nursing is discouraged in women who are on lithium. Mothers whose mood is stable are encouraged to continue taking their lithium and to bottle-feed their babies. On occasion, lithium is continued during breast-feeding if the benefits to the mother clearly outweigh the risks to the child.

Depakote concentrations in breast milk can run as high as 10 percent of the concentration in the mother's blood. Depakote may be administered with caution during breast-feeding, but effects on nursing infants are not known.

Tegretol concentrations in breast milk are roughly 60 percent of the concentration in the mother's blood. Tegretol has the potential for causing serious adverse effects in nursing infants.

PSYCHOTHERAPY AND FAMILY COUNSELING

On one hand, the discovery of medications for the treatment of bipolar disorder, research findings on the genetic, neurological, and biochemical underpinnings of the illness, and the ineffectiveness of psychoanalytic treatment in the disorder have caused psychological treatments to fall into disfavor. On the other hand, it is clear that even the most competent psychopharmacological treatment does not prevent relapse in a significant number of patients. Lithium and, to a lesser extent, anticonvulsants can have a number of unpleasant side effects, which discourage people from their use. Antidepressants carry a number of risks when used in bipolar disorder. As a result, specific psychosocial treatments based on a biomedical model of bipolar illness are drawing clinical and research attention. There is growing evidence that these treatments improve the outcome of bipolar disorder and decrease the incidence of hospitalization of manic patients when combined with medication. Following are descriptions of two therapies showing some promise in the treatment of bipolar disorder. These are undergoing clinical trials to test their efficacy.

Interpersonal and Social Rhythm Therapy (IP/SRT)

Inconsistencies in the timing of daily activities, the level of social stimulation, and sleep/wake times contribute to mood instability. IP/SRT is geared toward helping the patient learn how to solve interpersonal problems and keep daily activities and sleep/wake times on a consistent schedule.

Patients are helped to see how their mood disorder can contribute to interpersonal problems and how interpersonal problems may disrupt their schedules. It is also designed to help the patient balance the desire for social stimulation with the need to maintain stability in his social life.

The patient is helped to mourn the loss of the mentally healthy person he may once have been or wished he could be. This helps the patient accept the diagnosis of bipolar illness and improves adherence to medication regimens.

Finally, in later stages of treatment, the patient and therapist explore how specific kinds of interpersonal problems tend to recur in the patient's life and are connected with manic or depressive episodes. The patient is guided toward an understanding of how he may contribute to these difficulties and how to alter the course of developing interpersonal problems.

Behavioral Family Management (BFM)

Spouses and parents of bipolar patients can contribute to relapse by being critical, hostile, or emotionally overinvolved with the patient. This is referred to as negative expressed emotion (EE). The patient can contribute to this problem as well by his own critical, complaining demeanor or by becoming involved in escalating cycles of criticism and countercriticism with relatives. Research has consistently shown that bipolar patients from families with high EE have a greater incidence of relapse. This dovetails with findings about expressing undue anger and irritability. Expressing irritation does not ease it. It merely inflames the feelings. Suppressing undue irritation or learning how to calm oneself with cognitive and behavioral techniques or breathing exercises is better.

What if the relative's negative EE is due to his own mood disorder and not just a response to the stresses of dealing with the mood-disordered patient? That may not be so easy to modify with psychosocial treatments alone. The relative may need pharmacological treatment as well.

BFM is designed to help bipolar patients and families reduce the expression of angry and critical feelings, which can precipitate relapse in the bipolar patient. Patients and their families are taught communication, conflict-resolution, and problem-solving skills. Patients are encouraged to apply these skills at work with colleagues and in other relationships.

A family or spouse's conflicts with a patient are often based on the mistaken notion that the patient is choosing to act in an irritated, complaining, critical, or provocative manner and that the patient, rather than the illness, is to blame. This does not imply that the patient must be stripped of responsibility for his behavior. There needs to be a balance. Families learn that problem behaviors are symptoms of an illness. The patient needs to be held responsible for attempting to gain a perspective on what is illness behavior and what is not. If the patient can learn to make the distinction, then some degree of conscious control is often possible. Another critical element of BFM is the patient and family learning the signs of re-lapse and agreeing ahead of time how they should be dealt with.

COMMON ELEMENTS OF EFFECTIVE
PSYCHOSOCIAL TREATMENT FOR BIPOLAR ILLNESS

Therapists should know how to intervene with the patient and his family based on an understanding of the stage of the patient's illness and recovery. With a bipolar I patient recently released from the hospital, a therapist's first goals include forming a relationship with the patient and his family and monitoring the risk of self-destructive or violent behavior. Monitoring compliance with medication is cru-cial. In this regard, therapists should discuss the patient's and fam-ily's feelings about the diagnosis of manic-depressive illness and concerns or misconceptions about the use of medications. This is important in preventing relapse. Education about the nature of bipolar illness and its treatment should begin immediately.

The therapist should next work on making sure the patient and family or spouse are working on gaining the skills necessary to re-duce angry, critical exchanges with each other. The patient and family need to learn new interpersonal and problem-solving skills for managing stress.

Additional goals for a patient and his family include helping pa-tient and family deal with the stigma and fear of relapse.

In individual therapy, therapists should be careful not to chal-lenge defenses early on. Doing so might contribute to relapse. Therapy should be focused on dealing with practical problems.

In later stages of treatment and with bipolar II and cyclothymic patients, it will be important for therapists to notice and interpret how hypomanic or hyperthymic moods and attitudes cover and de-fend against depression, low self-esteem, guilt, and shame.

CHAPTER 10

NATURAL COMPOUNDS AND ALTERNATIVE PROCEDURES FOR THE TREATMENT OF MOOD DISORDERS

There are a number of natural compounds for depression that have not been well researched or publicized, at least in part because there is little money to be made from them.

Pharmaceutical companies put huge amounts of time, money, and human resources into creating antidepressant drugs and proving they are safe and effective. When they have succeeded in getting a drug approved for sale, they then spend huge sums of money promoting its use.

Ads for antidepressant drugs, for instance, appear in some journals read by psychiatrists just as ads for cars appear in *Time* magazine. The drug companies give away a lot of free samples to doctors. They pay sales representatives to knock on the doors of doctors and encourage them to give their drug a try. They give money to psychiatric organizations for free lunches, symposiums, and lectures to doctors. Research supporting the safety and efficacy of their drug may well be mentioned at these gatherings. The research may have been conducted at their laboratories or by researchers they supported financially. A drug company will pay the publisher of a psychiatric journal to print a supplement devoted to the treatment of a specific kind of mood disorder. The usefulness of their drug in treating the condition may be highlighted.

One reason the drug companies do all this, of course, is because they stand to make a huge profit. They get the exclusive right to sell the drug for seventeen years.

All of which is not meant to imply that this is a bad system. In fact, it is a great system for what it does. It encourages companies to do necessary research. Drug companies would not spend millions of dollars and ten to twenty years researching a drug and getting it approved if it did not have some chance of making money.

But the system the drug companies and doctors are a part of has its limitations. The drug companies will probably never invest in research on natural compounds with possible antidepressant properties, no matter how promising the compounds may be. The reason is that there is no money to be made: The compounds cannot be patented and sold at a premium.

Only a modest number of government and academic institutions have done well-designed research on natural compounds and alternative procedures for the treatment of mood disorders. Most of the research has been done on only a few compounds and most research has not been done in this country. No one has had the money to advertise to doctors or the public the results of what little research there is. As a result, until recently, natural compounds have gotten little medical or public attention. This is unfortunate, because some of them are promising.

Why are these compounds now coming to our attention? It's certainly not because they are new. The possible antidepressant properties of St. John's wort, 5-HTP, and SAM have been known for decades. The main reason that we are hearing so much more about these compounds is that a change in U.S. law in 1994 made it possible for nutritional supplement companies to market these compounds as long as they do not claim that the compounds treat illness. Suddenly, there was money to be made. As a result, the nutritional supplement companies have spent a lot of money in the last few years bringing these products to the public's attention. They have used the existing research to lend legitimacy to the substances.

CAUTIONS

- Do not self-diagnose or self-treat what you believe to be depression without an evaluation by a professional. You should be especially sure to have a thorough physical exam and several different blood tests to rule out medical illness and sleep disorders such as sleep apnea. Medical illnesses contribute to anywhere from 10 to 30 percent of problems with depression. A doctor should review your use of prescription or over-the-counter medications. Some can contribute to depression. If alcohol or drug use is a problem, that should be addressed first. Many depressions clear up on their own when substance abuse is treated.

- There are types of depression which require special forms of treatment. It takes an expert to be able to diagnose the milder forms of bipolar disorder. Treating bipolar depression with some natural alternatives meant for unipolar depression may precipitate a hypomanic episode or worsen the course of a bipolar illness. Please see chapter 1 for information on distinguishing unipolar from bipolar depression, chapter 2 for information on cyclothymia (a mild form of bipolar illness), and chapter 3 for information on bipolar II disorder (major depressive episodes with a history of at least one hypomanic episode).

- The alternative treatments listed here are not as sure a bet as psychotherapy and medication in terms of effectiveness. Are you willing to take the time to experiment with these alternative approaches? If you have moderate to severe depression, are suicidal, feeling overwhelmed or are having trouble functioning, you should be seriously considering the use of prescription medication as your first treatment. While you may worry about the risks of using prescription drugs (which are actually relatively risk-free), you need to weigh carefully the risks of not using antidepressants or mood-stabilizing medications in these circumstances.

- Natural or nutritional supplements may need to be combined with a number of diet and lifestyle changes to be maximally effective. You have to ask yourself if you are ready to or have the energy to make those changes to support recovery from depression. Understandably, many depressed people do not. You also have to ask yourself if you are able to afford the cost of supplements. They are not covered by insurance the way medications are. Although some, such as St. John's wort, are inexpensive, others will cost a great deal.

- Finally, while the supplements to be described in this book appear to be relatively safe, there has not been much research done on their safety. Natural does not automatically mean safe. Sunlight and butter are natural but too much of either can be dangerous. An amount fine for one person may be too much for another. Safety questions need to be answered about many of these supplements. Is it safe to take huge doses of substance X? Can a diabetic use it safely? What about a pregnant woman? Is it a problem to take substance X with other prescription drugs or over-the-counter medications? See, for instance, the information in the section on St. John's wort. One could reasonably argue that the prescription drugs are safer, because most of the important questions about effectiveness and safety have been answered (with the exception of possible long-term or rare risks).

As you look over the material on alternative approaches described later and ponder what might be helpful for you, consider what George Lundberg, M.D., a former editor-in-chief of the *Journal of the American Medical Association*, has written: "There is no alternative medicine [or conventional medicine for that matter]. There is only scientifically proven, evidence-based medicine supported by solid data, or unproved medicines for which scientific evidence is lacking . . . "

I will begin by describing compounds for which some scientific evidence exists. You should keep in mind, however, that I have not thoroughly evaluated the quality of the research done on most of these compounds. I can say, however, that most of the studies done on these compounds do not meet the gold standard for research: multicenter, large numbers of patients, placebo-controlled, and double-blinded (neither the researcher nor the subjects know whether they are getting the compound being studied or a placebo). I will comment on the evidence for a particular compound when I can.

For suggestions on a comprehensive alternative treatment plan for mild to moderate unipolar depression, see chapter 11, "Putting it All Together."

NATURAL COMPOUNDS

B Vitamins, Minerals, and Essential Fatty Acids

See chapter 11 on self-help.

Amino Acids

Amino acids, such as tryptophan, are the building blocks from which brain neurotransmitters are made. Tryptophan is a precursor of serotonin, a neurotransmitter implicated in depression. Used by itself, however, it does not seem to have a great impact. Tryptophan may be more useful as a supplement in treatment-resistant depression and in manic-depressive illness. Simply increasing serotonin brain levels temporarily can have a sedative effect, but it probably has little effect on depression. Some studies suggest the lack of efficacy in other research may be due to use of inappropriately high doses of tryptophan. Tryptophan may be effective only at low to moderate doses.

Or it may also be that in these studies, tryptophan was given with substantial quantities of other amino acids. Tryptophan and other amino acids compete to get taken up into the brain. When they all arrive at the brain at the same time, tryptophan does not get in.

In any case, tryptophan is not available over the counter. It was taken off the market when some people who were taking it developed a deadly illness. This was possibly due to contamination of the product and not to the tryptophan itself.

Tyrosine, phenylalanine, and methionine are other amino acids that may be helpful for some people with depression. They are available over the counter. A handful of studies done in the late 1970s indicated that phenylalanine was useful for depression. All the studies had methodological shortcomings that cast doubt on the results. Five of nine depressed patients got better using tyrosine in a double-blind placebo controlled study conducted in 1983. That is a very small number of patients to draw conclusions from. The typical dosage is a gram or two per day or more on an empty stomach, at least thirty to forty-five minutes before a meal (when other proteins will not be competing for uptake into the brain). Be sure to eat adequate sources of protein at other times.

Amino acids are generally safe when used in *modest* quantities. Large doses overwork the kidneys and liver. Some amino acids can be toxic in large doses. If you have any history of kidney disease, you may not be able to use amino acids. The metabolic products of phenylalanine and tyrosine may contribute to kidney failure. You should also be cautious about using amino acids if you have liver disease or cardiovascular disease, including high blood pressure.

You may not be able to use tyrosine, phenylalanine, or methionine if you have a bipolar disorder or problems with temper outbursts. They may worsen these conditions. Check with your psychiatrist. Do not take phenylalanine if you suffer from diabetes or phenylketonuria—an inborn inability to metabolize phenylalanine. Do not take tyrosine if you are on an MAOI antidepressant. To be safe, check with your psychiatrist before taking amino acids if you are on any antidepressant drug.

If you and your doctor decide you should try amino acids, be sure to obtain pharmaceutical-grade amino acids. Pharmaceutical-grade amino acids will have the letters USP (United States Pharmacopoeia) on their label. Also make sure you get what is referred to as L-form amino acids. Amino-acid molecules are rotated to either the left or the right. L-form amino acids are rotated to the left and are the ones that make up human tissue.

5-HTP

A possible alternative to tryptophan is 5-HTP, which is available over the counter. Tryptophan is converted to 5-HTP in your body, and 5-HTP is then converted to seratonin. It is particularly good for helping anxious and agitated depressed people get a good night's sleep (at a dose between 50 and 200 milligrams a half hour before bed).

In his book *5-HTP: The Natural Way to Overcome Depression, Obesity, and Insomnia*, Michael Murray, a naturopathic doctor, suggests that taking 5-HTP is just as effective as taking SSRI medications (the Prozac class of antidepressants). But he cites only one study done in Switzerland in 1991 that supports this conclusion. There were a number of problems with the study as well: It was not placebo controlled. The researchers in the study used only a modest dose of medication. The study lasted only six weeks (SSRI drugs sometimes take up to eight to twelve weeks to show full benefit). Although the researchers judged that the 5-HTP did better than the prescription antidepressant, more patients reported dramatic improvement from the medication than from the 5-HTP.

Although Murray states that 150 to 600 milligrams per day of 5-HTP is an effective dosage, I have seen studies suggesting that very large and prohibitively expensive doses may be needed (up to

1,600 milligrams per day), since much of 5-HTP is metabolized before it gets to the brain. In addition, Murray states that 5-HTP passes easily from the bloodstream into the brain, but I have come across at least one study that suggests otherwise.

Even at high doses, 5-HTP may not be the best treatment for depressions characterized by lethargy, oversleeping, and lack of motivation.

S-Adenosyl-Methionine (SAM)

SAM is perhaps one of the most promising natural antidepressants. It is intimately involved in the biochemistry of the neurotransmitters. Several studies have demonstrated clear antidepressant efficacy for this substance. It appears to have a more rapid onset of antidepressant effect than tricyclics (which can take four weeks to begin working).

Because of the possibility of nausea and vomiting early in treatment, dosing is started at 200 milligrams twice a day for the first two days and gradually increased to 400 milligrams four times a day after twenty days. Other side effects, such as dry mouth, thirst, headaches, and blurry vision, are usually mild and transient. It may be helpful if SAM is taken with a B-vitamin complex, calcium, and magnesium. Unfortunately, as of mid-1999, a 1,600-milligram-per-day regimen of SAM costs between $250 and $400 per month. The price may come down as more companies offer SAM for sale.

You may have noticed that methionine was mentioned above in the section on amino acids and that it is a component of SAM. Can taking methionine do what SAM can do? Maybe. There may be a problem in the conversion of methionine to SAM, however, that may prevent methionine supplements from being useful.

SAM's use in bipolar depressed patients is not recommended, since it may induce hypomania.

Inositol

Inositol is found in small quantities in many of the foods we eat, including vegetables, whole grains, milk, and meat. It is available over the counter.

Inositol is composed of the same number and kinds of elements as glucose, a simple sugar. The difference lies in the way the elements are arranged and connected in each substance (somewhat analogous to the way graphite and diamond are both made of carbon atoms arranged in different ways).

Inositol is a so-called "second messenger" in the nervous system's transmission network. The neurotransmitter serotonin is a "first messenger," which relays signals *between* one nerve cell and another. As a second messenger, inositol relays signals from serotonin to other chemicals *within* a nerve cell. In many ways, inositol therefore plays as important a role in nerve-signal transmission as does serotonin.

In a double-blind, placebo controlled study (neither patient nor doctor knew if the patient was receiving inositol or the placebo), 12 grams of inositol per day (a little less than half an ounce) improved patients' depression to a significantly greater degree than did the placebo after four weeks of treatment. Inositol had no side effects.

The only drawback to this study was the relatively small number of patients. The study has not yet been replicated.

At 12 grams a day, a month's worth of inositol would cost between $75 and $125.

Dehydroepiandrosterone (DHEA)/Pregnenolene

DHEA is the most abundant naturally occurring hormone produced by the human adrenal glands. Its level declines with age. One open-label (nonblinded, no placebo control) study with six depressed patients aged fifty-one to seventy-two years showed DHEA improved memory and mood. When it is taken in modest doses (up to 25 milligrams), there appear to be few side effects. High doses can lead to headache, irritability, and insomnia. In women, high doses can lead to the development of facial hair and acne.

Although DHEA is available over the counter, you should not take it without having your doctor check your current blood level of the hormone. If you take DHEA, you should have your blood level monitored periodically. Do not take DHEA if you are under forty or if you have been diagnosed with prostate cancer. Using it in large quantities may suppress the body's own production of DHEA. Also check with your doctor before using it if you are on an antidepressant, thyroid medication, insulin, or estrogen.

It is possible that the precursor of DHEA—pregnenolone—may also have antidepressant effects.

Phosphatidylserine (PS)

PS is one of a class of substances known as phospholipids. The permeability of brain-cell membranes depends on adequate amounts of the substance. Cell membrane function is closely linked to neurotransmitter function. PS may also work by suppressing the production of cortisol, a naturally occurring steroid hormone in the body. Cortisol levels are typically elevated in depression.

The body manufactures PS but not if there is insufficient SAM or folic acid, or if the body is deficient in another class of substances known as fatty acids (see the nutrition section in chap. 11).

Some good studies have shown PS to be an effective antidepressant in the elderly. But PS, like inositol, is expensive. It is available over the counter. It may be just as effective to take B vitamins and essential-fatty-acid supplements, the metabolic precursors of PS.

Medicinal Plants

St. John's Wort This oddly named plant with attractive yellow flowers has garnered more research evidence for effectiveness in the treatment of depression than any other natural substance. There have been at least fifteen placebo-controlled trials of St. John's wort. Results of these trials showed that it is significantly superior to placebo for mild to moderate depression. It is commonly prescribed for depression in Europe.

For many years, the usual recommendation was to take 300 milligrams three times per day of a preparation containing 0.3 percent hypericin. Hypericin was thought to be the active ingredient in St. John's wort. New studies suggest the active ingredient may be a compound called *hyperforin*. St. John's wort is available over-the-counter and is inexpensive.

The first U.S. clinical trial of St. John's wort for depression, sponsored by the National Institutes of Health (NIH), began in the spring of 1998 at Duke University Medical Center. The study includes patients with major depression of moderate severity. Some patients are being treated with St. John's wort, some with an antidepressant medication, and some with placebo. Results of the study were not available at the time of printing.

Minor gastrointestinal irritation may occur in a small percentage of patients. A study out of Fordham University indicated that the use of St. John's wort could lead to the formation of cataracts in individuals exposed to ultraviolet light (the part of the sun's rays that cause sunburn). A study at Loma Linda University School of Medicine in California found that St. John's wort had a variety of ill effects on sperm and eggs. St. John's wort also caused mutation of a tumor suppressor gene that can lead to an increase in the risk of breast and ovarian cancer. The Loma Linda researchers noted that these were laboratory findings only. The results are not from clinical trials with patients. The actual risk to users of St. John's wort is unknown.

Ginkgo Biloba The ginkgo tree is an extremely hardy ornamental tree introduced into the United States from China in the late 1700s. It may be the oldest living tree species known.

A possible mood-elevating effect of ginkgo was first noted in studies on the use of the plant for treating elderly patients with symptoms such as dizziness, ringing in the ears, and loss of mental abilities, including loss of memory. Its effectiveness as an antidepressant has not been well studied, but case examples and animal models suggest it may be useful, especially for people over fifty. There is some evidence that it may enhance the effectiveness of antidepressant medications in people over fifty as well.

Side effects are rare but may include gastrointestinal discomfort and headache. One study found that ginkgo had a number of ill effects on sperm and eggs in the lab. How much a risk ginkgo poses in patients who use it is not clear. Recommended dosage is 80 milligrams three times a day. It should be used for twelve to sixteen weeks before judging its efficacy. It is available over the counter.

Other remedies A variety of other remedies have been mentioned as useful in treating depression. These include tetrahydrobiopterin, phenlethylamine (a metabolite of the amino acid phenylalanine), rubidium, Bach flower remedies, homeopathic preparations, aromatherapy, wild oats, lemon balm, ginseng, and Chinese herbal medicines. However, there is no substantial body of scientific evidence to support the use of these as first-line treatments.

ALTERNATIVE TREATMENTS

Electroconvulsive Therapy (ECT)

Commonly referred to as shock therapy, this treatment has gotten even more bad press than Prozac and virtually no good press. (When was the last time you heard someone at a party talk in glowing tones about how much ECT had changed his personality for the better?) The public tends to view it as a barbaric, torturous procedure—as punishment and mind control perpetrated by sadistic doctors. Many people mistakenly believe a patient is turned into a zombie with ECT and that he loses all memory or sense of individuality and identity.

The facts are much different. ECT is painless, works more quickly and with fewer side effects than medication, and is safer than medication overall. ECT is safer than medication for severely depressed, pregnant patients. An older, severely depressed patient, especially one with other medical illnesses, will almost certainly have fewer problems with ECT than he would with antidepressant medication. More important, *ECT is the single most effective treatment for severe depression and mania.*

Here is how ECT works: A patient is given an anesthetic and put to sleep. He is given a muscle relaxant. Many patients are given oxygen. An electrode is placed on one side of the head. This is referred to as unilateral ECT. Unilateral ECT causes less posttreatment confusion and memory loss than the older technique of placing electrodes on both sides of the head (bilateral ECT). Some doctors will try bilateral ECT if unilateral is not effective. A small amount of current is administered in order to induce a seizure. The seizure is the therapeutic element in ECT. Doctors now use what is referred to as briefpulse ECT. Brief-pulse ECT uses less energy, which further reduces the risk of posttreatment confusion and memory loss.

A seizure needs to last at least twenty-five to thirty seconds to be effective. It generally stops on its own, but if necessary, a doctor is prepared to bring it to an end with medication. A patient does not feel the current, and with the muscle relaxants, his body does not convulse. He wakes up a few minutes after the seizure is over. A patient will generally require between five and twelve ECT treatments at two- to three-day intervals. The number of treatments and the time between them is highly variable, however.

A patient typically does awake with some confusion and memory loss for recent events, which usually lasts for an hour or less. With repeated treatment, some memory loss may persist for several months after the completion of treatment, but it often clears up with time. The risk of permanent memory loss is low. In fact, since severe depression adversely affects memory, quite a few patients report that their memory is improved after ECT.

The only other major risk associated with ECT is the risk of brain damage or death involved with anesthesia. But the risk is no worse than the risk shared by any patient anesthetized for a medical procedure.

Who is a candidate for ECT? Any patient who is severely depressed or manic, who is actively suicidal or violent, who is psychotic, or who cannot eat, sleep, or function. Typically, however, ECT is reserved for patients who do not respond to medication.

Transcranial Magnetic Stimulation (TMS)

This is a procedure originally used as a research and diagnostic tool for neurological disorders. Depression appears to be associated with lowered functioning of the white matter in the brain's left frontal lobe (the area under your forehead). By repeatedly passing an electromagnet over the left frontal lobe, the neurons in this part of the brain are activated. (Your brain operates chemically and with weak electrical currents. Magnetic fields affect the electrical current in your brain.) A study done at the National Institute of Mental Health found that six patients who had not responded to a number of medications for depression all improved over the course of several weeks with daily TMS. Two patients showed profound improvement; one of them became completely well for the first time in three years. Subsequent studies have also shown TMS to be effective in treating depression.

Treatment is done three to five times a week for twenty minutes. Researchers report that patients undergoing TMS feel few sensations, except for mild contractions and tension in the scalp muscles.

TMS may have to be used with caution in patients on medications that increase the risk of seizure. TMS may itself induce a seizure. This is an unwanted side effect but apparently not a problematic one, since seizure induction is the goal of ECT treatment. Unlike ECT, TMS produces no memory loss or posttreatment confusion.

This is a promising procedure, about which we will be hearing much more in the coming years. It is being actively investigated by several groups of researchers.

Bright-light Therapy, Dawn Simulation, and Tinted Glasses

Exposure to bright light for thirty minutes per day can be effective in treating seasonal affective disorder—a mood disorder characterized by depression beginning in the fall and ending in the spring in the Northern Hemisphere. The depressions can be severe (see the section on seasonal affective disorder). Light therapy is believed to work by stimulating the production of the neurotransmitter serotonin, but the exact mechanism of action is unclear. Some studies have found that overeating and oversleeping predict response to bright-light therapy, while one found that only the consumption of sweets during the latter half of the day predicted a good response. At least one study failed to show bright-light therapy was more effective than a placebo treatment.

The exposure is typically accomplished by having the patient sit in front of a box with bright fluorescent lights (incandescent lights work just as well). Full-spectrum light (light containing all wavelengths characteristic of the sun's light) is not necessary and is potentially harmful, since it contains ultraviolet rays. The lights are covered with a translucent material to cut down on glare and reduce eyestrain. Light is measured in units called lux. Normal indoor lighting is about 300 to 500 lux. The light box puts out 10,000 lux. This amount sounds bright, but it is not blinding.

There is some conflicting evidence about the need for high-intensity light, but most studies have found bright light to be more effective than low-intensity light. The patient sits fairly close to the light—about a foot and a half away.

Patients may read, eat, or do whatever else they would like as long as they stay roughly a foot and a half away from the light. They are instructed to keep their eyes open and not sleep. However, another device, the dawn simulator (see below) may work while the person is sleeping and light is filtering through their eyelids. So it may be that some patients could sleep while sitting in front of the light. Patients are instructed not to stare at the light but to glance at it from time to time. There is some disagreement about the time of day patients should sit in front of the light, but most are encouraged to do so in the morning as soon as they get up. Late-night exposure is discouraged, since it can lead to insomnia. Most people begin to respond within two to four days with thirty minutes of exposure. The full effect may take one to two weeks.

Some light-box users get mild headaches or minor eyestrain. These problems can be easily remedied by reducing exposure time or sitting farther away from the light. Others may experience some hypomanic symptoms: feeling "wired," irritable, or euphoric. The treatment should be stopped in such cases.

Overall, the treatment appears to be safe. The long-term effects of bright-light therapy on the eyes are not known, however. Some doctors recommend eye exams to make sure patients do not have any problems with their retinas. Others suggest eye exams only if the patient has a preexisting condition. Some drugs can make patients highly sensitive to bright light. These patients may not be able to use bright light. Patients should check with their doctor and pharmacist if they are taking medications.

Light boxes are commercially available (see the appendix). Some patients like to use a light visor, because it gives them freedom to move around. The light in the visors is much less intense, but the patient is much closer to the light source. Some clinicians and researchers believe they may not be as effective as 10,000-lux light boxes. It may be best to start with the light box. If that works, you can try switching to the visor.

A dawn simulator gradually increases the intensity of light while the patient is sleeping to simulate a summer dawn. The final intensity is surprisingly low at 250 lux, but the device appears to be effective.

Bright-light therapy may also be effective as a treatment for some depressed patients without seasonal variation in their symptoms. If a patient has early-morning awakening as part of her depression, it may ease depression to use bright light at night. For a depressed patient who has trouble going to bed at a reasonable hour and has to drag herself out of bed in the morning, bright light in the morning might help. These strategies are based on the idea that depression is at least partially due to differences between the body's natural rhythms and the patient's sleep-wake schedule. Bright light resets the body's rhythms.

Some insurance companies cover the cost of light boxes and visors.

One researcher found that a subgroup of people with severe symptoms of seasonal affective disorder who did not respond to bright light therapy responded to the use of glasses with either rose or blue-green tinted lenses. Many of the patients who responded had migraine headaches.

Sleep Deprivation Combined with Sleep Phase Advance or Bright Light

After one night of total sleep deprivation (TSD) or late, partial sleep deprivation (PSD, in which the patient is woken up three or four hours earlier than normal), about 60 percent of severely depressed patients reported a pronounced decrease in symptoms. This approach appears to be especially effective when a patient has lost all ability to experience pleasure, has early-morning awakening, and has lost appetite and weight. It may be useful in a smaller percentage of patients with atypical symptoms. Interestingly, even the briefest of naps the day after a night of SD will cause an immediate relapse. The really bad news is that 80 percent or more of patients who respond to SD will relapse following the next night of full sleep. Most patients with mild depression do not respond to SD.

Some patients have been able to maintain improvement by continued intermittent use of sleep deprivation (once a week or so). Sleep deprivation may also help speed the response to antidepressant medication and may help a patient respond to an ineffective medication.

Another possible solution to the problem of relapse after a night of sleep deprivation involves moving patients' bedtimes back to five hours or so earlier in the evening. European researchers have reported this can prevent relapse in up to two-thirds of those treated with sleep deprivation. This is referred to as sleep phase advance (SPA). The person's normal sleep-wake cycle is restored gradually over the following week. SPA has been tried alone—with mixed results—and in conjunction with antidepressants.

Bright-light therapy following a night of partial sleep deprivation may also be useful in preventing relapse.

Although sleep deprivation sounds like a simple method to try on your own, you should not conduct this treatment by yourself. Some patients who respond—particularly those with atypical symptoms—feel even worse after SD than before it, following the next night of full sleep. SD may precipitate mania and rapid cycling in vulnerable individuals.

Any clinician who proposes sleep deprivation or phase advance therapy should be experienced in their use, stay in close contact with the patient, and be fully prepared to deal with a psychiatric emergency should one arise.

Acupuncture and Electroacupuncture

Acupuncture is an ancient Chinese healing method. Wire-thin needles are inserted into the skin at specific sites on the body depending on a patient's problems. In electroacupuncture, mild electrical current is then passed through the needles. Electroacupuncture appears to be more effective for depression than traditional acupuncture.

A few studies have found that electroacupuncture is as effective as a tricyclic antidepressant.

Neurofeedback (EEG Biofeedback)

In this method, sensors that detect the electrical activity of the brain are attached to the patient's scalp. The patient is able to monitor her brain electrical activity with the help of special equipment. The patient is then taught to modify this electrical activity to alleviate depression and stabilize mood. Although there has been no controlled research on this method that I am aware of, I believe it has the potential to be helpful to many people suffering from mood disorders. The procedure can be expensive.

Negative Ion Therapy

An ion is an atom or group of atoms that has gained or lost negatively charged particles called *electrons*. As a result, the atom or group of atoms has either a negative or positive charge. There are machines available that generate large quantities of negative ions from the elements and compounds in the air. These negative ions may have mood enhancing and mood-stabilizing effects. See the appendix for the name of a company that sells negative ion generators.

Eye Movement Desensitization and Reprocessing (EMDR)

EMDR was first developed in the late 1980s, as a treatment for patients who were left emotionally scarred by combat, childhood physical and sexual abuse, violent crime, and accidents.

The patient is asked to keep the image of a trauma in mind, along with any bodily sensations and negative thoughts accompanying the trauma. The therapist holds his first two fingers vertically, about 12 inches or so in front of the patient's face. The patient, with her head held motionless, is then asked to track the movement of the therapist's fingers with her eyes. The therapist rapidly moves his fingers from side to side eighteen or more times before stopping.

Patients generally experience a change in the image of the trauma, the thoughts that attend it, and some diminution in painful emotions associated with the memory of the trauma. The therapist then has the patient repeat the eye movements with whatever new images and thoughts come up. This basic procedure is often repeated many, many times in one session with the therapist. The goal of EMDR is to eliminate the emotional pain and other symptoms associated with the trauma.

EMDR has not been adequately researched as a treatment for use in depressive illness. It should not be considered a primary treatment modality. However, it may well have an adjunctive role to play in a comprehensive treatment plan. Depressed patients who experienced traumas as a child would probably benefit from it. It may also be useful in helping patients eliminate the cognitive distortions associated with depressive illness.

A therapist who proposes using EMDR to treat your depression should have received formal training in the procedure.

Other Psychotherapy Techniques

Hypnosis and techniques from a system of psychotherapy referred to as neurolinguistic programming (NLP), while not considered primary forms of treatment for depressive illness, may be useful when combined with medication and biologically informed psychotherapy.

In traditional hypnosis, the therapist guides the patient into a relaxed and focused state of consciousness called the hypnotic trance.

In this state, a patient is more suggestible than when in a normal state of consciousness and may be more easily influenced to alter cognitive distortions.

There are a variety of nontraditional forms of hypnosis that do not necessarily involve having the patient enter a formal trance. Nontraditional forms of hypnosis and NLP employ a wide variety of verbal and nonverbal techniques to help patients alter symptoms, cognitive distortions, emotional blocks, or behavior patterns that interfere with personal growth.

Natural Compounds and Alternative Procedures for the Treatment of Bipolar Disorder

Choline   Choline is a naturally occurring substance. Large doses of choline added to lithium have produced good results with treatment-resistant bipolar patients, especially rapid-cyclers. Choline has virtually no side effects.

Choline can be bought over the counter in raw form or as phosphatidylcholine (PC). Both PC and its relative phosphatidylserine, which may have antidepressant properties, are members of a group of substances known as *phospholipids* (phosphorous-containing fats) that are critical to nerve cell membrane functioning. Lecithin, a naturally occurring food product, is also a good source of choline.

EPA   EPA is a fatty acid found in coldwater fish. The human body can generally make EPA if sufficient quantities of the essential fatty acid linolenic acid (found most abundantly in flaxseed oil) are consumed in the diet. A few studies have indicated that 9 grams of EPA per day can have mood-stabilizing effects in manic patients who are already taking, but have not responded to, mood-stabilizing prescription drugs. EPA is available over the counter, but taking large quantities involves swallowing at least ten capsules a day. See chapter 11 for more information on the importance of essential fatty acids.

Magnesium Nerve cells are dependent on magnesium for helping control release and reuptake of neurotransmitters such as serotonin. Patients should take between 300 and 500 milligrams per day of elemental magnesium from magnesium chloride, glycinate, or citrate. If you develop diarrhea, you should decrease the dose. At least one pilot study has shown that magnesium aspartate was as effective as lithium in 50 percent of rapid-cycling bipolar patients. This may mean little, however, since rapid-cycling patients typically respond poorly to lithium. Check with your doctor before taking magnesium supplements if you have kidney disease.

Tryptophan Especially when combined with other mood stabilizers, the amino acid L-tryptophan—the dietary precursor of serotonin—appears to be a useful antimanic agent in doses between 1.5 grams and 3 grams per day. It is available by prescription only.

Reducing vanadium and suppressing its effects The proper functioning of certain enzymes are critical to cell membrane chemistry and therefore to release and reuptake of neurotransmitters. It is thought that abnormalities in the activity of these enzymes may lead to bipolar disorder. Vanadium is an element that interferes with the workings of one of these critical enzymes. Diets low in vanadium (meat and grains are some of the main sources of vanadium) have been reported to be useful in treating bipolar disorder. Vitamin C suppresses the effects of vanadium and has been found useful in manic-depressive disorder in high doses (3 grams per day or more). These results have not been replicated, however.

The drugs methylene blue and EDTA also suppress the effects of vanadium.

Melatonin Melatonin is a hormone normally produced by the human body in the dark. One study showed that patients in manic episodes began producing melatonin one and a half hours earlier than they did when in depressive episodes.

Researchers are looking into the possibility that giving patients melatonin at specific times of the day during manic and depressive episodes might relieve symptoms of bipolar disorder.

Neurofeedback and negative ion therapy   See the section on alternative treatments for depression.

THE INTEGRATED MEDICINE APPROACH TO MOOD DISORDERS

Alternative medicine used to be practiced largely by people who did not have a medical degree: Chiropractors, naturopaths, herbal therapists, and the like. Now a growing group of traditionally trained and well-respected medical doctors has begun to embrace an approach to health care referred to variously as alternative, complementary, or integrated medicine.

Integrated medicine involves much more than simply treating symptoms with natural alternatives rather than prescription drugs. It's a different way of looking at a patient's problems. Doctors who practice this approach put less emphasis on attempting to explain a patient's problems by fitting the symptoms into a traditional disease or diagnostic category. This is especially the case with those patients whose conditions are chronic and for which there is no readily discernible cause. They point out that many of these diagnoses are, in fact, just labels and do not explain anything about the cause of a patient's problems. They argue that lumping all patients with similar symptoms into a diagnostic category obscures our understanding of what may be uniquely wrong with a particular person. Lumping people into categories usually leads to treatment that is aimed, not at underlying causes, but at the suppression of symptoms. Integrated medicine doctors prefer to locate and correct each patient's unique biochemical and metabolic abnormalities, even if these might not be obviously connected to the patient's symptoms.

Take the diagnosis and treatment of unipolar depression, for instance. An integrated medicine doctor would point out that unipolar depression is not an entity. The label does not explain what may be at the root of a particular patient's fatigue, insomnia, depressed mood, and other symptoms. Antidepressant drugs are effective at relieving symptoms, but are not a treatment of a particular patient's biochemical problems. The treatment of depression with antidepressant drugs is more like the use of aspirin to treat a fever than the use of antibiotics to treat an infection. Antidepressant drugs relieve symptoms of depression just as aspirin relieves fever. But neither aspirin nor antidepressants cure an underlying problem the way an antibiotic cures an infection.

Doctors practicing integrated medicine do not pretend to know what causes symptoms of depression in general. But they do believe that an investigation of each individual patient's biochemistry and metabolism may reveal abnormalities that, if corrected, could support recovery.

What sorts of abnormalities do these doctors look for? Following is a partial list. There are a number of tests that help integrated medicine doctors detect these abnormalities.

- Yeast overgrowth in the intestines
- Allergies, including food allergies
- Food intolerances such as intolerance of gluten and casein (found in grains and milk)
- Vitamin and mineral deficiencies
- Leaky gut
- Fatty acid abnormalities
- Subtle viral infections
- Heavy metal or pesticide toxicity
- Parasites
- Problems in liver detoxification chemistry
- Sulfur amino acid chemistry defects

Once these abnormalities have been detected, the patient is usually treated through diet modifications and with nutritional supplements. Prescription medications may be used to treat yeast overgrowth, parasites, or viral infections.

Keep in mind that there are no controlled studies of the effectiveness of this diagnostic and treatment approach for symptoms of depression. In addition, this approach can be very expensive and time consuming. Doctors who practice integrated medicine often charge $750 to $1,500 for a one and a half- to two-hour consultation. This does not include the cost of tests. Many insurance companies will not pay for these services.

If you have moderate to severe depression, are suicidal, feeling overwhelmed, or are having trouble functioning, you should not turn to integrated medicine as the first treatment. You should be seriously considering the use of prescription medication. After you have recovered, you can then safely and comfortably explore the integrated medicine approach.

If you would like to contact a medical doctor in your area who practices integrated medicine, try contacting the American College for the Advancement of Medicine at (714) 583-7666 or the American College of Alternative Medicine at 1-800-532-3688. You might also read *Power Healing* by Dr. Leo Galland or *Detoxification and Healing* by Dr. Sidney Baker to get a better idea how these doctors work. Information on Dr. Galland and his approach can be found on the web at http://www.healthy.net/bios/galland/index.html. Dr. Baker has a web site at http://www.sbakermd.com.

CHAPTER 11

SELF-HELP AND SUMMARY GUIDELINES FOR THE PROSPECTIVE PATIENT

There are many things a patient can do to help himself once medical treatment and psychotherapy have begun.

1. *Learn as much as you can about mood disorders and their treatment. Urge your family to learn about mood disorders, too.* If you suffer from depression or manic-depressive illness, one of your most powerful weapons is knowledge. The most important reason to learn about your illness is that your mood disorder will tend to override your ability to see yourself, your life, and your future accurately. Once you come to know the myriad subtle manifestations of your particular illness, you will be less likely to become a prisoner in the war against it.

Depression can be a relentless and persuasive torturer. It may scream at you at times, or it may merely whisper. But what it tells you about yourself, your life, and your future are lies. If you are taken prisoner, at least some small part of you may be able to remember this. It may make the pain more bearable until help arrives. It may help you survive.

Knowledge may also help you limit the damage your illness does to relationships. For the cyclothymic patient, for instance, being aware that she can be unduly irritable may allow the patient to exert some measure of conscious control over the irritability. Although the patient may feel certain that the irritation is warranted, she will learn to inhibit it because it may cause more problems than it's worth. If the patient lets time pass, the irritation often passes, too.

The old advice of "getting your feelings out" can be bad advice. Anger expressed in the service of self-protection or appropriate assertiveness is useful and healthful. Expression of undue irritation leads to more irritability. Researchers have found that there is a physiological basis for this. Learning to suppress irritation is also important if the mood-disordered patient's spouse has an irritable temperament. Two irritable people can end up having a bad marriage. This happens more frequently than you might think. In a process known as "assortative mating," a person with a mood disorder frequently marries someone else with a mood disorder.

Knowledge helps you become a partner with your therapist and doctor. When you are able to mark some of your experiences as symptoms, this helps you and your doctor gain a fuller understanding of the specific manifestations of your illness. You and your doctor are then able to formulate the best possible plan for treating your depression.

Knowledge of the true nature of mood disorders will help you accept that it is indeed an illness, for which you need bear no shame. This cannot be learned quickly. It often takes months or even years of grappling with the diagnosis and its implications, along with a willingness to be open about the illness to friends and relatives.

Knowledge of the best treatments available helps you choose the doctors, therapists, and treatments best for you. Unfortunately, the people treating you may not check thoroughly for or may miss the presence of a mood disorder, particularly the milder varieties. They may not have kept up on the latest developments in diagnosis and treatment. They may have a theoretical bias against some treatments for depression. They may make treatment recommendations that make little sense in light of what we know about mood disorders. You need to be an informed consumer.

You should become an expert in your mood disorder. The time and effort necessary to do so will provide you with some of the best medicine for what ails you.

2. Consider adding nutritional supplements to your diet. If you have not already done so, please read the information in chapter 10 on the scientific evidence regarding the effectiveness of natural compounds in treating mood disorders.

CAUTION: Do not treat yourself for what you believe to be depression with these supplements. You first need to get a mental-health diagnostic evaluation, physical exam, and blood workup. Women who are pregnant or breast-feeding, those who are on medications or being treated for an illness, and the elderly should be especially careful to consult a physician prior to their use. Specific cautions are listed for some of the supplements. Keep all supplements, including vitamins, out of the reach of children.

Vitamins and minerals. The B vitamins have been touted as a cure for depression for some patients. If you have a deficiency in any one of several B vitamins, you may well develop symptoms of depression. Treating the deficiency with B-vitamin supplements can obviously be useful.

Some studies have suggested that depressed patients have a greater incidence of B-vitamin deficiency than does the general population. If this is true, it is difficult to tell whether it is a cause of depression or an effect. Depressed people do not eat balanced meals and sometimes they do not eat much at all. So you would expect them to have nutritional deficiencies. To be on the safe side, your therapist or psychiatrist should ask for a serum folate (folic acid) and vitamin B_{12} test as part of the blood workup any patient seeking help for depression should get.

The real question with the B vitamins is whether large doses of them have druglike antidepressant effects when blood tests show no deficiencies or only marginal deficiency. While some studies have suggested that this may be the case for some depressed patients, the evidence is not convincing.

Given how inexpensive vitamins are, however, and the crucial role played by B vitamins in cerebral metabolism, it makes sense for depressed patients to take B-vitamin supplements.

You do not have to take scores of pills to get the vitamins and minerals you need. A good multivitamin/mineral formula should have all that you need, except for magnesium and calcium. You have to be careful not to take too much vitamin A or D—only 10,000 IU (international units) of vitamin A per day and 800 IU of vitamin D per day. These vitamins can be toxic in high doses. Keep in mind that you will be getting vitamins and minerals through your normal diet. Since just two cups of fortified milk give you a quarter of the RDA of vitamin D, for instance, you really do not have to take a lot in supplement form.

There's little reason to take more than 50 milligrams of vitamin B$_6$, unless your doctor is attempting to treat premenstrual syndrome. The RDA is only 1.6 milligrams per day for women and 2.0 milligrams per day for men. B$_6$ is one of the few B vitamins that can be toxic in high doses. The human body can use B$_6$ only in the form of pyridoxal-5-phosphate (P5P). Normally, the body converts B$_6$ to this compound. Some people may have trouble with the conversion, however, so it is probably best to take B$_6$ as P5P, if possible.

Take no more than 75 milligrams of vitamin B$_3$ (niacin) unless otherwise directed by your doctor (sometimes used in higher doses to treat high cholesterol). Excessive B$_3$ can produce abdominal pain and cramping.

Vitamin C, in doses of 3 grams (3,000 milligrams) per day, has been reported by one group of researchers to be effective in manic-depressive illness. If you want to take extra vitamin C, you should increase the dosage slowly. It can cause gastrointestinal distress and diarrhea in some people at doses as low as 500 to 1,000 milligrams per day.

Supplements of calcium up to two and a half grams per day are probably safe, but there is no reason to take that much. Stick to no more than 1,500 milligrams per day. If you suffer from bipolar illness, you might want to try *lowering* your intake of calcium. Patients with bipolar disorder tend to have too much calcium in their cells.

Men who eat meat regularly should not use supplements with iron, at least not on a regular basis. Concentrations of iron stored in the body can reach toxic levels if too much is ingested. Women should use no more than 10 to 15 milligrams per day unless they are pregnant. Check with your obstetrician if you are pregnant.

Take up to 500 milligrams of elemental magnesium per day, with adequate calcium intake. Adequate magnesium is important, since low levels of it may be linked to mood disorders. Check with your doctor if you have Addison's disease, myasthenia gravis, or kidney problems.

Essential fatty acids. Linolenic acid, a so-called omega-3 fatty acid, and linoleic acid, an omega-6 fatty acid, are referred to as essential fatty acids (EFAs). You have to include them in your diet because your body cannot manufacture them. Low intake of EFAs and high intake of saturated fats and cholesterol—the typical American diet—has been linked to many health problems, including cardio-vascular disease and cancer. Some preliminary studies now suggest a link between low EFA intake and depression as well. Others suggest that EFA supplements are useful in the treatment of premenstrual syndrome, chronic fatigue syndrome, and other disorders.

That EFAs might be effective in depression makes some sense in light of the role that cell-membrane structure and function play in mood disorders. Optimal functioning of the neurotransmitter systems in the brain (and all the body's biochemical processes, for that matter) is dependent upon proper cell-membrane function. Proper functioning is, in turn, dependent to a large extent upon the fatty composition of the membrane. Functioning of cell membranes may be compromised when you take in a lot of saturated fat and neglect EFAs in your diet. At least one group of researchers has suggested that prescription antidepressants may work by helping correct problems in cell-membrane function.

The EFAs are precursors to hormonelike substances referred to as prostaglandins, which have also been implicated in mood disorders. Prostaglandins may function as neurotransmitters. There are different types of prostaglandins. Some have sedative, tranquilizing, anti-inflammatory, and anticonvulsant properties. Other forms have adverse effects.

Prostaglandin levels—particularly the prostaglandins with adverse effects—are frequently well outside the normal range in people with mood disorders. It is not clear whether this is a cause or an effect of depression. However, when depression is effectively treated with medication, prostaglandin levels return to normal.

Even if you do not have signs of EFA deficiency (dry and dull hair, dry skin, dandruff, and cracked nails), it makes sense to restrict your intake of saturated fats and take an EFA supplement. The modest cost of the supplements, their overall health benefits, and the *possible* link to depression make it worthwhile.

Various commercially available vegetable oils contain essential fatty acids. But you should not look to the supermarket shelf for your EFA supplement. Supermarket oils are usually highly refined. Many of the nutrients have been removed or destroyed in the process. In addition, the best oils—flaxseed or linseed oil, evening primrose oil, and fish oils—are not generally available at the market.

You will need to get high-quality, unrefined oils from a health-food store or nutritional-supplement supply house (see appendix). Most of these oils will be organic, meaning that the grain they were made from was grown without the use of chemical fertilizers and pesticides. Oils should be manufactured in ways designed to minimize damage to them: cold-pressed in the absence of oxygen and bottled with inert gases such as nitrogen.

Flaxseed oil is by far the best source of the omega-3 fatty acids and a good source of omega-6 fatty acids. The human body can *generally* make other needed fatty acids—such as gamma-linoleic acid (GLA), docosahexaenoic acid (DHA), and eicosapentanoic acid (EPA)—from these two essential fatty acids. Although it has not been convincingly demonstrated, some people's bodies *may* have trouble making these metabolic conversions. If so, then it may make more sense to take other oils in addition to or instead of flaxseed oil to get the needed GLA, DHA, and EPA. Borage oil is a good source of GLA and has, in fact, been used to treat PMS. Fish-oil capsules are an excellent source of DHA and EPA.

There are commercially available products that combine a number of oils into one capsule so that you can get a complete profile of the fatty acids. You may pay a premium for the convenience, however.

If you do decide to use these oils, there is some indication that you should take them in a certain proportion for best results. You can start off by taking equal amounts of GLA and EPA. The products with combined oils are formulated with proper ratios in mind. You may have to adjust the balance as you go. Here again, there is no good science to guide the way this should be done. However, Barry Sears, M.D., who has done extensive work with the EFAs, has suggested that diarrhea, flatulence, and increased appetite are signs that you need to lower EPA intake. Constipation, lack of appetite, and irritability are indications, he believes, for less GLA and/or more EPA. You should be sure to take a multivitamin/multimineral formula, which includes at least magnesium, vitamin B_6, zinc, niacin, and vitamin C, since these nutrients increase the conversion of fatty acids to prostaglandins.

You may also wish to consider changing what and how you eat to get more foods naturally high in the EFAs and to reduce surges of insulin, which can adversely affect the balance of prostaglandins.

Check with your doctor if you are epileptic, diabetic, manic-depressive, or if you are taking aspirin or Coumadin on a regular basis.

Follow label directions with regard to amounts of these oils you should use.

3. *Consider modifying your diet.* This is a particularly good idea if you have anxiety or irritability after a meal high in carbohydrates or if you tend to overeat sweets and gain weight when depressed. You may be having fluctuations in blood-sugar levels that contribute to your symptoms. Keep in mind, however, that these fluctuations are not the cause of your depression. The dietary recommendations are not considered treatment for depression.

Eat several smaller meals rather than fewer large ones. Do not let yourself get so busy that you do not take time to eat. Eliminate all processed foods, junk food, white flour, sugar, and foods containing sugar. It is best not to have any of these in the house if you struggle with cravings. When you shop, do not even go in the aisle where these items are located. If possible, let someone else shop for you if you cannot resist buying them. Avoid alcohol and caffeine. Eat complex carbohydrates that cause less of an insulin response. These are referred to as low- to moderate-glycemic-index foods: whole-grain pastas, beans, oatmeal, most vegetables, and some fruits, such as grapefruit, apples, pears, and oranges. Lower-glycemic-index breads include rye and pumpernickel. For a complete list, consult nutrition and diet books as well as books on diabetes and hypoglycemia.

Some nutritionists and clinicians have claimed that even meals with *complex, low- to moderate-glycemic-index* carbohydrates cause a lot of problems, at least for some people who are carbohydrate cravers (binge eaters, bulimics, and patients with seasonal affective disorder or atypical depression). They claim that they can cause excessive insulin release, increase the production of those prostaglandins with adverse effects, cause reactive hypoglycemia, weight gain (insulin causes your body to store fat), and cycles of carbohydrate craving and binge eating. They recommend severely limiting carbohydrates, eating very small meals, and increasing the amount of protein and fat you eat.

It is difficult to know what to make of these recommendations. However, it is probably best if you do not dump a meal loaded with carbohydrates (even complex ones) into your body every time you eat. This is especially the case with breakfast, which should contain a substantial amount of protein. Each meal should contain a moderate amount of protein and some fat in addition to carbohydrates. Limit the amount of fruit you eat at one sitting.

There are nutritionists who claim that you can stop binges by separating your carbohydrate from your protein intake. In a protein-packed meal, many amino acids will be competing to get taken up into the brain. Tryptophan (the serotonin precursor) always loses this competition. When you eat a carbohydrate meal, tryptophan will get taken up into the brain, thereby increasing serotonin.

Athletes and others who use protein powders may want to hold off using them until their depression clears up. If you have been successfully treated with antidepressants and want to take protein powder for any reason, make sure it has some naturally occurring tryptophan in it. Introduce the protein supplement into your diet slowly and monitor your mood.

4. *Follow these mood-hygiene recommendations.* Those suffering from mood disorders, especially bipolar disorders, should strive to maintain consistency in work hours, sleep, eating and exercise habits, and social contacts. Sleep is probably the most critical. You should go to bed and get up at roughly the same time each day, even on the weekends. *If you are being treated for bipolar illness, trying to get more done in a day by forgoing sleep can trigger or worsen manic episodes.* Oversleeping can trigger or worsen depression.

Ideally, it would be best in the early stages of recovery for the mood-disordered individual to avoid people and events likely to stir up strong emotions like anger, guilt, anxiety, or worry. This probably even includes strong feelings brought up in therapy. These things can kindle problematic brain biochemistry changes that can contribute to relapse or at least make it harder for you to recover. Treatment will help the mood-disordered individual become more tolerant of stress. But even with good medical and psychotherapeutic care, some mood-disordered people may remain more vulnerable to stress-induced relapse than will others. Of course, patients suffering from mood disorders are going to have to accept the fact that the world is under no obligation to avoid dumping stress on them. To get unduly irritated about misfortune will only worsen matters. You do not want to get stressed out thinking you should not have to be stressed! You must take responsibility for how you cope with life's problems.

Family education and counseling is doubly important for this reason. Bipolar individuals whose families have been counseled on how to deal with the manifestations of the illness are much less likely to get involved in explosive emotional conflicts, which may contribute to a patent's relapse.

Mood-disordered patients very often seek treatment in the midst of some interpersonal crisis. The relationship problem is intricately enmeshed with their depression. One of the thorniest problems concerns a patient who is involved in a relationship with someone who is not completely available. The cycles of hope and frustration these create can keep the affected individual in a state of turmoil.

Patients should break off or suspend these relationships, but nearly always that feels like Mission Impossible until the mood disorder is treated with medication. Antidepressants decrease the obsessive longing for the lover and make the patient feel more emotionally capable of getting along without him or her. Without medication, people can stay wrapped up in these frustrating relationships for months and years. They then feel stupid and weak for "putting up with" the lover's lack of commitment and end up more depressed. Sometimes it can help the patient ease up on the self-criticism to know that being "locked into" a relationship like this is a symptom of depression and not a sign of weakness. Many of these people may get stuck in long-term psychotherapy, trying to figure out how their parents' behavior made them a sucker for bad partners. Not infrequently, the patient will stay stuck until their depression ends of its own accord. They will then be able to move on. Therapists can easily mistake this spontaneous remission for a "cure."

Minimal use of alcohol and avoidance of drugs is critical, even if the patient does not have an alcohol or drug problem. Social use of small amounts of alcohol for those with well-controlled unipolar depression will not be a problem for most people. But if the depression is resistant to treatment or there are frequent relapses, or if there are bipolar elements to the illness, alcohol should be avoided entirely.

5. *If you suffer from any type of bipolar illness, chart your moods, daily routines, and significant life events.* It will help your doctor monitor

the effectiveness of treatment. It will show the relationship be-tween stressful events and mood changes. This will help you tackle similar problems in the future. It will also help convince you that making changes in your sleeping and other habits or medication is closely linked to changes in your symptoms. There are a number of such charts available. The book *Overcoming Depression* has an excel-lent chapter on the topic (see appendix).

6. *Sometimes it is better to keep active than to let yourself be inactive.* In milder to moderate cases of depression or atypical depression, it is best to force yourself to do things you may not initially feel like doing (such as exercising, going out with friends, doing a project around the house or at work). Depressed people typically find themselves held back by what are referred to as "task-interfering cognitions." As you contemplate doing something, you may find yourself making a pre-diction: "I would not enjoy it" or "I would get nothing out of it." Per-haps you might think "It is too much to do; it would take too much time and energy." As a result, you sit around doing nothing, watching TV, or sleeping, and wind up feeling worse as a result.

Try an experiment. Make yourself do something you used to enjoy. Test your prediction! Unless you are severely depressed, once you get going, you will notice your motivation growing. You may also notice that you have a sense of accomplishment.

What happens if you feel absolutely no boost in your mood or sense of accomplishment? Well, the experiment is still a success, because you just came up with important information: You are probably depressed to the point where it makes no sense to push yourself right now. Let yourself off the hook. You are going to have to take it easy until you are better. It is odd how our culture sup-ports the person with a bad case of the flu staying in bed but not the person with a bad case of depression.

The fact is, many profoundly depressed patients find they simply *cannot* get themselves to muster up the energy or motivation to push themselves to do anything. This is a hard concept to understand for someone who has not known depression. The difficulty the patient has in getting going is not a matter of laziness or a lack of willpower. The problem is not under voluntary control. The usual advice from friends and family members to the severely depressed patient to "get busy" can be harmful. It makes the patient feel terrible about himself. He starts viewing the problem as a personal weakness.

It is best if families of severely depressed patients allow their loved one to be sick and out of commission for awhile. Families and helping professionals worry that allowing the patient to be ill in this sense will encourage the patient to remain sick and dependent. This is rarely a concern with a severely depressed patient who has a history of reasonably good functioning prior to the illness.

Being sociable is a big problem area for depressed individuals. The more severe the depression, the less likely it is that you will want to be around people. Others may urge you to "get out and meet some new people." If you do force yourself to go out, you may feel very pressured to "act happy" when you are in social situations. You may feel that you'll have to work too hard to hide the fact that you are depressed. You may also feel guilty and ashamed of your inability to be more lively and talkative. But you worry that if you do not socialize, people may start asking you why or pushing you in ways you find uncomfortable. What should you do? A lot depends on accurately judging the severity of your depression and on what you *want* to do.

All these concerns are manageable. I am going to give you some ways you can tackle them. But please keep in mind as you read that it is *perfectly okay to choose not to tackle the problem at all.* If you are severely depressed, you may not have the energy to think about all I am about to say, let alone put it into action. If this is the case, just forget about all this until you are feeling better. That day will come.

If you want to tackle the problem, the first step is to realize you do not *have* to act happy when you are not. Who says you must hide your depression or the fact that you are on medication for it? Where is it written that you must pretend to be happy when you actually feel miserable? You do not have to wear a sign saying you are depressed (although that would be one way to deal with the problem), but you don't have to keep it a closely guarded secret, either. It is the depression itself that makes you feel that you need to hide your condition. It is saying that you have something to be embarrassed about and ashamed of. These feelings do not die easily. Just because you are told a couple of times that depression is an illness does not mean you will feel that way about it immediately. Someday you will, but you have to argue with yourself lots of times before it sinks in.

Your depression will create all sorts of awful scenarios about how people will react if they learn you suffer from depression. Are you really convinced it would be terrible if someone knew the truth? If you are up for it, try another experiment. Tell someone about your depression! Put your fear to the test. You will probably be surprised at the sympathetic response you get. With a bit of luck, the person you tell will be suffering from depression, too, and on the latest medication, or know someone who is.

The more important issue, of course, is what your depression is causing you to think about yourself: If you find, as you probably will, that you are feeling ashamed of yourself, you may be helped if you read more about depression or the life stories of famous people who were depressed. You may feel less shame if you join a support group where you openly talk about your depression.

You may be concerned that you will make others uncomfortable or "ruin their good time." That is unlikely. Do you really believe the music will stop and people will decide to sit around in a circle feeling miserable because you are glum?

Not only do you not need to hide your depression, but you also do not need to get into it with anyone if you choose not to. Just because someone comments on your mood or asks you questions does not mean you have to explain yourself. Say as little or as much as you would like.

Have you gotten unwanted advice about how to deal with your depression from in-laws who do not know what they are talking about? Stop them in midsentence and say you do not want to hear it. Or pretend not to hear it. Or change the subject. Or excuse yourself to go to the bathroom.

7. *Try to get regular exercise.* There is good scientific evidence that regular exercise is an effective antidepressant for those with mild unipolar depression. The exercise should probably be aerobic. That is, it should get you breathing deeply and your heart working at a particular pace. Walking fast, jogging, bicycling, and dancing are all good ways to get aerobic exercise. Some evidence suggests that other forms of exercise not typically aerobic, such as weight lifting or yoga, may also be beneficial.

To get an antidepressant effect *and* cardiovascular benefit, you should do any exercise that gets your heart beating at around 75 percent of capacity, which is calculated by subtracting your age from 220. You should exercise with your heart beating at that rate for at least twenty minutes at least three times a week. If you are thirty years old, for example, your maximum heart rate would be 190 (220 minus 30). You would need to get your heart going at about 142 beats per minute (75 percent of 190 beats) for twenty minutes. Such sports as tennis, volleyball, or downhill skiing may not do the trick, since they involve a lot of starting and stopping.

To get the antidepressant effect alone from exercise probably requires somewhat less intensity. This is good news, because if you have been sedentary for a while or have any cardiovascular problems, you are going to need to take some time to build up your endurance. Always warm up with light exercise and stretching prior to beginning your workout. Check with your doctor before you begin any exercise program if you have been sedentary or have cardiovascular disease.

The problem with this approach to depression is *getting started.* If you are depressed and have been sedentary for a while, you are probably not going to *feel* like exercising. But if you wait to feel like exercising before you begin, you probably never will exercise.

8. *Distract yourself and let time pass.* Your friends and family may admonish you to get your mind off your problems, put them out of

your head, not think about them, or stop worrying about them. What they do not understand is that active efforts like this are doomed to failure when you are depressed. Your brain is in a rut.

Active efforts to combat unpleasant thoughts are not just ineffective, they are likely to make things worse when you are depressed. They do this for two reasons, the first of which is very simple. If you try not to think about something, you are thinking about not thinking about it! In other words, your mind is still on the subject. Second, depressed people are overly self-critical. Rather than think, "Oh, my friend's advice to stop thinking about my problems was wrong," the depressed person will think, "There is something wrong with me. I am mentally weak. I should be able to pull myself out of this rut." The result is demoralization and more depression.

A gentler and more passive approach may be helpful for some people. *If the following does not work well for you, please keep in mind it is not your fault.* It may simply be weak medicine. The approach starts with this premise: *Until your depression is adequately treated, you cannot prevent unrealistic worries, nagging self-doubts, painful self-criticism, irritable feelings, and gloomy thoughts from popping into your head. This is a symptom of depression, just as a fever is a symptom of the flu.* That may sound discouraging, but at least you will not be holding yourself unreasonably responsible for something over which you have little control.

Next, at least some small part of you needs to know when you are feeling *unduly* gloomy, worried, or irritable. You need that small amount of rationality to be able to make use of distraction. Otherwise, why would you want to distract yourself if you really felt you should be thinking about your problems?

Once you accept the presence of unpleasant thoughts and feelings and can mark them as symptoms, you can attempt to gently distract or refocus yourself. You may not be able to stop the thoughts from popping into your head, but you may have more luck in keeping yourself from dwelling on them. Be aware, however, in depression, a voice inside you will keep trying to convince you it is important to pay attention to something you are worried, depressed, or irritated about. The voice may be quite persuasive. Do not believe it for a minute! The less attention you pay to unpleasant or obsessive thoughts or feelings, the more likely they are to go away—at least for a while. Do not expect to distract yourself one time and be done with it. Initially, it will be something you will need to do frequently. You will distract yourself and then suddenly become aware that your mind is back on a worry or unpleasant image or feeling.

If you are mildly to moderately depressed and retain the ability to experience pleasure, try to direct your energy and attention to anything that gives you enjoyment, helps you feel good about yourself, or enhances your sense of well-being. If, for instance, you have children and you are feeling painfully preoccupied with how little success you have achieved in life, play with them. Notice little things: their smile, the way they run, or the silly things they say or do. When you catch your mind back on your worries or your bad feelings about yourself, accept that as the way depression works and then gently refocus your attention on your kids. If you do not have kids or there is not much that gives you pleasure, focus your attention on getting a chore done. Keep in mind that you will have to repeatedly refocus yourself when your attention is drawn back to your worries. This is normal. Keep going! It usually gets easier the more you do it.

Talking to trusted friends, family, or your therapist may be useful if you are not sure if the depression is making you unduly worried, gloomy, or irritated. Depressive thinking can be insidious. You may not realize that your thoughts and feelings are actually symptoms of the depression. Getting someone else's perspective can help a great deal.

Depressed people, even when adequately treated, may be more susceptible than they would like to having unpleasant moods triggered by stress. Remember that mood disorders are basically an inborn defect in buffering against stress. Homeostatic mechanisms normally operative in most people are not quite up to the task of keeping your mood level. Brain biochemistry is more easily knocked off kilter. Talking to others can help keep things in perspective.

9. *Learn stress-reduction techniques.* High levels of stress hormones are associated with depression. It is possible, although not proven, that meditation, self-hypnosis, relaxation training, and other stress-reduction methods, by reducing the level of stress hormones in the body, may reduce depression. Although you should not pin your hopes strictly on meditation to cure your depression, it is another one of those self-help methods that have a lot of other health benefits.

If you are extremely obsessive and guilt-ridden or have trouble concentrating, you might find some relaxation techniques difficult and possibly unpleasant. You might not be able to focus your attention or keep your mind from dwelling on painful memories or current problems.

10. *Join a patient-run support group.* Although many depressed and manic-depressive individuals will resist going to a support group out of embarrassment and shame, it can be very helpful in terms of the education, the boost in morale, and the reduction of shame it provides. The National Depressive and Manic-Depressive Association (NDMDA), the National Foundation for Depressive Illness (NAFDI), the National Depression and Related Disorders Association (DRADA), and a number of local organizations support these groups. Every patient is urged to attend one of these groups for at least a few sessions. Telephone numbers for DMDA, NAFDI, and DRADA can be found in the appendix.

PUTTING IT ALL TOGETHER

It is best for you, as a patient, to seek out a therapist who is knowledgeable, open-minded, willing to discuss the pros and cons of several approaches to your mood disorder, and willing to use whatever means appropriate to help you.

Here are some guidelines to help you in your decisions about treatment.

1. You should not attempt to make a diagnosis or decide on treatment without guidance from a mental-health professional who

is an expert in the diagnosis and treatment of mood disorders. The professional you consult should be willing to consider all biological, emotional, and interpersonal factors in understanding your depression. He should have, however, a biologically informed perspective on mood disorders, since the weight of the scientific evidence suggests that this is the most accurate model.

If you are seeking help for symptoms of depression, make sure your doctor or therapist takes the time to consider whether your symptoms are due to unipolar depression or are part of a bipolar disorder. Critical treatment decisions hinge on this diagnostic distinction.

2. You should have a complete physical exam with blood workup and urinalysis.

3. If this is your first episode of mild to moderate depression, you have no family history of mood disorder, your symptoms are emotional (depressed mood) and not physical (sleep, appetite disturbance), and the episode has been relatively brief, you might wish to discuss using just psychotherapy with your doctor or therapist. If you are not doing considerably better in two to four months, however, consider the use of other treatments. If your therapist disagrees, seek a second opinion with a biologically informed therapist.

4. If you have mild to moderate depression and are opposed to the use of antidepressants, you can consider the following alternative treatment program.

Four nutritional supplements should form the foundation of any alternative treatment program:

a. One to two tablespoons of cold-pressed, unrefined flax oil per day to provide omega-3 essential fatty acids. Or take borage *and* fish oil capsules. Patients with diabetes should check with their doctor before using these products.

b. High-quality multivitamin, multimineral formula (which should include zinc and selenium) with ample doses of the B vitamins. Get a brand that you take at least twice and preferably three times per day with meals. Make sure it does not contain iron.

3. A special form of vitamin B$_6$ called pyridoxyl-5-phosphate (50 milligrams per day).
4. Extra magnesium: 350 to 500 milligrams per day of elemental magnesium. Do not use magnesium oxide. It is poorly absorbed. Magnesium glycinate, citrate, or chloride are all acceptable. If you get diarrhea after starting magnesium supplements, decrease the dose. If you do not eat dairy products regularly or if you are a woman, take supplemental calcium as well. Check with your doctor before taking magnesium supplements if you have kidney disease.

Once this foundation is in place, I suggest to most of my patients with mild unipolar depression who opt not to take antidepressants that they take St. John's wort or 5-HTP. The advantage of St. John's wort is that it is the least expensive and best-studied alternative treatment. It should be a preparation that has been standardized to contain a high level of the ingredient hyperforin. The disadvantage of St. John's wort is that it can take six to eight weeks to begin working. In my opinion, women with a family history of breast cancer or women attempting to conceive should not use St. John's wort. Husbands of women who are attempting to conceive should not use St. John's wort either. Please review the information on health risks with St. John's wort in chapter 10.

If it is going to work, 5-HTP will produce results in a shorter period of time than St. John's wort. 5-HTP may be especially good for patients who are agitated or anxious and cannot sleep. The disadvantage of 5-HTP is that the dosages required may be prohibitively expensive. Some alternative medicine practioners have claimed good results with as little as 200 milligrams per day of 5-HTP, but I have also seen reports that some patients need as much as 1,600 milligrams per day.

If a patient can afford it, I have them start on SAM instead of St. John's wort or 5-HTP.

Although I suggest starting with either St. John's wort, 5-HTP, or SAM, other options patients can consider include bright light therapy (even if the patient does not have seasonal affective disorder), EEG biofeedback, or acupuncture.

What if a combination of psychotherapy, the nutritional supplements, and one of the treatment options noted above is not effective? If the patient wants to continue with alternative treatments, I will suggest they try adding 5-HTP and the amino acid tyrosine (2 to 6 grams per day) if they have been using St. John's wort, St. John's wort and tyrosine if they have been using 5-HTP, or they can switch to inositol. There is no research evidence whatsoever indicating that the combinations suggested or that switching to inositol will do the trick, but it may be worth a try if someone is adamantly opposed to using antidepressant medication.

Those over fifty might also want to try taking DHEA or gingko biloba. The use of gingko could have adverse effects on sperm or on eggs.

If you can do it, you may also want to consider:

- Changing your diet so that it consists of a balance of high-quality, lean protein foods (chicken, turkey, lean red meat, or for the vegetarian, combinations of foods to provide all essential amino acids), and complex carbohydrates (the bulk of which should come from vegetables, some fruits, and moderate amounts of low-glycemic grains). Sugar and saturated and trans-fatty acids (margarine, partially hydrogenated oils used in baked goods) should be avoided. Each meal should contain protein, fat, and moderate amounts of carbohydrates.
- Engaging in moderate exercise three times per week.

5. If you have moderate to severe depression that is interfering with your ability to function and to get enjoyment out of life, if it is disrupting sleep, affecting your appetite and weight, or contributing to interpersonal problems (with irritability, impatience), you should be in therapy with a biologically informed therapist and should be seriously considering the use of medication. You should

use medication if you have persistent thoughts of suicide. If you are very anxious and feel suicidal, ask your doctor about using a tranquilizing drug for a few weeks until antidepressants take effect.

6. If you have had two or more episodes of depression in your lifetime or have been chronically depressed for some time (dysthymic) and have a family history of mood disorder, you should be seeing a biologically informed therapist and should seriously consider medication.

If you are strugggling with whether to try psychotherapy or medication first, you should consider the following argument in favor of at least giving medication a try. Psychiatrists Paul Wender and Donald Klein pointed out over fifteen years ago that treating a depression or other psychiatric illness that may respond best to medication with psychotherapy first could waste a lot of your time and money. You might also wind up suffering needlessly. It makes more sense to first try treating a depression of suspected biological origin with medication. You will find out fairly quickly if you are on the right track (usually within two to four weeks). If you start with psychotherapy alone, you might have to wait considerably longer (two to four months) before finding out if you are treating it properly.

CHAPTER 12

DIAGNOSIS AND TREATMENT OF MOOD DISORDERS IN THE TWENTY-FIRST CENTURY

If you suffer from a mood disorder or are concerned about your children's vulnerability to a mood disorder, you can look forward to many diagnostic and treatment advances in the coming years.

Improved diagnosis will come, in part, from medical imaging techniques, such as CAT scans (computerized axial tomography), which produce a detailed cross section of tissue with X rays and MRI (magnetic resonance imaging), which makes images of tissue through the use of a magnetic field. Researchers are using CAT scans and MRI to search for brain abnormalities in groups of patients known to have depression and bipolar illness. If characteristic abnormalities can be identified, then CAT scans and MRIs might someday be able to diagnose mood disorders in individual patients undergoing evaluation.

Technology also exists to take pictures, not only of brain structure but of active brain functions, such as blood flow, glucose metabolism, and the activity of neurotransmitter receptors. PET (positron emission tomography), which uses mildly radioactive substances to make images of the brain at work, and SPECT (single-photon emission computed tomography), a variation of CAT, and functional MRI (fMRI), are revealing commonalities in the brain processes of depressed patients. For instance, studies have found sluggish use of glucose in the frontal lobes of depressed patients' brains. The more severely depressed the patients were in these studies, the more sluggish their frontal lobes' use of glucose. When successfully treated with antidepressants, the glucose metabolism returned to normal. If researchers discover problems in brain activity typical of a group of depressed patients, then a test for the abnormal activity can be used as a diagnostic tool in individual patients.

Identification of substances in blood, urine, and spinal fluid that are unique biological markers of depressive illness will almost certainly be used routinely in the not-too-distant future to identify specific subtypes of depression. This will help a doctor choose the medication most likely to be effective for a particular patient. A lot of the guesswork currently involved in treatment will be avoided.

In addition to providing more accurate diagnoses, all of these methods will help researchers understand the underlying biochemical dysfunctions responsible for mood disorders. The first antidepressants and the mood stabilizer lithium were all discovered by accident. A greater understanding of the biochemical roots of depression will eventually lead to more rationally designed and effective drug treatments. That is, researchers will be able to design drugs that target the specific biochemical abnormalities involved in depression. Rationally designed drugs will have increasingly fewer and less troublesome side effects.

There are already at least eighteen new antidepressant medications in various phases of development. Many of these work on the same neurotransmitters as the older antidepressants, but with fewer side effects.

For instance, Reboxetine is a selective norepinephrine reuptake inhibitor that has been in use in Europe since 1997 and will probably become available in the United States in 2000. It may be especially useful for severe depression and will not cause the gastrointestinal upset and sexual dysfunction typical of Prozac and the other SSRIs.

Flesinoxan, a drug that works on the serotonin system, is under development for both depression and anxiety.

Researchers are working on the first-ever skin patch delivery system for an antidepressant—an MAO inhibitor. The reader may recall that this class of medication is highly effective, especially for depression with atypical symptoms. When taken orally, however, it can cause a rapid and potentially life-threatening rise in blood pressure if the patient eats certain foods. Since the patch delivers the antidepressant directly to the blood, this problem is eliminated. In one study, all eighty patients on the patch showed improvement within a week.

The makers of Prozac have entered a licensing deal with another pharmaceutical company to produce a form of Prozac that should have fewer side effects than the original drug.

Antidepressants with unique mechanisms of action are also under development. Some of these will work on neurotransmitter systems and brain chemicals that have previously received little attention but are probably implicated in depression. Drugs that affect the glutamate system are one example. Drugs that block a brain chemical called substance P are another.

In the twenty-first century, researchers will identify the hereditary foundations of mood disorders. Hereditary information is carried on structures in the nucleus of our cells called chromosomes. We have twenty-three pairs of chromosomes in virtually every cell in our body. The chromosomes are made up of roughly 80,000 discrete pieces of hereditary information called genes. The entire collection of genes is referred to as our genome. Genes carry instructions for making and assembling proteins, the building blocks of all the tissues in our body, including brain tissue. Genes also have a great deal of influence on all the biochemical processes in the body, including those linked to mood regulation. Erroneous genetic instructions result in structural and biochemical abnormalities in the brain.

Since the 1980s, researchers have been searching for the genes responsible for manic-depressive illness. Recently, researchers have found two areas on chromosome 18, which appear to confer a vulnerability to manic-depressive illness. There are, however, hundreds and perhaps thousands of genes in the region identified. It will take a great deal of work to identify the location of the specific genes that are linked to manic-depressive illness.

If only one gene were responsible for producing bipolar illness, it would be relatively easy to find it with only a small number of affected individuals. But there are probably many genes that interact in complex ways to produce bipolar illness. Researchers need to have genetic data from a large number of families with at least two affected individuals in order to be able to find the genetic commonalities among the families responsible for bipolar illness.

In 1989, the National Institute of Mental Health (NIMH) began a project to find such families. As of the date of this book, roughly one hundred families with four hundred affected individuals have come forward to take part in the project. Researchers may ultimately need 500 or more families to have an adequate data base. Blood samples are drawn from family members. Their genetic material is stored at very cold temperatures and, theoretically, could be kept available to qualified researchers for hundreds of years.

Once the specific genes that confer a vulnerability to bipolar illness are discovered, researchers will need to determine the function of each of the genes. The door will then be open to curing or even preventing mood disorders by inserting corrected genetic information into the appropriate cells. A number of methods of inserting genetic material into cells have already been developed. Eventually, doctors may be able to eliminate vulnerability to mood disorder in a depressed or bipolar patient's future offspring by inserting correct genetic information into sperm or egg cells.

We must keep in mind, however, that heredity is not the only factor involved in mood disorders. Traumatic life stress can trigger the vulnerability to depression or manic-depressive illness by causing biochemical reactions in the body that change which genes are active. Stress turns particular genes on and off. Nervous system structure and biochemistry are thereby altered in ways that produce symptoms.

It has been discovered that the stress of childhood sexual or physical abuse can produce profound and lasting changes in a brain structure and function and in the workings of the hormonal system. These changes can contribute to the later occurrence of clinical depression. A unique class of antistress medications is being developed that may soon help victims of childhood abuse. Called CRF antagonists, the drugs will block the action of the naturally occurring brain chemical that causes the release of stress hormones.

On the one hand, it may seem that we know little about the brain and the causes and cure of mood disorders. On the other hand, it is apparent that we have made great progress in a very short time. Until the early 1900s, there was no systematic identification or description of the various mood disorders. As recently as the 1950s, we had few clues about the causes of mood disorders and virtually no effective treatments. It was not until the 1970s that research into the causes and cures of mood disorders really took off. And it was not until the late 1980s and the 1990s that we began to make rapid progress in understanding the workings of the brain and the biochemical basis of mood disorders. The rate at which researchers are making new discoveries is accelerating.

Research on mood disorders in the twenty-first century will begin to reveal how the influences of genetics, biochemistry, personality, and stress come together to create illness in an individual patient. By the last half of the twenty-first century, we may well have the elusive cure for mood disorders we seek.

APPENDIX

PSYCHIATRISTS
American Society of Clinical Psychopharmacology, Inc. (ASCP)
P.O. Box 2257
New York, NY 10116
(212) 268-4260

ASCP will provide you with the name of a psychiatrist specializing in the medical treatment of depression and other psychiatric disorders.

Society of Biological Psychiatry
(904) 953-2842

CHILD AND ADOLESCENT PSYCHIATRISTS
American Academy of Child and Adolescent Psychiatry
3615 Wisconsin Avenue NW
Washington, DC 20016
(202) 966-7300

Information on psychiatric disorders in children and adolescents. Referrals to child psychiatrists in your area.

ORGANIZATIONS
Mood Disorders
All of the following organizations will send you information on mood disorders. They also offer the other services listed.

National Foundation for Depressive Illness (NAFDI)
P.O. Box 2257
New York, NY 10116
1-800-248-4344

List of doctors and support groups in your area. Newsletter.

National Depressive and Manic-Depressive Association
(NDMDA)
730 North Franklin Street, Suite 501
Chicago, IL 60610
1-800-826-3632

List of support groups in your area. Guidelines on how to start a
support group. Annual conference. Book catalogue. Newsletter.

National Mental Health Association (NMHA)
1021 Price Street
Alexandria, VA 22314
1-800-228-1114

Information on all psychiatric disorders. Information on how to
find treatment in your area.

National Alliance for the Mentally Ill (NAMI)
2101 Wilson Boulevard, Apt. 302
Arlington, VA 22201
(703) 524-7600

Information on all psychiatric disorders. Information on how to set
up a support group. Newsletter.

Depression and Related Affective Disorders Association, Inc. (DRADA)
Johns Hopkins Hostel, Meyer 4-181
1601 North Wolfe Street
Baltimore, MD 21205
(410) 955-4647

Annotated bibliography of publications on mood disorders. Support group handbook.

National Association for Research on Schizophrenia and Depression (NARSAD)
60 Cuttermill Road
Great Neck, NY 11021
(516) 829-0091

Newsletter with the latest on depression research. NARSAD accepts donations for research on depression.

Stanley Foundation Bipolar Network
5430 Grosvenor Lane, Suite 200
Bethesda, MD 20814
1-800-518-SFBN

Newsletter, which includes the latest information on research in bipolar illness.

Other Disorders

Obsessive Compulsive Foundation (OC Foundation)
(203) 878-5669

Referral to a specialist in the treatment of obsessive-compulsive disorder in your area.

Anxiety Disorder Association of America
6000 Executive Boulevard, Suite 200
Rockville, MD 20852

Publishes the *National Treatment Directory.* Newsletter.

Attention Deficit Disorder Warehouse
1859 Pine Island Road, Suite 185
Plantation, FL 33322
(954) 792-8100

Information on attention-deficit hyperactivity disorder.

Lithium Information Center/Obsessive Compulsive
Information Center
Dean Foundation for Health, Research and Education
8000 Excelsior Drive, Suite 302
Madison, WI 53717
(608) 836-8070

Provides bibliographies and single photocopies of articles on any topic relating to lithium, Depakote, Tegretol, or obsessive-compulsive and related disorders. Physician referral and support-group referrals. Excellent patient information booklets available for antidepressants, lithium, Tegretol, Depakote, obsessive-compulsive disorder, ECT, hyperactivity medications, stimulants, and other drugs.

National Clearinghouse for Drug and Alcohol Information
P.O. Box 2345
Rockville, MD 20847
(301) 468-2600
1-800-729-6686

This federal center provides videotapes and literature on drug and alcohol abuse.

BOOKS

There are many, many books on the market about mood disorders. Listed here are just a few of them.

Lonely, Sad and Angry: A Parent's Guide to Depression in Children and Adolescents, by Barbara Ingersoll and Sam Goldstein (Doubleday). Good information on the diagnosis, causes, and treatments of depression in youngsters. Information on suicide and hospitalization.

Overcoming Depression, by Demitri and Janice Papolos (Harper Collins). Good chapters on the biochemistry and genetics of mood disorders and on mood charting.

The Good News About Depression: Breakthrough Medical Treatments That Can Work for You, by Mark Gold (Bantam Books). Descriptions of many medical illnesses mimicking depression. Discussion of cutting-edge methods for diagnosing subtypes of depression.

Mind, Mood & Medicine: A Guide to the New Biopsychiatry, by Paul Wender and Donald Klein (Meridian). Published in 1981 but way ahead of its time. Excellent comparison of the biological and psychological models of mood disorders and other psychiatric illnesses.

Understanding Depression: A Complete Guide to its Diagnosis and Treatment, by Donald Klein and Paul Wender (Oxford University Press). Straightforward and concise. The authors demonstrate their intimate understanding of the subtle expressions of mood disorders.

You Mean I Don't Have to Feel This Way? by Collete Dowling (Bantam Books). Engaging and well-researched book on depression and the interesting links among mood disorders and eating disorders, panic attacks, and substance abuse. Especially good for women who suffer from one or more of these illnesses. The author's husband and daughter suffered from depression.

An Unquiet Mind, by Kay Redfield Jamison (Alfred Knopf). A psychologist who suffers from manic-depressive illness describes her own battle with the condition. Also contains information on symptoms and treatment. Jamison is one of the world's foremost authorities on manic-depressive illness. She coauthored the standard medical text on the subject with psychiatrist Frederick Goodwin.

Winter Blues: Seasonal Affective Disorder: What It Is and How to Overcome It, by Norman Rosenthal (Guilford Publications). Good basic information on SAD from one of the world's experts on the topic.

This Isn't What I Expected: Overcoming Postpartum Depression, by Karen Kleiman and Valerie Raskin (Bantam Books).

Feeling Good: The New Mood Therapy, by David Burns (Avon Books). Lively, well-written, and fun to read. Chock full of information on cognitive-behavioral tactics for managing depression. Contains a good chapter for men to read on the (false) connection between self-esteem and success. Has another good chapter on handling perfectionism. Also has an excellent chapter addressing the misconceptions patients have about medication. If you are moderately to severely depressed or have suffered chronic depression, do not expect this book to fix you. It is useful, however, as a supplement to formal medical and psychotherapeutic treatment.

Mastering Depression: A Patient's Guide to Interpersonal Psychotherapy, by Myrna Weissman (Graywind Publications).

A Brilliant Madness: Living with Manic-Depressive Illness, by Patty Duke and Gloria Hochman (Bantam Books). The author's personal experiences with bipolar illness combined with an engaging presentation of technical information about all forms of bipolar illness.

We Heard the Angels of Madness: A Family Guide to Coping with Manic Depression, by Diane and Lisa Berger (William Morrow). Personal accounts, plus technical information about the illness.

VIDEOS

The following two videos are available from the Depression and Related Affective Disorders organization:

A Patient's Perspective—Dick Cavett. The talk-show host discusses his experiences with depression.

A Patient's Perspective—Mike Wallace. The CBS correspondent discusses his experiences with depression.

Available from the National Depressive and Manic-Depressive Association:

Dark Glasses and Kaleidoscopes: Living with Manic-Depression. Information on manic-depressive illness and its treatment. Advice for patients and their families.

Available from Fanlight Productions at 1-800-937-4113: *Four Lives: Portraits in Manic-Depression.*

Support Groups

Would you like to get into a support group, but do not want to leave home? Have a seat at your computer! If you have a commercial on-line service, they are sure to have forums on mood disorders. You can also tie into an internet Usenet newsgroup using any internet access provider. Try the group *alt.support.depression.*

Discount Nutritional Supplies

There are scores of nutritional supply houses. If you decide to use vitamins or the other supplements mentioned in this book on a regular basis, you can save a substantial amount of money by ordering them by phone from a discount supplier rather than buying them at a retail store.

You will find advertisements for several companies in health, fitness, or weight-training magazines. Pick a few suppliers with toll-free telephone numbers who will send you free catalogs. Compare prices and shipping charges. Look for a supplier who has a number of brands of a supplement from which you can choose. You need to be aware that there are few controls on the quality of the products sold. It might help to stick with brand-name products. Some manufacturers claim their products are produced in laboratories certified by the Food and Drug Administration. You may wish to ask the supplier about this when you call for a catalog.

BRIGHT LIGHT THERAPY UNITS FOR SEASONAL AFFECTIVE DISORDER

Enviro-Med: 1-800-222-3296
SunBox Company: 1-800-548-3968

DAWN SIMULATORS

SunBox Company: 1-800-548-3968
Seventh Generation: 1-800-456-1177 (Sunrise Alarm Clock)

NEGATIVE ION GENERATORS

Bionic Products of America: 1-800-634-4667

FREE PRESCRIPTION MEDICATION

If you do not have insurance nor the money to pay for prescription medications, you may be eligible to get free medication from manufacturers. Write to:

PhRMA
1100 Fifteenth Street NW
Washington, DC 20005
or call (202) 835-3400

INDEX